D0491796

Literacy in Context
for GCSE

John O'Connor

General editor **Joan Ward**

CAMBRIDGE
UNIVERSITY PRESS

PUBLISHED BY THE PRESS SYNDICATE OF THE UNIVERSITY OF CAMBRIDGE
The Pitt Building, Trumpington Street, Cambridge, United Kingdom

CAMBRIDGE UNIVERSITY PRESS
The Edinburgh Building, Cambridge CB2 2RU, UK
40 West 20th Street, New York, NY 10011-4211, USA
477 Williamstown Road, Port Melbourne, VIC 3207, Australia
Ruiz de Alarcón 13, 28014 Madrid, Spain
Dock House, The Waterfront, Cape Town 8001, South Africa

http://www.cambridge.org

© Cambridge University Press 2002

This book is in copyright. Subject to statutory exception and to the provisions of relevant collective licensing agreements, no reproduction of any part may take place without the written permission of Cambridge University Press.

First published 2002

Printed in the United Kingdom at the University Press, Cambridge

Typefaces Bembo, Legacy Sans   *System* QuarkXPress®

A catalogue record for this book is available from the British Library

ISBN 0 521 52715 5 paperback

Prepared for publication by Pentacor Book Design plc

ACKNOWLEDGEMENTS

Thanks are due to the following for permission to reproduce copyright textual material:

pp. 8–9, *The Amber Spyglass*, by Philip Pullman © Philip Pullman, 2000, the third book in the *His Dark Materials* trilogy, published by Scholastic Children's Books, reproduced by permission of Scholastic Limited; pp. 20–1, Ben Elton/Time Warner Books UK; p. 26, Grant Naylor/Penguin Books; pp. 28–9, Extract from *Last Act in Palmyra* by Lindsey Davis, published by Century. Used by permission of The Random House Group Limited; pp. 32–3, Reprinted by kind permission of the Author's Estate, Linda Smith, acting in conjunction with The Dorian Literary Agency; p. 33, Reprinted by permission of PFD on behalf of: The Estate of Catherine Storr; p. 34, Lee Krystek/The Museum of Unnatural History; p. 35, p. 39, Paul Stonehill; pp. 40–1, pp. 52–3, p. 58, pp. 112–13, © the *Guardian*; p. 47, p. 99, p. 106, pp. 114–15, pp. 120–1, *Daily Mail*; p. 54, Michael Benton; p. 55, Extract from *Walking with Dinosaurs* – by Tim Haines reproduced with the permission of BBC Worldwide Limited. Text © Tim Haines; pp. 60–1, Plan UK, 5–6 Underhill Street, London NW1 7HS, Tel: 0207 4829777, Fax: 0207 4829778, www.plan-uk.org; p. 67, © William Jefferson Clinton; p. 72, p. 73, p. 77, Thames Valley Police – CP Keith Raw and Crime Services Agency – CSO Roy Townsend; p. 78, The Living Rainforest; p. 79, Rainforest Concern, Tel: 0207 2292093, Fax: 0207 2214094, 27 Lansdowne Crescent, London W11 2NS, www.rainforestconcern.org; pp. 80–1, GAP Activity Projects (GAP UK Ltd), a not-for-profit organisation, is the UK's leading year out provider for the 18–19 age range, sending up to 2000 school leavers annually on fixed-term overseas voluntary work experience placements in 34 countries worldwide. Programmes range from heritage and conservation to community management; p. 85, Natural History Museum; pp. 86–7, Cheryl Stonehouse/Express Newspapers; pp. 92–3, the *Mirror*/Mirrorpix.com; p. 93, Anabel Inge, pupil at The Latymer School, a grammar school in North London; pp. 98–9, Tony Parsons/Mirror Syndication International; p. 103, Extracted from article by Deborah Orr, first published in the *Independent* 14 January 2002; pp. 104–5, *Unreel*; p. 107, Adam McQueen/*Big Issue*; pp. 122–3, *Channel 4 News*/ITV; p. 136, p. 137, p. 138, p. 139, © RNLI; pp. 144–5, Warwick Castle; p. 145, Tower Bridge Experience; p. 146, Bletchley Park Trust; p. 147, Cabinet War Rooms; p. 153, p. 154, p. 155, Department of Health; p. 174, Reprinted by permission of Harper Collins Publishers Limited © Pamela Stephenson 2002; p. 175, Sally Morgan, Time Warner Books UK.

Thanks are due to the following for permission to reproduce photographs:

Cover (from left), Department of Health, Cabinet War Rooms, RNLI/Rick Tomlinson, Plan UK; p. 14, p. 15, p. 19, Donald Cooper/Photostage; p. 34, p. 38, Fortean Picture Library; p. 41 *l*, p. 45, p. 55, p. 70, p. 71, p. 72 *t*, p. 73 *l*, pp. 120–1, p. 142, p. 160, p. 162, p. 166, p. 174, p. 177, Corbis; p. 41 *r*, Magrath Photography/Science Photo Library; p. 51, p. 72 *b*, p. 73 *r*, Getty Images; p. 86, Express Newspapers; p. 101, PA Photos; pp. 104–5 © Ted Nasmith/Harper Collins Publishers Ltd; p. 113, © South Tyrol Museum of Archaeology, Italy, www.iceman.it, Photo: Augustin Ochsenreiter; p. 122, p. 123 *b*, British Antarctic Survey; p. 123 *t*, MODIS images courtesy of NASA's Terra satellite, supplied by Ted Scambos, National Snow and Ice Data Center, University of Colorado, Boulder; p. 128, p. 129, p. 130, p. 131, p. 132, Lowe.

Every effort has been made to reach copyright holders. The publishers would be glad to hear from anyone whose rights they have unknowingly infringed.

The publisher has tried to ensure that the URLs for external websites referred to in this book are correct and active at the time of going to press. However, the publisher has no responsibility for the websites and can make no guarantee that a site will remain live or that the content will remain appropriate.

Literacy in Context for GCSE is a collection of texts and activities – with a strong focus on non-fiction and media – which will prepare you for a major part of your English GCSE.

It is not a course book which requires you to work through from page one to the end: you can dip into the various units in any order, focusing on film reviews one day and television advertisements the next, moving from websites to campaign leaflets, newspapers to political speeches.

● Each unit gives you a **text** – an example of writing in a particular genre, such as an information article, a review or a factual report. These texts cover a wide variety of subjects, from famous executions to blockbuster films, dinosaurs to 'Bigfoot'.

In some units you will be given the opportunity to **compare** two or three texts. This will help you to understand the way texts work much more clearly.

● Each unit then focuses on three or four key **language features** typical of that genre – such as paragraphing or the use of quotes. You will read a clear explanation of each of these features, and then work through a range of **activities** which will help you to understand them.

● Finally you have a choice of **tasks** which are closely modelled on the kind of question you will be given in your GCSE exam. There are four tasks at the end of each unit: two at **foundation level**, two at **higher level**. Your teacher will advise you on which are the most useful tasks for you to attempt.

● To help you assess your **progress**, every section gives you a chance to check that you feel confident about each of the new skills you have acquired.

I hope you enjoy using *Literacy in Context for GCSE* and understanding more about the fascinating range of texts that we come across in our daily lives.

John O'Connor

Contents

Contents

Analyse, review and comment

Media texts

Multi-genre texts

Literary non-fiction

KEY LANGUAGE FEATURES	FOUNDATION TIER TASKS	HIGHER TIER TASKS
• emotive vocabulary • paragraphing • presentation of both sides of the argument	• summarise the article • write two short speeches, one for and one against	• explain how the writer uses language to illustrate particular issues • write an analysis of a chosen issue
• appropriate register • personal perspective • first and third person • the language of criticism	• summarise a writer's opinions • explain how a writer uses language to express opinions	• write a film, television or music review • explain and comment on the two reviews
• colloquial language • slang and neologisms • language to express opinions	• summarise opinions • comment on the articles	• compare three articles • write a comment article
• the language of analyse, review and comment texts • plot summaries • quotations	• summarise an article • explain how a writer uses language to express opinions	• write an analysis of a film • compare the three kinds of writing
• photograph, headline and intro • paragraphs • pyramid writing	• write a summary • write a tabloid newspaper article	• analyse the two articles • write a tabloid newspaper article
• the language of writing to inform • adjectives • quotes	• summarise the reports • write a speech	• analyse the two texts • plan a web-page on a news item
• moving-image techniques • awareness of target groups • message and slogan	• summarise the advertisement • create a storyboard for a television advertisement	• analyse the Aero advertisement • write an advertising brief
• genre • purpose and audience • register	• write an account of the RNLI • write a magazine advertisement	• analyse the RNLI website • plan pages for a charity website
• imperatives • vocabulary • combination of text and image	• summarise a leaflet • write a letter to a friend	• compare the leaflets • plan an advertising leaflet
• use of narrative • typography • graphic novel techniques	• write a report, summarising a narrative • write a letter to your MP	• analyse the three advertisements • plan an advertisement in a graphic novel style
• emotive reporting • factual reporting • audience and purpose	• create a storyboard • write a letter to a newspaper	• compare and contrast the two reports • write a report of the execution
• emotive language • irony • polemical writing	• summarise an argument • write a polemical letter to a newspaper	• write to a newspaper in character • compare and contrast the texts
• direct speech • juxtaposition • biographical and autobiographical writing	• write a short biography • write about an episode from your own life	• analyse the language of biography and autobiography • write a section from a biography

The vulture woman

In this unit you will:

- read an extract from a novel
- examine the language of fantasy
- write an episode from a novel in a chosen genre

This extract comes from *The Amber Spyglass*, the third novel in Philip Pullman's trilogy, *His Dark Materials*. Lyra and Will have travelled to the land of the dead, accompanied by Tialys and Salmakia, two Gallivespians – tiny warriors who ride on the backs of dragonflies.

The Amber Spyglass

They stood still and listened. The only sound was an endless drip-drip-drip of water from the leaves, and as they looked up they felt one or two drops splash coldly on their cheeks.

"Can't stay here," said Lyra.

They moved off the wharf, keeping close together, and made their way to the wall. Gigantic stone blocks, green with ancient slime, rose higher into the mist than they could 5 see. And now they were closer, they could hear the sound of cries behind it, though whether they were human voices crying was impossible to tell: high mournful shrieks and wails that hung in the air like the drifting filaments of a jellyfish, causing pain wherever they touched.

"There's a door," said Will, in a hoarse strained voice. 10

It was a battered wooden postern under a slab of stone. Before Will could lift his hand and open it, one of those high harsh cries sounded very close by, jarring their ears and frightening them horribly.

Immediately the Gallivespians darted into the air, the dragonflies like little war-horses eager for battle. But the thing that flew down swept them aside with a brutal blow from 15 her wing, and then settled heavily on a ledge just above the children's heads. Tialys and Salmakia gathered themselves and soothed their shaken mounts.

The thing was a great bird the size of a vulture, with the face and breasts of a woman. Will had seen pictures of creatures like her, and the word *harpy* came to mind as soon as he saw her clearly. Her face was smooth and unwrinkled, but aged beyond even the age of 20 the witches: she had seen thousands of years pass, and the cruelty and misery of all of them had formed the hateful expression on her features. But as the travellers saw her more clearly, she became even more repulsive. Her eye-sockets were clotted with filthy slime, and the redness of her lips was caked and crusted as if she had vomited ancient blood again and again. Her matted, filthy black hair hung down to her shoulders; her 25 jagged claws gripped the stone fiercely; her powerful dark wings were folded along her back, and a drift of putrescent stink wafted from her every time she moved.

Will and Lyra, both of them sick and full of pain, tried to stand upright and face her.

"But you are alive!" the harpy said, her harsh voice mocking them.

Will found himself hating and fearing her more than any human being he had ever known. 30

"Who are you?" said Lyra, who was just as repelled as Will.

For answer the harpy screamed. She opened her mouth and directed a jet of noise right in their faces, so that their heads rang and they nearly fell backwards. Will clutched at Lyra and they both clung together as the scream turned into wild mocking peals of 35 laughter, which were answered by other harpy-voices in the fog along the shore. The jeering hate-filled sound reminded Will of the merciless cruelty of children in a playground, but there were no teachers here to regulate things, no one to appeal to, nowhere to hide.

He set his hand on the knife at his belt and looked her in the eyes, though his head was 40 ringing and the sheer power of her scream had made him dizzy.

"If you're trying to stop us," he said, "then you'd better be ready to fight as well as scream. Because we're going through that door."

The harpy's sickening red mouth moved again, but this time it was to purse her lips into a mock-kiss. 45

Then she said, "Your mother is alone. We shall send her nightmares. We shall scream at her in her sleep!"

Will didn't move, because out of the corner of his eye he could see the Lady Salmakia moving delicately along the branch where the harpy was perching. Her dragonfly, wings quivering, was being held by Tialys on the ground, and then two things happened: 50 the lady leapt at the harpy and spun around to dig her spur deep into the creature's scaly leg, and Tialys launched the dragonfly upwards. In less than a second Salmakia had spun away and leapt off the branch, directly on to the back of her electric-blue steed and up into the air.

The effect on the harpy was immediate. Another scream shattered the silence, much 55 louder than before, and she beat her dark wings so hard that Will and Lyra both felt the wind, and staggered. But she clung to the stone with her claws, and her face was suffused with dark-red anger, and her hair stood out from her head like a crest of serpents.

Will tugged at Lyra's hand, and they both tried to run towards the door, but the harpy launched herself at them in a fury and only pulled up from the dive when Will turned, 60 thrusting Lyra behind him and holding up the knife.

The Gallivespians flew at the harpy at once, darting close at her face and then darting away again, unable to get in a blow but distracting her so that she beat her wings clumsily and half-fell on to the ground.

Lyra called out, "Tialys! Salmakia! Stop, stop!" 65

The spies reined back their dragonflies and skimmed high over the children's heads. Other dark forms were clustering in the fog, and the jeering screams of a hundred more harpies sounded from further along the shore. The first one was shaking her wings, shaking her hair, stretching each leg in turn and flexing her claws. She was unhurt, and that was what Lyra had noticed. 70

The Gallivespians hovered, and then dived back towards Lyra, who was holding out both hands for them to land on. Salmakia realized what Lyra had meant, and said to Tialys: "She's right. We can't hurt her, for some reason."

Language in context

The power of language

Key features of the writing are:

1 genre

2 comparisons

3 language that appeals to the senses

 GENRE

> **Genre** is the name given to a particular kind of writing with its own typical features.

a) *The Amber Spyglass* can be placed in the **fantasy** genre. In pairs, brainstorm the titles of books and films which belong to each of the following popular fiction genres: **fantasy**, **horror**, **crime** and **science fiction**. Think up four or five titles for each genre heading.

b) Each genre has its own recognisable features to do with characters, plot, themes and language. Copy the table below and, using the list you have just made, add examples of the characteristic features of each genre. Features of *The Amber Spyglass* and *The Lord of the Rings* by JRR Tolkien have been inserted as examples of the fantasy genre.

c) The first book of Tolkien's *The Lord of the Rings* trilogy opens with the following paragraph. In pairs discuss how you would guess that it was the introduction to a fantasy.

When Mr Bilbo Baggins of Bag End announced that he would shortly be celebrating his eleventy-first birthday with a party of special magnificence, there was much talk and excitement in Hobbiton.

d) Write a similar opening to a book in a different genre such as horror, crime or science fiction. Include as many features of the chosen genre as you can.

FEATURES	GENRES			
	fantasy	**horror**	**crime**	**science fiction**
	examples *The Amber Spyglass, The Lord of the Rings*			
characters	including imagined creatures with strange powers: e.g. *Gallivespians, orcs, wizards*			
settings	other worlds with their own 'rules': e.g. *parallel universes, Middle-earth*			
plots	journeys, quests: e.g. *to destroy the One Ring*			
events	encounters with terrifying creatures: e.g. *the harpy, the balrog*			
themes	major themes: e.g. *innocence and experience, Good v Evil*			
language	strange names: e.g. *Salmakia, Gandalf*			

2 COMPARISONS

Fantasy writers use familiar language in order to describe the unfamiliar. **Comparisons** help the reader to picture the scene.

These might be:

- **literal comparisons:** *Will's face was like his father's…* or
- **impressions:** *his features brought to mind an old, lined map…*

They might also be:

- **similes:** *it glowed as brightly as a holly berry in the dimness…* or
- **metaphors:** *her face lit up…*
  her eyes were dark pools of mystery…

(A **simile** is a means of comparing things in an unusual or unexpected way in which the writer creates an image in the reader's mind. A simile uses the words *like* or *as*. A **metaphor** serves the same purpose, but does not involve the use of *like* or *as*: the person or object is described as though they *really were* something else.)

a) In pairs, find the following lines in the extract. Then discuss what kind of comparison each one is (not all of them are clear-cut), and how effective it is in the context of the description:

wails that hung in the air…

like the drifting filaments of a jellyfish, causing pain wherever they touched.

like little war-horses eager for battle.

the word harpy *came to mind as soon as he saw her clearly.*

as if she had vomited ancient blood again and again.

reminded Will of the merciless cruelty of children in a playground…

and her hair stood out from her head like a crest of serpents.

b) Write a short description of a landscape in a fantasy or science fiction novel, using all four types of comparison.

3 LANGUAGE THAT APPEALS TO THE SENSES

A writer will call on a variety of language skills in order to create powerful descriptions. In this extract Philip Pullman uses **language that appeals to our senses**.

Philip Pullman's descriptions of landscape and character are not just visual descriptions: he also asks us to use our senses of hearing, touch and smell.

a) Write down the following quotations from the extract. Next to each, state which of our senses is being appealed to.

they felt one or two drops splash coldly on their cheeks.

one of those high harsh cries sounded very close by, jarring their ears and frightening them horribly.

and a drift of putrescent stink wafted from her every time she moved.

b) Using the three quotations above, and others that you can find, write a paragraph about the effect that Philip Pullman achieves in his description by appealing, not only to the sense of sight, but to the senses of hearing, touch and smell.

Writing to imagine

FOUNDATION TIER TASKS

1 WRITING ABOUT THE NOVEL

Write a short description in two sections, describing:

- the harpy's appearance and behaviour
- Lyra's and Will's reactions to it

Write 200–250 words.

Planning and drafting

The task is in two parts. Use these points in order to make preparatory notes:

Part 1: describe the harpy's appearance and behaviour

Look at:

- the creature's first appearance *The thing was … time she moved.* lines 18–27
- its reaction to being spoken to by the children *For answer … nowhere to hide.* 33–9
- its reaction to Will's threats *The harpy's sickening … her sleep!* 44–7
- its response to being attacked by the Lady Salmakia *The effect on the harpy … serpents.* 55–8

> You could begin:
> *Their first impression was that the creature was a cross between a vulture and a woman…*

Part 2: describe Lyra's and Will's reactions to the harpy

Look at:

- the children's first reactions on seeing the creature *Will and Lyra … repelled as Will.* 28–32
- their reactions to the harpy's scream *Will clutched … nowhere to hide.* 34–9

- Will's thoughts about using the knife *He set his hand … that door.* 40–3
- what they learn after the harpy is attacked by Lady Salmakia *She was unhurt … for some reason.* 69–73

> You could begin:
> *The children felt sick at the sight of the harpy…*

2 WRITING YOUR OWN EXTRACT

Write an extract from a story, beginning:

As they approached the massive iron gates, they were aware of a shadow…

Write 200–250 words.

Planning and drafting

Remember that you are writing an *extract* from a story – not the complete story.

You could follow the structure of the extract from *The Amber Spyglass*:

- description of the characters arriving in a new and frightening place
- sudden appearance of a terrifying creature or human figure
- the characters' reactions to the creature's behaviour and appearance

You might want to use:

- comparisons (look back at page 11):
    literal comparisons
    impressions
    similes
    metaphors
- language which appeals to different senses (page 11)

HIGHER TIER TASKS

1 WRITING ABOUT THE NOVEL

What are your impressions of this extract from *The Amber Spyglass*?

Write about:

● the feelings this extract arouses in you
● what might be found frightening or horrifying in it

Support your answer by reference to details from the text.

Remember to put quotation marks round any words or phrases from the story that you have used.

> You could start:
> *My first emotion on reading this extract was one of…*

2 WRITING YOUR OWN EXTRACT

Write an extract from a novel in a particular genre.

Planning and drafting

Choose a genre that you enjoy.

Look back at page 10 to remind yourself about the typical features of your chosen genre, in terms of:

● characters
● settings
● plots
● events
● themes
● language

You might want to use:

● comparisons (page 11):
  literal comparisons
  impressions
  similes
  metaphors
● language which appeals to different senses (page 11)

> You could start with any of the quotations on this page.

Western

'I don't like it. It's too quiet,' whispered Jed, reloading his Winchester and squinting up at the ridge…

Crime

'The explanation is simple,' said Battersby, lighting his pipe. 'Only one person had a cast-iron alibi…'

Horror

The thing which crawled from the coffin bore no resemblance to the body which had been placed in it…

Romance

'His voice, when he spoke, was husky and surprised. 'You're… beautiful,' he whispered, gazing down into the blueness of her eyes.

Fantasy

Eldan felt old: even for a wizard, eleven hundred years was an advanced age…

Supernatural

The candles flickered and she felt a sudden drop in temperature…

Science Fiction

'Anxiety is illogical,' declared Zarn, reading her thoughts. 'These are merely different life-forms…'

Thoughts of murder

In this unit you will:

- read extracts from three plays by Shakespeare
- examine Shakespeare's language
- write a scene from a play

A number of Shakespeare's plays show people plotting murder.

KING RICHARD III

In this extract from *King Richard III*, Richard is seen plotting the deaths of his wife Anne (who later dies mysteriously) and his two royal nephews, now known as the Princes in the Tower. He orders one of his supporters, Catesby, to spread rumours that Anne is extremely ill, and then meets James Tyrrel, whose job it will be to kill the Princes…

RICHARD	Come hither, Catesby. Rumour it abroad	51	
	That Anne my wife is very grievous sick.		
	I will take order for her keeping **close**.		*shut up*
	. . . .		
	Look how thou dream'st! I say again, give out		
	That Anne my queen is sick and **like** to die.		*likely*
	About it, for it **stands me much upon**		*is of great importance to me*
	To stop all hopes whose growth may damage me.	60	
	I must be married to my brother's daughter,		
	Or else my kingdom stands on brittle glass.		
	Murder her brothers, and then marry her:		
	Uncertain way of gain. But I am in		
	So far in blood that sin will pluck on sin.	65	
	Tear-falling pity dwells not in this eye.		
	Enter TYRREL		
	Is thy name Tyrrel?		
TYRREL	James Tyrrel, and your most obedient subject.		
RICHARD	Art thou indeed?		
TYRREL	Prove me, my gracious lord.		
RICHARD	Dar'st thou resolve to kill a friend of mine?	70	
TYRREL	**Please you**.		*if it please you*
	But I had rather kill two enemies.		
RICHARD	Why then thou hast it: two **deep** enemies,		*deadly*
	Foes to my rest and my sweet sleep's disturbers		
	Are they that I would have thee deal **upon**.	75	*with*
	Tyrrel, I mean those bastards in the Tower.		
TYRREL	Let me have open means to come to them,		
	And I'll soon rid you of the fear of them.		
RICHARD	Thou sing'st sweet music. Hark, come hither, Tyrrel.		
	Go by this **token**. Rise, and lend thine ear. *Whispers*	80	*[possibly a ring]*
	There is no more but so; say it is done,		
	And I will love thee and **prefer** thee for it.		*promote*
TYRREL	I will **dispatch it straight**.	*Exit*	*see it done straightaway*

King Richard III, Act 4 Scene 2, lines 51–83

MACBETH

The following extract is taken from *Macbeth*. Like Richard, Macbeth has already killed in order to gain the crown; and, also like Richard, he will not feel secure until more rivals and opponents are dead…

MACBETH	**How sayst thou** that Macduff **denies his person** At our great bidding?		*what do you make of Macduff staying away?*
LADY MACBETH	Did you send to him, sir?		
MACBETH	I hear it **by the way**, but I will send.	130	*on the grapevine*
	There's not a one of them but in his house		
	I keep a **servant fee'd**. I will tomorrow –		*i.e. a paid spy*
	And **betimes** I will – to the weird sisters.		*early*
	More shall they speak. For now I am **bent** to know		*determined*
	By the worst means, the worst; **for mine own good**,	135	*to get what I want*
	All causes shall give way. I am in blood		*I will sacrifice everything*
	Stepped in so far that should I wade no more,		
	Returning **were** as tedious as **go o'er**.		*would be going across*
	Strange things I have in head that will to hand,		
	Which must be acted ere they may be **scanned**.	140	*thought about*
LADY MACBETH	You lack the **season** of all natures, sleep.		*seasoning, preservative*

Macbeth, Act 3 Scene 4, lines 128–41

JULIUS CAESAR

Julius Caesar is based on actual events which took place in ancient Rome. A group of conspirators, led by Caesar's supposed friend, Brutus, have plotted to assassinate Caesar, believing him to have grown too powerful. In this scene they have come to collect him from his house and lead him to the Capitol, where the assassination is planned to take place. As the conspirators enter, Caesar welcomes them…

CAESAR	Welcome, Publius.		
	What, Brutus, are you stirred so early too?	110	
	Good morrow, Casca. Caius Ligarius,		
	. . .		
	Now, Cinna, now, Metellus. What, Trebonius,	120	
	I have an hour's talk in store for you.		
	Remember that you call on me today;		
	Be near me **that** I may remember you.		*so that*
TREBONIUS	Caesar, I will. [*Aside*] And so near will I be		
	That your best friends shall wish I had been further.	125	
CAESAR	Good friends, go in and taste some wine with me,		
	And we, like friends, will straightway go together.		
BRUTUS	[*Aside*] That every like is not the same, O Caesar,		
	The heart of Brutus **earns** to think upon.		*yearns, grieves**
	Exeunt		

Julius Caesar, Act 2 Scene 2, lines 109–29

*Brutus comments sadly on the difference between the appearance and the reality: they will accompany Caesar 'like' friends, while planning to kill him.

Language in context

The power of language

Key features of the writing are:

1 the metre

2 wordplay

3 imagery

---

1 THE METRE

> The pattern of light and heavy stresses in a line of poetry is known as the **metre**.

Regular metre

a) The metre of the following three lines is totally regular. To hear this regular metre in Shakespeare's verse, read the lines out loud, emphasising the heavily stressed syllables (in **bold**):

- That **Anne** my **wife** is **very grievous sick**.
- I **hear** it **by** the **way**, but **I** will **send**.
- What, **Brutus**, **are** you **stirred** so **early too?**

b) To become more familiar with Shakespeare's metre, copy out the following lines and underline the stressed syllables:

- That Anne my queen is sick and like to die.
- Strange things I have in head that will to hand
- Good friends, go in and taste some wine with me

c) The six lines above are all totally regular in their metre. Write down what you notice in each line about

- the pattern of short and heavy stresses
- the number of syllables

Varying the pattern of stresses

It would be extremely boring if every line of verse in a Shakespeare play had the regular metre – dee-**dum**, dee-**dum**, dee-**dum**, dee-**dum**, dee-**dum**. That is why, unlike the six lines above, most of the lines in Shakespeare's plays will have an irregular stress pattern.

d) Find the final line of Richard's first speech (*Tear-falling…*) and write it down. Read the line aloud several times. Many actors choose to place the stress as follows:

*Tear-falling **pi**ty **dwells** not in this **eye**.*

Write a brief comment on the line, explaining how the stress pattern helps to convey the meaning and the speaker's mood.

Do the same with these lines from the extracts:

- ***Mur**der **her bro**thers, and then **marry her** (King Richard III)* What do you notice about the heavy stresses at the beginning of the line? What effect do they have on the meaning?
- *And **I'll soon rid** you of the **fear** of them (King Richard III)* Look for the section of the line that has a number of heavy stresses one after the other.
- ***Cae**sar, I **will**. [Aside] And **so near will** I **be** (Julius Caesar)* There are heavy stresses on three consecutive words: *so near will…* How does this help the actor get the meaning across?

Iambic pentameter

- Just as music has bars, so verse has **feet**. Shakespeare's verse has five feet in a complete line.
- A five-feet line is called **pentameter** (*pent* = five, *meter* = measure).
- A foot which contains an unstressed syllable followed by a stressed one (the standard beat – *dee-**dum***) is called an **iamb**.
- Verse which has five iambs per line as its standard rhythm is therefore called **iambic pentameter**. Iambic pentameter which does not rhyme is also known as **blank verse**.

e) Make up some regular iambic pentameter newspaper headlines. For example:

Milan to sell their Irish striker, Byrne
United Nations aids Afghanistan
Election set for June the twenty-first

2 WORDPLAY

> The meanings of Shakespeare's language often come through the sounds of the words he chooses. This is particularly noticeable in **wordplay**.

Shakespeare frequently plays on a word's multiple meanings. For example, when Romeo's friend Mercutio is at the point of death, he says:

*Ask for me tomorrow and you shall find me a **grave** man. (Romeo and Juliet,* Act 3 Scene 1, lines 89–90)

a) Write a paragraph to explain and comment upon the effect of the two examples of wordplay in the *Julius Caesar* extract (playing on the words *near* and *like*).

For example:

● What does Caesar mean by *Be near me...* and what kind of 'nearness' does Trebonius have in mind?

● What does Brutus realise about the different meanings of the word *like*? Think about the difference between *he has been like a father to me* (his behaviour has been genuinely fatherly), and *margarine is like butter* (it seems like butter but in reality is very different).

3 IMAGERY

> Metaphors and similes (see page 11) are often referred to collectively as **imagery**. An **image** in poetry is a picture in words which helps to get across an idea.

We use images all the time in day-to-day speech. For example, we might describe somebody as 'a tower of strength'. The image, based upon the idea of an impregnable castle, was invented by Shakespeare when he wrote *King Richard III* (Act 5 Scene 3, line 12).

a) There are a number of images in the Shakespeare extracts. Copy the following grid, adding the origin of each image, an explanation of the meaning and a comment on how effective the image is, in your opinion. Two of the boxes have been filled in to start you off.

b) In pairs, talk about which of the images you find most effective and why.

Image	Its origin, what the image brings to mind	Its meaning and effectiveness
KING RICHARD III		
To stop all hopes whose growth may damage me.	*Origin: plants; it brings to mind a parasite such as ivy which can damage a tree's growth*	
Or else my kingdom stands on brittle glass.		
Thou sing'st sweet music ... Tyrrel		
MACBETH		
I am in blood / Stepped in so far that should I wade no more, / Returning were as tedious as go o'er.		
You lack the season of all natures, sleep.	*Origin: food; sleep is like a seasoning or preservative to keep us fresh*	

Writing to explore

FOUNDATION TIER TASKS

1 WRITING A SCENE

In *King Richard III*, *Macbeth* and *Julius Caesar* Shakespeare has taken events from the history books and used them to make an exciting play.

Choose one of the extracts and redraft it so that it becomes a scene from a novel.

Planning and drafting

Make sure that you write the scene in your own words, using Shakespeare's story, but adding details of your own.

> For example, you might begin:
>
> *Richard had some planning to do. First, he needed to get rid of his wife: with Anne alive, he could never feel really safe…*
>
> or
>
> *Macbeth poured a drink and handed it to his wife. Half to himself he said: 'So… Macduff refused to come…'*
>
>   *'You did invite him?'*
>
>   *'Of course I invited him!'*
>
> or
>
> *As the conspirators entered Caesar's house, the man they were planning to kill welcomed them one by one. Publius was the first to take Caesar's hand. They smiled at each other.*

2 ANALYSING THE LANGUAGE

Reread the extract from *King Richard III*. Explain how Richard's language helps us to form a picture of the king.

Remember to use quotation marks for any lines taken from the extract.

Planning and drafting

Find quotations which show what kind of person Richard is.

For example, many people would say that he was:

- unscrupulous (look at lines 51–2)
- cold-hearted (53)
- short-tempered (57–9)
- self-centred (61–3)
- insecure (62)
- recklessly violent and bloody (64–5)
- without remorse or conscience (66)
- changeable in his friendships (81–2)

> For example, you might begin:
>
> *Richard will stop at nothing.*
> *His unscrupulousness shows in the way in which he ruthlessly plans ahead, sowing the seeds of his wife's disappearance and death by ordering Catesby to spread rumours that she is 'very grievous sick'…*

HIGHER TIER TASKS

1 ANALYSING THE LANGUAGE

Using the three extracts as examples, explain how Shakespeare uses the verse to express meanings and create dramatic scenes.

Planning and drafting

Make preparatory notes by thinking about the effect of:

- **the metre**
  compare some regular iambic lines (see question 1a, page 16) with ones that have an irregular stress pattern (see question 1d)
- **rhyming couplets**
  for example, *King Richard III*, lines 64–5; *Macbeth*, lines 135–40
- **wordplay**
  for example, *near* and *like* in *Julius Caesar*, lines 123–9
- **imagery**
  use the notes that you have entered in the table (page 17)

For example, you could say:

The regularity of the metre in Richard's line

That Anne my wife is very grievous sick (52)

helps to show how smoothly it trips off his tongue. It is as though he were issuing a normal, everyday order. But the heavy stress on the first syllable of

Murder her brothers… (63)

underlines the seriousness of what he plans to do.

2 WRITING BLANK VERSE

The three plays from which the extracts are taken – *King Richard III*, *Macbeth* and *Julius Caesar* – are all based upon actual events from history.

Pick a moment from history or legend and write a brief Shakespearean scene in blank verse based upon it.

Planning and drafting

Try to include examples of

- stress patterns that help to convey the meaning
- rhyming couplets that make particular statements stand out
- wordplay
- imagery

Pick a dramatic moment (such as the interrogation of Guy Fawkes immediately after his arrest, the battle of the Somme, or the first moon-landing).

You could start:

ARMSTRONG *This may well be one tiny step for me,*
But for mankind it seems a mighty
leap…

Big Beard

In this unit you will:

- read an extract from a comic novel
- examine the language of comedy
- write a description of a comic character

This extract comes from *Gridlock*, a novel by Ben Elton. A party political conference is taking place in a large hotel, and in every meeting-room are groups of people who have come together to discuss their favourite cause so that they can 'lobby' their MPs – try to persuade them to support their point of view. The major political topic of the day is traffic congestion. And the most fanatical lobbyist of them all is Big Beard…

BIG BEARD

Deep deep down in the bowels of the hotel, where the ancient, groaning heating system shuddered and hissed and made sounds which wandered round the pipes, giving the impression that a ghost was being sick in the radiator, there stood one man alone. Deep down in the forgotten underworld of an English hotel, with the great piles of mouldering leaflets from failed 50s advertising campaigns (Isn't sunshine all the nicer for not having too much of it?) stood one solitary fellow with a bottle of rum in his hand. He was a huge, wild-looking man with great gnarled fists and great gnarled arms. Everything about him was gnarled – the story of how his inside thighs came to be gnarled delighted the lads at the Frog and Gherkin every time he told it.

The man was clearly mad. His wild eyes sparkling over his huge beard. A beard which gave him the appearance of a man who was trying to swallow an Old English Sheepdog and not getting very far; a great tousled mass of steel-grey hair which was a sort of Bermuda triangle for combs and brushes. A great, strong, noble-looking man, with a fearful, savage dignity – but mad. That's what they said.

'Old Big Beard,' the hotel porters said, 'bloody mad.'

And they were right, but not mad as in insane, mad as in angry. Old Big Beard was angry as a man with no head who gets a collection of balaclava helmets for Christmas.

'He hasn't come!' Big Beard roared in a voice so filled with passion that even the boiler stopped gurgling and listened.

'Another year goes by! and still he hasn't come!'

This was the annual conference soirée of the canal lobby.

'Hear me! Hear me!' thundered Big Beard, pulling mightily at his bottle and grabbing up thirty or forty cheesy nibbles in his hamlike fist. 'Britain has hundreds and hundreds of miles of canals! Dug with sweat and blood and … and … shovels,' he continued, slipping from his oratory peak for a moment. 'Dug two centuries ago, to transport goods about the country. Today, we carry coal by road!!!' Tears stood in the huge man's eyes. 'Are we mad! A hundred million years coal lay still in the Earth! and we take it on its last journey at seventy miles an hour! Burning oil all the while! Choking the sky! Scarring the land! Squashing the hedgehogs!' The tears began to dive out of the old beardy's eyes, making elaborate somersaults and pirouettes as they fell and bounced off his oilskin coat – just to make their point absolutely clear.

Behind Big Beard, mostly obscured by his huge gnarled tummy, was a map of the British Isles. A map which nobody but Big Beard ever saw. On it were marked the canals of Britain and on each canal was drawn a chain of barges covering its entire length.

The point was, that although the very first barge at the front of the queue might take weeks to reach its destination, from that point on, if the chain were not broken, barges might arrive every fifteen minutes. This clearly would not do for perishable products, but for coal, concrete, brick, wood…

'Imagine it,' the visionary screamed, 'a great, noble shire-horse, running on high octane grass and bramble, slowly plodding along, pulling perhaps thirty barges! No fuel consumption, no pollution, except the kind you can put on your roses…!'

'Listen to me! Listen to me!'

Of course there would be pretty considerable practical problems, you certainly could not get that volume of traffic through locks as they are currently designed. But then there are considerable practical problems to building motorways, and that never stopped anyone. Anyway, Big Beard was an idealist. He knew nothing of practical problems, mainly because nobody had ever bothered to discuss them with him.

Big Beard took another great sorrowful pull on his bottle and loosened his bow-tie. He fell over. The canal lobby soirée was over for another year.

'He hasn't come!'	Every year Big Beard invites Digby Parkhurst, the Minister of Transport, to attend the meeting… and every year he fails to turn up.
soirée of the canal lobby	evening get-together of the action-group in favour of using canals

Language in context

The power of language

Key features of the writing are:

1. comic character description
2. comic dialogue
3. comic narrative

1 COMIC CHARACTER DESCRIPTION

A writer can create a comic character by describing or commenting on their visual **appearance**, their **speech**, their **actions** and their **inner make-up**.

For example:

He was a huge, wild-looking man… (appearance)
'Squashing the hedgehogs!' (speech)
grabbing up thirty or forty cheesy nibbles… (actions)
Big Beard was an idealist. (inner make-up)

a) Write down four further quotations from the extract to illustrate the four types of description listed above.

Big Beard's appearance

b) Fantasy writers often use **comparisons** in order to describe the unfamiliar (see page 11). Writers of comedy sometimes create comparisons which are comic in themselves.

- Write a paragraph to comment on four of Ben Elton's comparisons – his descriptions of:

    the noises made by the heating system
    (*sounds which wandered round the pipes*)

    Big Beard's beard
    (*A beard which gave him the appearance…*)

    the beard's hair
    (*a great tousled mass*)

    Big Beard's anger
    (*Old Big Beard was angry as…*)

- Which of these is the most effective as a comic comparison in your opinion? Select your favourite and add two or three sentences to explain why the comparison works and what it adds to our picture of Big Beard.

Big Beard's speech, actions and inner make-up

c) Ben Elton makes two key statements about Big Beard:

The man was clearly mad.
Big Beard was an idealist.

In pairs, talk about the ways in which the descriptions of Big Beard's speech and actions help to support the picture of a 'mad idealist'.

2 COMIC DIALOGUE

> What a fictional character says or does is usually more important in helping us to form an impression of them than their appearance. Big Beard's **dialogue** reveals a great deal about him.

Punctuation of dialogue

Dialogue needs to be punctuated clearly and correctly.

a) The following lines are from an earlier chapter of *Gridlock*. Copy them, leaving wide margins on each side:

> In another part of the hotel, a small forlorn group of men and women waited for Digby.
> 'I don't think he's coming,' said one.
> 'He never does,' said another.
> The forlorn group of people were the Chairman and senior management of Britain's railways.

In pairs, annotate your copy with notes to show the rules of punctuation which are followed when writing dialogue.

For example:

- Where are the **speech marks** actually placed?
- What is the rule about **capital letters**?
- When should you begin a **new paragraph**?
- What are the possible **punctuation marks** that can appear immediately before you close speech marks?
- Why does *said* begin with a small (**lower case**) *s*?

Exclamation marks

Exclamation marks can be used not only for exclamations (*Oh, no!*), but for strong assertions (*I will not!*) and emotions such as surprise (*I don't believe it!*) or powerful personal feelings (*I can't stand that music!*).

b) Why are exclamation marks used so frequently in Big Beard's speech? In pairs discuss what this tells you about him, his mood and his attitude in this scene.

Ellipsis points and suspension points

Ellipsis is the term given to an omission in language. **Ellipsis points** (three dots…) can show that something has been left out of a sentence or that it is unfinished. For example:

This clearly would not do for perishable products, but for coal, concrete, brick, wood…

Suspension points (also three dots…) are used to suggest a pause. For example:

Dug with sweat and blood and … and … shovels

c) In pairs, read aloud the section of the extract from *'He hasn't come!'* to *'Listen to me! Listen to me!'*, one person reading the narrative and the other performing Big Beard's speeches. Use the clues given by the exclamation marks, suspension points and ellipsis points to give a dramatic performance of Big Beard's speech.

3 COMIC NARRATIVE

> Writers use a number of devices to help them create a comic effect. These include **anticlimax**.

Many writers of comedy have used anticlimax (also known as **bathos**).

A good example is the description of Big Beard as:

A great, strong, noble-looking man, with a fearful, savage dignity – but mad.

a) Find two examples of anticlimax in Big Beard's speeches (they are to do with *shovels* and *hedgehogs*). Talk about how they contribute to our impression of Big Beard and his passion for canals.

b) Discuss the ways in which the whole extract leads to a comic anticlimax. (For example, the Minister never turns up; nobody but Big Beard ever sees the map; he has never considered the practical problems of canal transport; his passion ends in a drunken collapse.)

Writing to entertain

FOUNDATION TIER TASKS

1 ANALYSING THE LANGUAGE

How does Ben Elton manage to get across to the reader what Big Beard is like? Write three paragraphs to explain how the writer focuses on:

- appearance
- speech
- actions and inner make-up

in order to create his picture of Big Beard.

Write 200–250 words in total.

Remember to put quotation marks round any words or phrases taken from the passage.

Planning and drafting

Focus on each of these features in order to make preparatory notes:

- Appearance
  Reread the section beginning
  He was a huge, wild-looking man…
  Look back at the activities on comparisons (page 22)

- Speech
  Reread the speeches beginning
  'He hasn't come!'
  Look back at the activities on exclamation marks, ellipsis points and suspension points (page 23)

- Actions and inner make-up
  Look back at the activities on actions and inner make-up (page 22) and anticlimax (page 23)

You could start:
Ben Elton first of all concentrates on Big Beard's size, using words such as 'huge', 'great' and 'strong'…

2 WRITING A DESCRIPTION

Write a description of an unusual or eccentric person as though you were introducing the character in a novel or short story.

Write 200–250 words.

Planning and drafting

Choose a character who has a burning passion about something. For example, they might be an over-enthusiastic door-to-door salesperson, a passionate collector of old bikes, a fanatical protester.

When you plan your writing, make sure that each of the following adds to your picture:

- Appearance
  (You could use comparisons and repetition)

- Speech
  (Check the rules for punctuating dialogue)

  You could use exclamation marks, ellipsis points and suspension points to get across the way the character is speaking

- Actions and inner make-up

You could model your opening sentences on Ben Elton's introduction to Big Beard:

Deep down in the forgotten basement of a city school sat X. He was a tiny, shrivelled little man…

HIGHER TIER TASKS

1 ANALYSING THE LANGUAGE

Explain how Ben Elton creates a comic character.

Planning and drafting

Look at the way Ben Elton creates a setting for his character in the opening paragraph.

Note how he pays attention to Big Beard's:

- appearance
- speech
- actions and inner make-up

Study in detail:

- punctuation of dialogue (e.g. ellipsis points, suspension points, exclamation marks)

Consider his use of:

- anticlimax

You could begin:

In order to introduce Big Beard, Ben Elton first of all establishes the environment in which the character is to be found…

2 INTRODUCING A COMIC CHARACTER

Write a section from a comic novel in which a new character is introduced.

Use the model of Ben Elton's introduction of Big Beard: make your character someone who takes himself or herself very seriously, but whose whole appearance, behaviour and personality are presented comically.

You could structure the description so that it moves, as Ben Elton's does, towards anticlimax.

Aliens, ghosts & corpses

In this unit you will:

- compare three pieces of fiction
- examine the different functions of dialogue
- write to imagine, explore and entertain

WRITING TO IMAGINE

In this extract from the television comedy series *Red Dwarf*, the emergency shuttle
Starbug is pursuing its mother ship through space, crewed by Lister (a human), Rimmer
(once a human, now a hologram), the Cat (part human, part feline) and a robot, Kryten.

RED DWARF – Primordial Soup
by Grant Naylor

KRYTEN: Suggest we begin debriefing. Mr Rimmer?

RIMMER: Thank you, Kryten. Gentlemen, as we're all aware, we have lost Red Dwarf. This is not the time for small-minded, petty recrimination. The time for that is when Lister is court-martialled after we get back to Earth. 5

LISTER: I didn't lose it.

RIMMER: You're the one who parked it, Lister. You're the one who couldn't remember which planetoid you'd left it around.

LISTER: Yeah, but they all look the same, those little blue-green planetoids. They're all sort of little, blue-green and 10 planetoidy.

KRYTEN: Sirs, please, there's no advantage in finger-pointing. We didn't lose Red Dwarf. Red Dwarf was stolen. By persons … or life forms unknown.

CAT: Who would steal a gigantic red trash can with no brakes 15 and three million years on the clock?

KRYTEN: Rogue droids … Genetically engineered life forms … Figments of Mr Lister's imagination made solid by some weird space ray. Who knows? The important thing is, after two hundred years of following their vapour trail, 20 we have them.

LISTER: What d'you mean?

KRYTEN: *clears some breakfast things off the scanner screen.*

KRYTEN: They've been forced to make a massive detour to circumnavigate this asteroid belt. However, *Starbug* is small enough to negotiate its way directly through the middle. For 25 the first time in two centuries, we have the opportunity to head them off at the pass, as it were, and recover Holly.

CAT: Well, what are we waiting for?

RIMMER: Without deflectors? What about Space Corps Directive one-seven-four-two? 30

KRYTEN: One-seven-four-two? 'No member of the Corps should ever report for active duty in a ginger toupee'? Thanks for reminding us of that regulation, sir. But is it really that pertinent in this particular situation?

RIMMER: One-seven-four-*three*, then. 35

KRYTEN: Oh, I *see*. 'No registered vessel should attempt to transverse an asteroid belt without deflectors.'

RIMMER: Yes? God, he's pedantic.

LISTER: Rimmer, check out the supply situation. (*Indicates computer printout.*) Your hologram's on battery back-up. 40 We've only got oxygen for three months: water, if we drink re-cyc, seven weeks. And worst of all, we're down to our last two thousand poppadoms. We're in trouble, big time.

RIMMER: You know how unstable these belts are. Rogue asteroids … meteor storms. One direct hit on that plexi- 45 glass viewscreen, and our innards will be turned inside out quicker than a pair of Lister's old underpants.

LISTER: We're out of options, man. We're taking her in.

KRYTEN: Recommend the Cat pilots. His superior reflexes and nasal intuition will give us our best chance. 50

CAT, LISTER and KRYTEN *stand to leave.*

RIMMER: For pity's sake, one breach in that hull, and we're people paté.

CAT: There's an old Cat proverb: 'It's better to live one hour as a tiger, than a whole lifetime as a worm.'

RIMMER: There's an old human saying: 'Whoever heard of a 55 wormskin rug?'

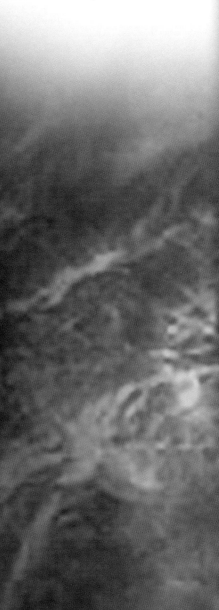

WRITING TO EXPLORE

This extract is near the opening of Oscar Wilde's short story *The Canterville Ghost*, published in 1887. Canterville Chase, an ancient country house in England, has been bought by an American, Hiram B Otis, despite warnings that the place is haunted. When the Otis family arrive to take possession, they are greeted by the housekeeper, Mrs Umney…

THE CANTERVILLE GHOST

Standing on the steps to receive them was an old woman, neatly dressed in black silk, with a white cap and apron. This was Mrs. Umney, the housekeeper, whom Mrs. Otis, at Lady Canterville's earnest request, had consented to keep on in her former position. She made them each a low curtsey as they alighted, and said in a quaint, old-fashioned manner, 'I bid you welcome to Canterville Chase.' Following her, they passed through the fine Tudor hall into the library, a long, low room, panelled in black oak, at the end of which was a large stained-glass window. Here they found tea laid out for them, and, after taking off their wraps, they sat down and began to look round, while Mrs. Umney waited on them.

Suddenly Mrs. Otis caught sight of a dull red stain on the floor just by the fireplace and, quite unconscious of what it really signified, said to Mrs. Umney, 'I am afraid something has been spilt there.'

'Yes, madam,' replied the old housekeeper in a low voice, 'blood has been spilt on that spot.'

'How horrid,' cried Mrs. Otis; 'I don't at all care for bloodstains in a sitting room. It must be removed at once.'

The old woman smiled, and answered in the same low, mysterious voice, 'It is the blood of Lady Eleanore de Canterville, who was murdered on that very spot by her own husband, Sir Simon de Canterville, in 1575. Sir Simon survived her nine years, and disappeared suddenly under very mysterious circumstances. His body has never been discovered, but his guilty spirit still haunts the Chase. The bloodstain has been much admired by tourists and others, and cannot be removed.'

'That is all nonsense,' cried Washington Otis; 'Pinkerton's Champion Stain Remover and Paragon Detergent will clean it up in no time,' and before the terrified housekeeper could interfere he had fallen upon his knees, and was rapidly scouring the floor with a small stick of what looked like a black cosmetic. In a few moments no trace of the bloodstain could be seen.

'I knew Pinkerton would do it,' he exclaimed triumphantly, as he looked round at his admiring family; but no sooner had he said these words than a terrible flash of lightning lit up the sombre room, a fearful peal of thunder made them all start to their feet, and Mrs. Umney fainted.

'What a monstrous climate!' said the American Minister calmly, as he lit a long cheroot. 'I guess the old country is so overpopulated that they have not enough decent weather for everybody. I have always been of opinion that emigration is the only thing for England.'

'My dear Hiram,' cried Mrs. Otis, 'what can we do with a woman who faints?'

'Charge it to her like breakages,' answered the Minister; 'she won't faint after that;' and in a few moments Mrs. Umney certainly came to.

There was no doubt, however, that she was extremely upset, and she sternly warned Mr. Otis to beware of some trouble coming to the house.

'I have seen things with my own eyes, sir,' she said, 'that would make any Christian's hair stand on end, and many and many a night I have not closed my eyes in sleep for the awful things that are done here.' Mr. Otis, however, and his wife warmly assured the honest soul that they were not afraid of ghosts, and, after invoking the blessings of Providence on her new master and mistress, and making arrangements for an increase of salary, the old housekeeper tottered off to her own room.

Lindsey Davis has written a series of crime novels set in ancient Rome and featuring a detective called Falco. In this extract from *Last Act in Palmyra*, Falco and his girlfriend Helena Justina have followed two men up a mountain path, only to discover one of them floating in a reservoir…

Last Act in Palmyra

If I had had any sense I would still have convinced myself he was just bathing peacefully. We could have turned away without staring too closely, then a rapid stroll downhill would have taken us back to our lodging. We should have done that anyway; I should have kept us out of it.

He was almost submerged. His head was under water.

Only something bulky, caught under his clothing, was holding him afloat.

We were both already running forwards. 'Unbelievable!'

Helena marvelled bitterly as she scrambled down from the sacrificial platform. 'Just two days here, and look what you've found.'

I had reached the rock-formed tank ahead of her. I lowered myself over the edge into the water, trying to forget I couldn't swim. The water came above my waist. The chill made me gasp. It was a large cistern, about four feet deep: ample to drown in.

The swirl of water as I entered caused the body to move and start sinking. I managed to grab at the garments that had helped buoy him up. Arriving a few moments later, we could have avoided this trouble. He would have been lying out of sight on the bottom as the drowned do – assuming, of course, that drowning was the real cause of his death.

Slowly I pulled my burden to the side. An inflated goatskin floated out from under his tangled cloak as I manoeuvred him. Helena leant down and held his feet, then helped me haul him half out of the water. She had the nice manners of any senator's daughter, but no qualms about helping out in an emergency.

I climbed out again. We completed the operation. He was heavy, but together we managed to remove him from the cistern and flop him face down. Without more ado I turned his head sideways. I leaned on his ribs for a respectable period, trying to revive him. I noticed my first shove seemed to expel air rather than water. And there was none of the froth I had seen with other corpses who had drowned. We get plenty in the Tiber.

Helena waited, at first standing above me with the wind blowing her clothes against her body while she gazed thoughtfully around the high plateau. Then she walked to the far side of the cistern, examining the ground.

As I worked I was thinking things through. Helena and I had been climbing quite slowly, and our pause for recreation had taken up time. But for that, we would have arrived at the crucial moment But for that, we would be sharing the fabulous windswept views with two men, both alive.

We had come too late for this one. I knew even before I started that my efforts would be useless. Still, I gave him the courtesy. I might need to be resuscitated by a stranger myself one day.

Eventually I rolled him over on his back and stood up again.

He was fortyish. Too fat and flabby. A wide, berry-brown face with a heavy chin and thuggish neck. The face looked mottled under its tan. Short arms; broad hands. He had not troubled himself with shaving today. Lank, rather long hair merged with coarse black eyebrows and dripped sluggishly on to the rock floor beneath him. He was dressed in a long, loose-weave brown tunic, with a more sun-bleached cloak tangled wetly around him. Shoes knotted on top of the foot, a toe-thong apiece. No weapon. Something bulky under his clothes at the waist, however – a writing tablet, not written on.

Helena held out something else she had found beside the cistern – a round-bottomed flask on a plaited leather cord. Its wicker casing, stained brown with wine, made me pull out the stopper: wine had been in it recently, though only a couple of drops shook out on to my palm. Maybe the goatskin had contained wine too. Being tipsy could explain how he came to be overpowered.

Language in context

The power of language

Key features of the texts are:

1 the language of *imagine*, *explore* and *entertain* texts

2 genre

1 THE LANGUAGE OF WRITING TO IMAGINE, EXPLORE AND ENTERTAIN

Writing to **imagine**, to **explore** and to **entertain** all involve the creative and literary use of language. They are the kinds of writing found, for example, in novels, short stories, poetry and play scripts.

Writing to imagine: characters and dialogue

Red Dwarf and *The Canterville Ghost* are good examples of the ways in which character can be revealed through dialogue.

a) Reread the *Red Dwarf* extract. Write down what we learn about:

- Lister, from his excuses (lines 6–11: *I didn't lose it … planetoidy.*)
- Kryten, from his interruption (12–14: *Sirs, please … unknown.*)
- Kryten, from his exchange with Rimmer (29–38: *Without deflectors?… pedantic.*)
- Lister, from his analysis of the situation (39–43: *Rimmer, check out … big time.*)
- Rimmer, from his response to the Cat's proverb (53–6: *There's an old … wormskin rug?*)

For example, you could say:
Lister's excuses show, firstly, that he is extremely careless and neglectful; secondly, that he is not the usual kind of expert hi-tech astronaut found in science fiction space adventures…

b) Reread the extract from *The Canterville Ghost*.

- What do Mrs Umney's speech and actions reveal about her attitude to the fact that Canterville Chase is haunted? Does she dislike the idea or rather enjoy it? Look, for example, at: *The old woman smiled… 'The bloodstain has been much admired…' Mrs. Umney fainted…. 'I have seen things with my own eyes'*

- Hiram has a very different perspective on the supernatural to Mrs Umney. How is this conveyed through what he says? Does he believe in ghosts; and does he sympathise with Mrs Umney's viewpoint? Look, for example, at: *'What a monstrous climate!'* *'Charge it to her … she won't faint after that'* *Mr. Otis … and his wife warmly assured…*

c) The extract from *The Canterville Ghost* is almost wholly in dialogue. The one significant exception is the concluding sentence (*Mr. Otis, however…*).

- Redraft that sentence as it might appear in a play version of the story. You might begin: HIRAM: *Let me reassure you, Mrs Umney…*
- Write a paragraph to explain why you think Wilde chose not to use dialogue in that concluding sentence.

Writing to explore: language and theme

Towards the end of the nineteenth century, when Oscar Wilde wrote *The Canterville Ghost*, many writers were exploring the differences between the 'Old World' of Europe, with all its history and traditions, and the 'New World' of the United States, with its fresh and upbeat way of looking at things.

d) Explain how this theme is brought out, by contrasting the language of Mrs Umney with that of Washington Otis.

For example, look at Mrs Umney's explanation of the bloodstain (*It is the blood … cannot be removed*) and contrast it with Washington's:

- optimism (*That is all nonsense…*)
- practicality (*he had fallen upon his knees…*)
- enjoyment of the language of advertising (*will clean it up in no time*)

How is this theme developed through Mrs Umney's and Hiram's different reactions to the thunder and lightning?

Writing to entertain:
sentences and narrative viewpoint

> A **simple sentence** contains only one **clause**.

Examples of simple sentences in the extract from *Last Act in Palmyra* are:
He was almost submerged.
Slowly I pulled my burden to the side.
I climbed out again.

> Sentences which do not conform to a regular pattern are called **minor sentences**.

Examples include:
Too flat and flabby.
A wide, berry-brown face with a heavy chin and thuggish neck.
No weapon.

e) Write a short paragraph to explain the effect of the simple and minor sentences in Falco's description of the body (*He was fortyish … not written on.*). For example, do they:

- make the account sound like the notes a detective might make?
- give the impression of Falco as a man of action?
- help us to gain a quick impression of the important details?

2 GENRE

> **Genre** is the name given to a particular kind of writing with its own typical features.

To remind yourself about genre, look back at page 10.

a) Write two or three paragraphs to explain which genre each of the extracts on pages 26–9 belongs to. In your answer, use the quotations below to show how (a) the language and (b) the plot are typical of each genre:

Red Dwarf
- *Rogue droids … Genetically engineered life forms*
- *some weird space ray.*
- *to circumnavigate this asteroid belt.*
- *Your hologram's on battery back-up.*
- *We've only got oxygen for three months*

The Canterville Ghost
- *and answered in the same low, mysterious voice*
- *'It is the blood of Lady Eleanore de Canterville'*
- *a terrible flash of lightning lit up the sombre room*
- *'I have seen things with my own eyes, sir'*

Last Act in Palmyra
- *If I had had any sense I would still have convinced myself he was just bathing peacefully.*
- *assuming, of course, that drowning was the real cause of his death.*
- *And there was none of the froth I had seen with other corpses who had drowned.*
- *Then she walked to the far side of the cistern, examining the ground.*
- *We had come too late for this one.*

Compare and contrast

1 WRITING DIALOGUE

Write a page of dialogue between three or four people that reveals something of the character and personality of each one.

Planning and drafting

- Think carefully about who the **people** are and what you want to reveal about their characters and personalities.

  Try to create people who are very different.

  For example, one might be bad-tempered, another cheerful; one young, another old.

- Place them in a particular **setting** and create a **situation** that they are faced with.

  Think up a setting and situation which are challenging or awkward.

  For example, a lift that has broken down between floors, a windswept station platform late at night, a surprise birthday party that is going horribly wrong…

> For example, you could start:
>
> *The lift had now been stuck for half an hour and the temperature in the cramped compartment was rising. Sir Toby Beamish, managing director of Beamish Enterprises, could contain his impatience no longer…*

2 WRITING IN A GENRE

One of the most popular of all genres is stories of the supernatural. Write the opening of a ghost story.

Planning and drafting

To give you some ideas, here are some openings of ghost stories. You could build your own writing around one of them, or use them for ideas.

- *The little green stoppered bottle had been waiting in the earth a long time for someone to find it. Ned Challis found it.* (The Shadow Cage, Philippa Pearce)
- *Such ordinary things make me afraid. Sunshine. Sharp shadows on grass. White roses. Children with red hair. And the name – Harry. Such an ordinary name.* (Harry, Rosemary Timperley)
- *The scene amidst which Clayton told his last story comes back very vividly to my mind.* (The Inexperienced Ghost, HG Wells)
- *'There's someone coming down in the lift, Mummy!' 'No, my darling, you're wrong, there isn't.' 'But I can see him through the bars – a tall gentleman.' 'You think you can, but it's only a shadow. Now, you'll see, the lift's empty.' And it always was.* (Someone in the Lift, LP Hartley)

1 WRITING ABOUT GENRE

Read the following extracts. They are both openings of tales from a genre which might be called ghost stories, or stories of the supernatural.

Write a passage of 200–250 words to show how both the language and the plot help to make clear to the reader which genre the extracts belong to.

> You could start:
>
> *There are a number of features which show that these extracts are from stories of the supernatural. To begin with…*

Housebound

R Chetwynd-Hayes

He, if indeed that which remained of Charlie Wheatland could be designated as he, was most happy when he was in the woodwork. The wainscoting, the picture rails, the large wardrobe, the dressing-table, and sometimes the floor-boards; the coarse-grained pine, the tough oak, enabled him to spread out, to become as water on blotting paper, to dim down his never-sleeping consciousness to a gentle twilight. The walls were not so kind, the bricks and plaster did not absorb him so easily, and the thoughts of the room's occupants clung to the faded wallpaper like flies on a hot day.

The Dream House

Catherine Storr

What she didn't tell her mother was about her other dreams, the dreams of the latest of her dream houses. Always before, she had looked forward to visiting these houses, she had felt that they were friendly, and there was the wonderful moment when she was on the verge of exploring the unexpected rooms in them. But the house which was haunting her dreams now, though it was beautiful, was not friendly. It had begun to take on the proportions of a nightmare.

In that very first dream, she hadn't had time to discover more than that it was old and impressive, and she had seen a wide staircase sweeping up from the linked rooms on the ground floor to the long gallery above.

2 IMITATING THE STYLE

Write a page of dialogue spoken by the characters in *Red Dwarf*, *The Canterville Ghost* or *Last Act in Palmyra*.

You could choose to continue the existing scene or create a completely new one.

> Possible openings are:
> - *Kryten leant forward and tapped Lister politely on the shoulder. 'I hesitate to mention this, sir, and I wouldn't wish to spoil your cornflakes with tabasco, but…'*
> - *'That's the problem with these British ghosts,' said Hiram, emitting another cloud of smoke from his cheroot, 'no sense of humour…'*
> - *As Helena entered the bath-house, a pungent smell assailed her nostrils. 'Is that what I think it is?' Falco nodded.*

Self assess

These are the main language features that you have learned about in this section. Decide how confident you feel about:

- explaining what **genre** is and picking out a genre's typical features
- understanding the different ways in which a writer can make **comparisons**
- commenting on the ways in which **descriptive writing** often appeals to **the senses**

- understanding terms such as **metre**, **iambic pentameter** and **blank verse**
- identifying the effects Shakespeare achieves by varying the **pattern of stresses** in a line of verse
- giving examples of Shakespeare's **wordplay** and talking about its effects
- understanding what **imagery** is and how it is used

- commenting on the ways in which writers **describe a comic character** through their appearance, speech, actions and inner make-up
- understanding how a writer creates **comic dialogue** and **comic narrative**
- picking out **simple** and **minor sentences** and commenting on their use

What do you feel you need to revise?

Snow monster

In this unit you will:

- read two website pages about the Bigfoot
- examine the language of information texts
- write an information article

The following extracts are taken from websites. Both give information about the mysterious creature known in different parts of the world as the *yeti, abominable snowman, Sasquatch* or *Bigfoot*.

Bigfoot of North America

by Lee Krystek

If the Himalayas of Asia has its Yeti, the Pacific Northwest of America has its Bigfoot: a hairy, ape-like biped that stands seven to nine feet tall and weighs between 600 and 900 pounds.

Bigfoot, or as it's often called in Canada, the Sasquatch, is mentioned in several native American legends. In fact, the term 'Sasquatch' is Indian for 'hairy giant'. The first sighting of a Sasquatch by a white man apparently came in 1811 near what now is the town of Jasper, Alberta, Canada. A trader named David Thompson found some strange footprints, fourteen inches long and eight inches wide, with four toes, in the snow…

Rumours about the Sasquatch continued through to the end of the century. Then, in 1910, the murder of two miners, found with their heads cut off, was attributed to the creatures, though there was little supporting evidence that the killing wasn't human in origin.

In any case, the place of the murders, Nahanni Valley, in Canada, was changed to Headless Valley, because of the incident.

The year 1924 turned out to be a banner year in Bigfoot history… According to a Canadian lumberjack named Albert Ostman, he had been prospecting near Tobet Inlet when he was captured by a family of Bigfoots. The father and daughter guarded him while the mother and son prepared the meals…

Interest in Bigfoot began to pick up in the United States in 1958 when a bulldozer operator named Jerry Crew found enormous footprints around where he was working in Humboldt County, California. Crew made a cast of the footprint. A local newspaper ran the story of Crew and his footprint with a photo. The story was picked up by other papers and ran throughout the country. It was the picture of Crew holding the 'Bigfoot' that made the name stick.

In 1967 Roger Patterson and Bob Gimlin, Bigfoot buffs, announced they'd captured Bigfoot with a movie camera. They filmed a few seconds of an ape-like creature, apparently female, moving across a clearing near Bluff Creek in northern California. While the film is not perfectly clear, there is no mistaking the creature in the film for a common animal. The movie shows either a real Bigfoot, or a man in a clever costume…

www.unmuseum.org/bigfoot

Bigfoot, Sasquatch, Yeti...

by Paul Stonehill

During the 1900s, the *Colonist* newspaper in Victoria, British Columbia, ran several stories about people spotting 'monkey-men' in remote wooded areas. In the 1920s, British Columbia schoolteacher J. W. Burns wrote extensively in newspaper and magazine articles about reports of giant hairy creatures. Burns's writings were responsible for popularising the term 'Sasquatch', which he identified as a derivation from the language of the Coast Salish Indians. Sasquatch quickly became known among the general public of western Canada, long before tales of such a creature ever found notoriety in the United States.

Following the publicity surrounding Eric Shipton's 1951 photograph of a Yeti footprint, interest in Sasquatch increased dramatically. John Green, a newspaper publisher in British Columbia, began reporting Sasquatch sightings in 1955... Green became genuinely captivated by the creature, and his extensive compilation of stories and sightings made him the leading Sasquatch authority of his day.

One Sasquatch spotter Green interviewed was William Roe, a trapper, who claimed to have a close encounter with a female of the species in 1955, while hunting on British Columbia's Mica Mountain.

'The thought came to me that if I shot it I would probably have a specimen of great interest to scientists the world over,' Roe said. But he couldn't bring himself to pull the trigger on his rifle. 'Although I have called the creature it, I felt now that it was a human being, and I knew I would never forgive myself if I killed it,' he said.

The publication of Roe's account would later inspire another man to step forward with his own Sasquatch experience, which he said had happened more than thirty years before. Albert Ostman, a 64-year-old retired lumberman from British Columbia, went public in 1957 with a tale he had kept to himself since 1924, for fear of being ridiculed. Ostman's story was the most dramatic report ever in the history of Bigfoot studies: a first-person account of abduction by Sasquatch.

While on a camping trip near Vancouver Island, Ostman found that something had disturbed his supplies and food on two nights in a row...

Then one night Ostman was shaken awake to find himself being indelicately carried away inside his sleeping bag. The opening of the sleeping bag was held shut, and Ostman had no choice but to be dragged along the forest ground for what he estimated to be 25 miles, nearly suffocating. After what seemed like a three-hour ordeal, he was thrown to the ground in a heap, and emerged to find himself in the company of four Sasquatches. Ostman described them as a family, with a father and a mother and their pair of offspring, one male and one female. He indicated that the adult male, his kidnapper, was over eight feet tall and powerfully built, covered in dark hair all over. The children, though smaller, were still about seven feet tall.

Ostman said the Sasquatches chattered amongst themselves in a seemingly intelligent language, and although they did not hurt or threaten him, they were determined not to let him leave. Their lair was inside a small valley enclosed by cliffs, and the adult male stood guard at the only apparent entry passage. Ostman suggested that he may have been selected as a prospective mate for the young female.

Ostman claimed that he was held captive for a period of six days. In that time he formed a tentative bond with the younger male, who became fond of sampling Ostman's snuff. That gave Ostman an idea. He offered his snuff to the adult male, which impulsively dumped the entire container into his mouth. The tobacco rush incapacitated the big Sasquatch in short order, making him writhe on the ground in overwhelming discomfort. Ostman seized the opportunity to escape...

www.n2.net/prey/bigfoot

in short order   very quickly

Language in context

The power of language

Key features of the texts are:

1. chronological writing
2. parenthesis
3. active and passive

1. CHRONOLOGICAL WRITING

Chronological writing organises events in the order in which they happened.

a) Reread both extracts and note down all the stages in the history of Bigfoot sightings and reports. Then draw up a **timeline** and enter dates and sightings from both extracts **in chronological order**.

- As the articles do not record sightings by native Americans, start off with David Thompson's in 1811.
- Albert Ostman's story could have two entries: one for when it took place, another for when he made it public.

b) Rate these different kinds of writing on a scale of 1 to 5 (1 lowest), according to how far they would organise their material **chronologically**. Add a comment to explain your decision in each case. For example, a booklet of bus timetables might have some sections arranged chronologically, and others not. One has been completed to start you off.

Kind of writing	1–5	Comment
a television and radio listings magazine (e.g. *Radio Times*)	4	*Although each day's programmes are listed chronologically, some of the magazine is devoted to articles and features.*
a set of instructions on how to set up and operate a video		
an encyclopedia article on eclipses		
a chapter on the First World War in a school History textbook		
a chapter on volcanoes in a school Geography textbook		
a write-up of a Science experiment in school		
an entry in a personal diary		
a police report on a road accident		
a newspaper report of an Olympic long-jump event		
a newspaper column headed *Yesterday in Parliament*		
a booklet giving timetables for a rail network		

2 PARENTHESIS

A **parenthesis** is a word, phrase or clause inserted into a sentence to provide additional information.

A parenthesis can be placed between **commas**, or **dashes**, or **brackets** (which are themselves sometimes known as **parentheses** – the plural form of the word).

Parenthesis is common in information texts like the two extracts about Bigfoot. It is used to add different kinds of information, such as:

- a more specific descriptive detail: *Jones,* **a retired police officer**, *was the first to spot the escape vehicle.*
- a time or date: *Two years later,* **in the middle of January**, *it suddenly collapsed.*
- an interesting fact: *The team,* **known locally as 'the Terminators'**, *is not noted for its skill.*

a) Use the two extracts to write a paragraph explaining and illustrating some of the uses that parenthesis can have in an information text. Look, for example, at the following sentences:

Lee Krystek

Bigfoot, or as it's often called…	(paragraph 2)
Then, in 1910…	(paragraph 3)
In any case, the place…	(paragraph 3)
In 1967 Roger Patterson…	(paragraph 6)
They filmed a few seconds…	(paragraph 6)

Paul Stonehill

John Green, a newspaper…	(paragraph 2)
One Sasquatch spotter…	(paragraph 3)
Albert Ostman, a 64-year-old…	(paragraph 5)
He indicated that…	(paragraph 7)

b) Write a brief (100 word) report for a local newspaper on a sporting event. Use parenthesis to add:

- specific descriptive details: *Rutherford, who usually plays in the back four, was substituted after…*
- times: *Then, ten minutes into the second half, came the moment…*
- interesting facts: *The Borough manager, whose sister captains the Northern Counties eleven, then took the bold step of…*

3 ACTIVE AND PASSIVE

In an **active** sentence, the subject performs the action; in a **passive** sentence, the subject is on the receiving end of the action.

For example:

The Sasquatch **dragged** Ostman through the forest (active).

The Sasquatch **was affected** by the snuff (passive).

The passive enables the writer to describe an action without stating who the subject is.

It can be used, for example:

- when the receiver of the action is more important than the doer (e.g. *she was struck by a car*)
- when the doer is not known (e.g. *the house was burgled during the night*)
- when the writer does not want to reveal who the doer is (e.g. *the handle was turned slowly from the inside*)
- when the doer is unimportant (e.g. *bicycles must not be left in the entrance hall*)
- when the doer is obvious (e.g. *Lincoln was re-elected*)
- in scientific writing which needs to be impersonal (e.g. *the substance was subjected to a battery of tests*)

a) Write down why you think the passive might have been used in each of the following sentences from Lee Krystek's article. For each sentence, think about the six reasons listed above and decide which ones apply.

Bigfoot, or as **it's often called** *in Canada, the Sasquatch,* **is mentioned** *in several native American legends.*

Then, in 1910, the murder of two miners, found with their heads cut off, **was attributed** *to the creatures*

In any case, the place of the murders, Nahanni Valley, in Canada, **was changed** *to Headless Valley, because of the incident.*

The story **was picked up** *by other papers and ran throughout the country.*

Writing to inform

FOUNDATION TIER TASKS

1 SUMMARISING THE BIGFOOT HISTORY

Use the two extracts to summarise the sightings and reports of Bigfoot.

Use your own words as far as possible. Write 200–250 words.

Planning and drafting

Use these points to help you plan your summary.

- Base your summary on the timeline that you created for question 1a on page 36.
- Begin with David Thompson in 1811.
- Do not go into too much detail about Albert Ostman's experience.

> You could start:
>
> *Although several legends of the native Americans contain stories of Bigfoot, the first recorded discovery of Bigfoot prints was in 1811…*

2 WRITING AN ACCOUNT

Rewrite the account of Albert Ostman's abduction by Sasquatches as it might appear in his autobiography, *Abducted by Sasquatches.*

Planning and drafting

- Write in the first person:
  In 1924 I was on a camping trip near Vancouver Island…
- Use the facts from Paul Stonehill's account:
  Suddenly I was awoken by someone shaking me…
- Add details of your own to make the account dramatic and gripping:
  My back was severely bruised by the journey…
- Let the reader know how you felt:
  Imagine my horror when it dawned on me that I might have been selected as a prospective mate for the young female…

HIGHER TIER TASKS

1 ANALYSING THE LANGUAGE

Explain how both writers, through their content and use of language, inform us about the history of Bigfoot.

Refer among other things to the use of chronological writing, parenthesis and the mixture of active and passive sentences.

You could start:
The two writers use a number of different methods to inform us about Bigfoot. Lee Krystek, for example…

2 EVALUATING THE EVIDENCE

Write an article for a magazine entitled *Does Bigfoot Exist?*

First, read the account below by Paul Stonehill about Bigfoot enthusiast Roger Patterson. Having written a book about Bigfoot, Patterson set off to film one.

Planning and drafting

Your article could contain:

- a history of claimed Bigfoot sightings (perhaps based on the timeline you drew up for question 1a, page 36)
- a summary of the Patterson story and the arguments which followed
- your conclusions, based on the evidence, as to whether Bigfoot exists

You could start:
Although there have been many claimed Bigfoot sightings, hard evidence has been in short supply…

On October 20, 1967, Patterson and his friend Bob Gimlin were riding on horseback in the wilds of California's Bluff Creek valley, with Patterson carrying a rented 16mm camera to shoot some atmospheric footage for his planned film. He ended up filming a lot more than just scenery. Patterson and Gimlin spotted a huge, dark-furred, bipedal creature hunched over in the middle of a creek. The beast rose to a full height that Patterson estimated at seven feet, four inches, and began walking toward the woods. Thrown to the ground after his horse reared up in fright, Patterson anxiously yanked the movie camera from his saddlebag and began shooting. The day's filming had left him with only 28 feet of film in the camera, but he managed to record the alleged Bigfoot's image briefly before it fled from view…

In the ensuing three decades, the 952 frames of Patterson's Bigfoot film have been submitted to all manner of examination and analysis… The creature has been classified as female, because of its apparent breasts… the exact way in which it moves its neck, and its unusual method of distributing its weight as it strided, have led many to conclude that this could not be a man in a suit.

But many others feel certain that Patterson's Bigfoot was a fake. Being established in the "Bigfoot business," Patterson stood to profit from fabricating film footage of the creature. Bigfoot expert John Napier pointed out that the footprint casts were physiologically inconsistent with the height of the creature and the length of its stride as shown in the film. If the creature was a fake, everyone agrees that it was a remarkably skilful one. The only known source of such a high quality of costume and makeup in 1967 was the movie special effects industry, and in fact there is strong evidence that this Bigfoot came from Hollywood.

After lengthy investigations and interviews, journalist Mark Chorivinsky has found that the consensus among the movie-effects industry professionals is that the film depicts a prankster in a skilfully crafted costume. In fact, many state that the falsity of the Patterson film has been common knowledge in the business for years.

Looking into deep space

In this unit you will:

- read an article about an astronomical telescope
- examine the language of explanatory texts
- write an explanatory article

The following article is from *Guardian Education*, 29 January 2002.

Earlier this month the partly British-owned Gemini South telescope in Chile came into operation. Ten times more powerful than Hubble, it will peer back to the birth of stars.

By **JOHN CRACE**

Looking into deep space

Situated on the summit of Cerro Pachon in the Chilean Andes, away from sources of terrestrial light and pollution, the Gemini South telescope is identical to Gemini North in Hawaii. The UK has an almost quarter share in the two telescopes, which allow astronomers to view the entire sky in both the northern and southern hemispheres. The Gemini telescopes produce images of the universe in the infrared waveband. This allows astronomers to see through the cosmic dust that obscures star-forming regions and galaxies to reveal the secrets of the birth of stars. Each telescope has an optical capacity with ten times the light-gathering power of the Hubble space telescope.

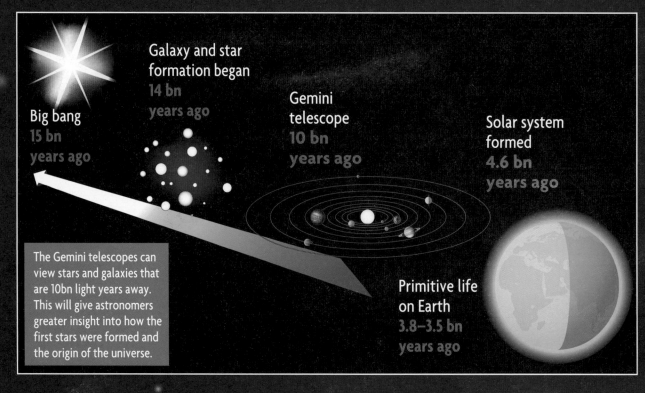

Big bang
15 bn
years ago

Galaxy and star formation began
14 bn
years ago

Gemini telescope
10 bn
years ago

Solar system formed
4.6 bn
years ago

Primitive life on Earth
3.8–3.5 bn
years ago

The Gemini telescopes can view stars and galaxies that are 10bn light years away. This will give astronomers greater insight into how the first stars were formed and the origin of the universe.

Adaptive optics

Gemini compensates for the blurring of images (star twinkle) caused by the Earth's atmosphere by using adaptive optics (AO) instruments. The Gemini AO system adjusts the shape of the mirror up to one hundred times per second to counteract the ripples in the lightwaves caused by atmospheric turbulence. This helps produce images as sharp as those from space.

Discoveries

Gemini North has revealed surprising conditions surrounding a supermassive black hole at the core of an active galaxy, and the gas and dust encircling stars where early planetary systems might be forming. Other observations have shown the centre of our Milky Way galaxy in unprecedented detail, unexpected conditions at the core of a distant active galaxy, the closest brown dwarf (or failed star) ever seen around a sun-like star, and a spectacular image dubbed 'the perfect spiral galaxy'.

Deepest-ever infrared picture of a section of the 'Trapezium' region of the Orion Nebula, taken by the Gemini South telescope

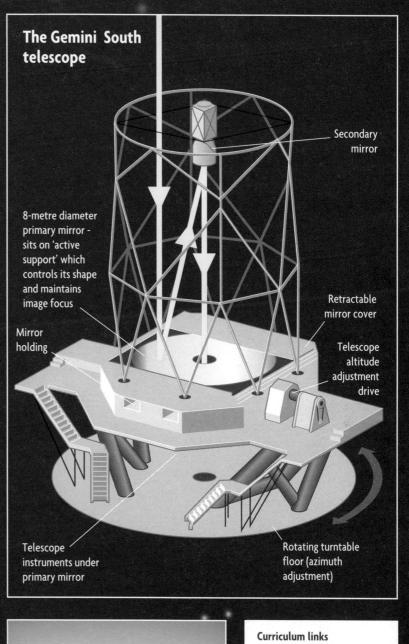

The Gemini South telescope

Secondary mirror

8-metre diameter primary mirror – sits on 'active support' which controls its shape and maintains image focus

Mirror holding

Retractable mirror cover

Telescope altitude adjustment drive

Telescope instruments under primary mirror

Rotating turntable floor (azimuth adjustment)

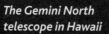

The Gemini North telescope in Hawaii

Curriculum links

Double Award Science KS4, SC4 Physical processes: The solar system and the wider universe

a)   the relative positions and sizes of planets, stars and other bodies in the universe [for example comets, meteors, galaxies, black holes]

b)   that gravity acts as a force throughout the universe

c)   how stars evolve over a long timescale

Language in context

The power of language

Key features of the text are:

1. the combination of text and image
2. nouns and determiners
3. awareness of audience

1   THE COMBINATION OF TEXT AND IMAGE

> Explanatory texts will often use a combination of **text** (words) and **image** (photographs and illustrations).

Looking into deep space can be divided into various sections. Each section contains a different style of illustration, using either artwork or photographs.

a) Study each of the four illustrations and write answers to the following questions:

- *the photograph, centre*
  Why is a photograph more effective than artwork to illustrate the main text?

- *the artwork, top-right*
  What are the advantages of representing the telescope in an annotated drawing, rather than a photograph?

- *the artwork, bottom-left*
  Explain how the artwork depicting the history of the universe helps to support and expand upon the text in the box, bottom-left (*The Gemini telescopes … of the universe*).

2   NOUNS AND DETERMINERS

> A **noun** is a word which labels a person, place or thing. The way a noun is used in a sentence is decided by **determiners** such as the **articles** *a*, *an*, *the* or words such as *some, those, this, that.*

Nouns

Explanatory writing such as *Looking into deep space* depends very heavily on nouns to convey the key ideas. Nouns are sometimes divided into **common nouns**, **proper nouns** and **abstract nouns**.

a) Copy this table and complete it with further examples from the text of each type of noun:

Type of noun	Definition	Examples from the text	Further examples from the text
common nouns	the labels given to people, places and things *in general*	*summit* *telescope*	
proper nouns	the names of *particular* people, places, things	*Cerro Pachon* *Andes*	
abstract nouns	concepts, ideas and emotions	*sources* *secrets*	

It is sometimes difficult to classify nouns in this way. For example, what decision did you make about words such as *hemispheres*, *universe* and *waveband*: are they common nouns in this text or abstract nouns? Compare your completed table with someone else and discuss your decisions.

Compare the main text (*Situated on … spiral galaxy*) with the text surrounding the illustration of the Gemini South telescope (*8-metre diameter…* etc). Which type of noun is used most often in each of the two sections of text – common noun, proper noun or abstract noun? Write a sentence or two to explain your findings.

Determiners

b) As you have seen, *Looking into deep space* can be divided into sections. Find the two sections of the page in which the nouns are not accompanied by determiners (such as the articles *a*, *an* or *the*). Write a short paragraph to explain the rule or convention which tells you where you normally do *not* use determiners in explanatory texts.

3 AWARENESS OF AUDIENCE

> **Audience** is the term given to the people who are expected to read or see a text – the group to whom that text is addressed. The term can refer to readers, listeners, film/television viewers, or users of information technology.

Anybody writing to explain a concept has to ask some basic questions about their audience. For example:

What can I expect my audience to **know and understand** already about this topic?

What can I expect them **not** to know or understand?

a) The writer of *Looking into deep space* expects that the audience will understand:

- some challenging vocabulary (such as *terrestrial*)
- certain difficult scientific terms (such as *infrared waveband*)
- important scientific references (such as *Hubble space telescope*)

In pairs, find further examples from the article of each of these three features of the text.

b) *Looking into deep space* was published on the back page of *Guardian Education*, a weekly supplement of a major national newspaper. In pairs, discuss who you think the intended audience are. For example, think about age groups and interest groups.

Take into account:

- the examples of vocabulary and references that you have just found
- the combination of text and image
- the box in the bottom-right of the page

Writing to explain

FOUNDATION TIER TASKS

1 SUMMARISING THE EXPLANATION

Study *Looking into deep space* again.
Then summarise in your own words:

- what the Gemini telescopes can do
- why they are better than other telescopes

Use your own words as far as possible.
Write 200–250 words in total.

Planning and drafting

The task is in two parts. Use these points in order to make preparatory notes:

Part 1: what the Gemini telescopes can do

Look at:

- the box, bottom-left
  (*The Gemini telescopes can…*)
- the information in the main text, to do with:

  viewing the entire sky (*…which allow astronomers to view…*)

  producing images in the infrared waveband (*This allows astronomers to see…*)

  achieving sharp images (*This helps produce images…*)

  the achievements of the telescopes so far (*Gemini North has revealed…*)

Part 2: why they are better than other telescopes

Look at:

- information in the main text, to do with:

  their power (*Each telescope has…*)

  the way they avoid the blurring of images (*Gemini compensates…*)

You could start:

In January 2002, a powerful new telescope came into operation…

2 COMBINING TEXT AND IMAGE

Study the artwork and text in the bottom left-hand corner of *Looking into deep space* which show how Gemini telescopes can view stars and galaxies that are 10 billion light years away.

Use that as a model to design a poster for a school classroom which explains **How fossils are formed**.

Planning and drafting

- First read the text below. This will provide you with the essential facts.
- Then do a set of rough sketches which can be combined with some text.
- Select the information you need and redraft it in your own words.
- Make sure that the text and the illustrations combine to explain clearly how fossils are formed.
- Produce a final version.

FOSSILS

Imagine a shellfish living on the seabed. After it dies, it is covered in sand. Soon its soft insides have rotted away, leaving only the shell. In the next few thousand years, more layers of sand build up on top of the shell, eventually forming sandstone. The shell is by this time deep inside the sandstone. Next, mineral solutions seep through the sandstone and harden the shell. At the same time, the empty space inside the shell (where the soft insides used to be) becomes filled up with crystal deposits. In time the shell is turned to rock.

Millions of years later the old seabed is now dry land. The sandstone is eroded or quarried, and the ancient shell is discovered, now a fossil.

mineral solution	liquid which will later form rock
seep	soak through
deposits	material that has collected there
eroded	worn away
quarried	dug up (for use in building etc)

HIGHER TIER TASKS

 ## 1 ANALYSING THE TEXT

How effective is the explanatory text *Looking into deep space*? Write an analysis of the article, giving your own opinions supported by close reference to the text and images.

Planning and drafting

In making preparatory notes, ask yourself the following questions:

- What were the **topic** and **purpose** of the page?
  (What did its creators want to explain?)
- Who were their intended **audience**?
  (What did they expect them to know and understand?)
- How effective was the chosen **form**?
  (Think about the combination of text and image.)

You could start:
The creators of Looking into deep space *set out to explain the workings of…*

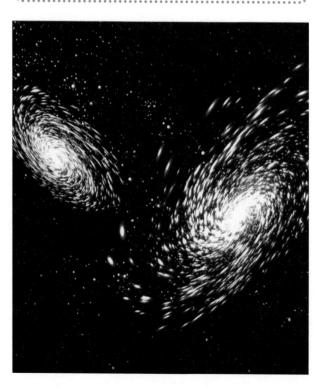

2 CREATING YOUR OWN EXPLANATORY ARTICLE

Select a topic that you are currently studying in one of your GCSE subjects and plan an explanatory article on it modelled on *Looking into deep space*.

- Write the text in full.
- Describe the illustrations that will be an important part of the page.
- Explain how the text and images will combine to maximum effect.

Planning and drafting

Purpose

- The purpose will be to give a clear and interesting explanation of a topic about which general readers will know only a little.

Topic

- Select a topic that you have already been studying. It could be from any subject: History (e.g. the Spanish Armada), Geography (e.g. the Great Barrier Reef), RE (e.g. the Eightfold Path in Buddhism), Science (e.g. evolution) or Art (e.g. Picasso).

Audience

- Decide who you want to address: the easiest audience would be students of your own age.
- If you aim your article at younger readers, think carefully about language level and what you can expect the audience to know and understand.

Form

- Think about the kind of article found in the education section of a newspaper; use *Looking into deep space* as a model.
- Remember the conventions to do with nouns and determiners in explanatory texts of this kind.
- Think carefully about the combination of text and illustration.

- Now use your text and notes to create your own explanatory article.

The finger of fate

In this unit you will:

- read a newspaper article
- examine the language of description and report
- write a report

This is the opening of an article by Michael Hanlon which appeared in the *Daily Mail* on 14 January 2002.

The finger of fate

Their end, when it came, was very different from that of their victims: swift and relatively painless. On the morning of May 23, 1905, Albert Stratton and his brother Alfred were taken to the gallows and blindfolded by the hangman.

Witnesses described Albert's death as instantaneous, his body becoming limp straight after the drop through the trapdoor.

In Alfred's case, according to a newspaper report, 'there was some muscular movement afterwards'.

Gruesome deaths, perhaps, but merciful compared with the savage butchery the brothers had inflicted just three weeks previously.

One Monday morning, a sales assistant called William Jones had turned up for work only to find the door to the shop – a paint suppliers in Deptford High Street, South London – locked.

The shop's elderly manager, Thomas Farrow, would normally have opened up a couple of hours earlier.

Puzzled, Jones broke in and discovered a horrific scene. Farrow lay face-down, his body crumpled in a bloody pile, his skull staved in by a crowbar. Upstairs, his wife Ann lay dying, her wounds also the result of a sustained bludgeoning with a metal implement.

Later that morning, when Scotland Yard's assistant commissioner Melville Macnaghten joined the policemen in the shop, he noticed a greasy smudge on the shop's empty cash box. Immediately, he had it sent to the Yard's Fingerprint Branch.

Meanwhile, a witness, Ellen Stanton, told police she had seen

It was the case that made history... the first time that a fingerprint had been used to catch a killer. But behind it lay a story of intrigue and bitter jealousy

by

Michael Hanlon

Alfred Stratton, a well-known petty criminal, and another man tearing at high speed away from the shop.

The Stratton brothers were arrested, and Detective Inspector Charles Collins of the Fingerprint Branch subsequently discovered that Alfred's right thumbprint matched the print on the cash box.

Though fingerprints had never been used before as evidence in a murder trial, Macnaghten decided to commit the case to prosecution.

The key question was: would a jury be willing to send two men to the gallows on fingerprint evidence?

Forensic evidence was still widely mistrusted. Until then, convictions for murder had relied on sworn testimonies from the witness box that placed the accused at the scene of the crime.

No one saw the Strattons commit the murder; eyewitnesses had merely seen them near the shop.

It took just two hours' deliberation for the jury to find the brothers guilty – and to change legal history for ever. The Strattons became the first men in England to be hanged for murder on the evidence of a fingerprint.

Michael Hanlon's article is based on a book by Colin Beavan, *Fingerprints – Murder and the Race to Uncover the Science of Identity* (published by Fourth Estate)

Language in context

The power of language

Key features of the text are:

1 non-chronological writing

2 adverbials

3 adjectives

1 NON-CHRONOLOGICAL WRITING

Non-chronological writing organises events in a different order from the one in which they happened.

Look back at page 36 to remind yourself about *chronological* writing.

a) The article describes a crime and its aftermath in the following **non-chronological** order:

Paragraph	Events
1–2	the execution of the Stratton brothers
3	a newspaper report of the execution
5–7	William Jones's discovery of the crime
7	the injuries inflicted on the victims
8–9	the police investigation
10	the arrests
11–14	preparing the prosecution
15	the trial

- Re-organise these eight sections chronologically – in other words, so that the events are described in the order in which they happened.

- Write a paragraph to explain what effect Hanlon achieves by his non-chronological account.

  For example:
  Why might he have opened the article with an account of the execution?
  Why do you think he leaves describing the trial until the end?

2 ADVERBIALS

Adverbials are words or phrases which add important information to a sentence. They can help us to answer questions such as When? How? and Where?

For example, the following sentence from the article contains three common types of adverbial:

*Meanwhile, a witness, Ellen Stanton, told police she had seen Alfred Stratton … tearing **at high speed away from the shop**.*

- **time adverbials** answer the question **When?**
  Meanwhile…

- **manner adverbials** answer the question **How?**
  …at high speed…

- **place adverbials** answer the question **Where?**
  …away from the shop.

Adverbials can be:

single words	*Immediately, he had it sent…*
phrases	*One Monday morning, a sales assistant called William Jones had…*
whole clauses	*Though fingerprints had never been used before as evidence in a murder trial, Macnaghten decided…*

Manner adverbials and place adverbials

a) In the first column of the following table are two of the three common types of adverbials: **manner adverbials** and **place adverbials**. Next to each type are two examples from the extract. Copy the grid and write down three more examples of manner adverbials and place adverbials, also taken from the extract.

Type of adverbial	Examples from the extract
Manner adverbials (answer the question How?)	• *Farrow lay **face-down**…* • *…tearing at **high speed**…*
Place adverbials (answer the question Where?)	• ***Upstairs**, his wife Ann lay dying…* • *…tearing … **away from the shop**.*

Time adverbials

b) Most of the adverbials in the extract are **time adverbials**.

- Pick out time adverbials in the phrases and sentences beginning:

  On the morning of… (lines 4–8)

  there was some muscular… (14–15)

  the savage butchery the brothers had… (17–19)

  One Monday morning… (20–5)

  The shop's elderly manager… (26–9)

  Later that morning… (38–43, there are two time adverbials in this sentence)

  and Detective Inspector Charles Collins… (53–7)

  Until then, convictions for murder… (67–71)

  and to change legal history… (77–8)

- Write a paragraph or two to explain why time adverbials should be so useful in a *non*-chronological description like this one. Quote examples to show their importance. (For example, if the account starts with the executions, it is important to let the reader know that the murders were committed *just three weeks previously*.)

3 ADJECTIVES

> An **adjective** is a word which gives us information about a noun or pronoun. A group of words which does this is called an **adjective phrase**.

Adjectives play an important part in Michael Hanlon's description of the crime and its aftermath. For example, he writes about *gruesome* deaths, *savage* butchery, a *horrific* scene.

a) Pick out:

- the adjectives from the opening four paragraphs (up to …*three weeks previously.*) Two of them have been quoted in the sentence above.
- the one adjective which describes the manager, Thomas Farrow (in the paragraph beginning *The shop's…*)
- the four adjectives from the description of what William Jones discovered upon entering the shop (in the paragraph beginning *Puzzled, Jones broke in…*)

b) Write a paragraph to explain how the adjectives you found in question 3a are used to draw a contrast between the savagery of the attack upon an innocent man and the law's treatment of the murderers.

To do this, compare:

- adjectives in the section from *The shop's…* to …*metal implement.*

with

- adjectives in the opening four paragraphs

c) There are fewer adjectives in the second half of the extract, but they play a key role.

For example, look at the two sentences which open and conclude the final section of the article:

Forensic evidence was still widely mistrusted.
The Strattons became the first men in England to be hanged for murder on the evidence of a fingerprint.

- Pick out the adjective in each sentence.
- Write a paragraph to explain how these two adjectives are essential in summing up the main point of the article.

Writing to describe

FOUNDATION TIER TASKS

1 RETELLING WHAT HAPPENED

Retell Michael Hanlon's account of what happened in chronological order.

Use your own words as far as possible. Write 200–250 words.

Planning and drafting

Retell the account in the order in which the events actually happened:

- the robbery and the injuries inflicted on the victims (lines 30–7)
- William Jones's discovery of the crime (20–37)
- the police investigation (38–51)
- the arrests (52–7)
- preparing the prosecution (58–74)
- the trial (75–81)
- the execution of the Stratton brothers (1–12)
- a newspaper report of the execution (13–19)

You could start your account:

One morning in May 1905, two brothers, Albert and Alfred Stratton, attacked and robbed Thomas Farrow, the elderly manager of a paint suppliers in Deptford High Street, south London…

2 WRITING AN ARTICLE

Write a newspaper report of a crime which was solved using fingerprints. To make it different from *The finger of fate*, choose any crime but murder.

Write 200–250 words.

Planning and drafting

Base your report on a crime which could be solved through the evidence of fingerprints, such as burglary, arson or handling stolen goods.

Include paragraphs on the following events:

- details of the crime (What happened? Who were the victims? Were they harmed?)
- the discovery of the crime
- the police investigation (How did fingerprints help police to solve the crime?)
- the arrests
- the trial (What was said? What sentence were the criminals given?)
- events following the trial (What comments have the victims or their families made?)

You could start with the most recent events and then explain the background, as Michael Hanlon does:

In the Old Bailey yesterday morning, George Bateson was convicted of … and sentenced to…

The trial had lasted…

Summing up, Justice Shannon had told the jury…

HIGHER TIER TASKS

1 ANALYSING THE LANGUAGE

Explain how Michael Hanlon, through his content and use of language, creates a gripping and informative article.

Planning and drafting

First, consider the subject matter. Why does it capture our interest? What makes it:

- important historically?
- dramatic?

Then, think about the language.
Comment on his use of:

- non-chronological writing
  (Why does he open with the execution, do you think?)
- adverbials
  (Why are time adverbials so important here?)
- adjectives
  (How have they been used to get across the essential points the writer wants to make?)

You could start:

In choosing to write an article based upon Colin Beavan's new book on the history of fingerprinting, Michael Hanlon has found a subject guaranteed to capture our interest…

2 WRITING A NON-CHRONOLOGICAL REPORT

Write a non-chronological newspaper report of any episode from history, legend, mythology or fiction.

Planning and drafting

- Select a story that interests you and that you know fairly well. For example, it could be from something you have been studying in History (e.g. the events of the Gunpowder Plot), or RE (e.g. Judas's betrayal of Jesus) or English (e.g. the story of Macbeth's rise and fall).
- Write out the main events (in note form) in chronological order.
- Plan a gripping non-chronological order of events, choosing a dramatic moment with which to open and conclude your report.

For example, you could start:

- *A pile of smouldering ashes is all that remains this morning of Guido Fawkes…*
- *Betrayed by a seemingly innocent kiss on the cheek in the Garden of Gethsemane, Jesus of Nazareth lies in prison this morning awaiting…*
- *The severed head spiked on the gatehouse of Dunsinane Castle today is dramatic evidence that the bloody reign of King Macbeth is finally over. After a conflict which lasted…*

Dawn of the reptiles

In this unit you will:

- compare three texts about dinosaurs and early reptiles
- examine the language of the texts
- write to inform, explain and describe

WRITING TO INFORM

THOUSAND-TOOTHED 'LAWNMOWERS' SCYTHED ACROSS WEST AFRICA

Plant eating hammerhead shark on legs was easy prey

Tim Radford
in Boston

It had the long neck of a Diplodocus. It had a mouth like a hammerhead shark. It had up to 1,000 teeth in its intricate jaws, and it would have swung its long neck to crop low-lying meadows of ferns like a mesozoic lawnmower, says Paul Sereno, dinosaur-hunter extraordinary.

It has been dubbed Nigersaurus, because it was discovered in Niger, and it could have been the prey of a 12 metre (40ft) long crocodile called Sarcosuchus, or super-croc, discovered and named by Dr Sereno, of the University of Chicago, in Niger last year. His other discoveries in Africa alone have included a giant predator, Carcharodontosaurus, a rival to T rex; a swiftcarnivore, Deltadromeus; and an 18 metre (60ft) long plant eater, Jobaria.

He and colleagues had been piecing together the life of Nigersaurus. "We are missing only a few bones of the skull, feet and the tip of the tail," he told the American Association for the Advancement of Science in Boston yesterday. It roamed a meandering African river valley 100m years ago and its way of life is still a puzzle.

Nigersaurus may have grown to 14 metres (45ft) long and three metres (10ft) high at the hip. "The teeth were narrow, needle shaped, not bigger than just a few millimetres in width and packed into an open groove in the jaw. There were stacks of eight or 10 teeth in line, erupting from a single point in the jaw: a huge number of small teeth, enamel covered, giving it more bite, because each small tooth has its own wrapping of enamel, and a lot more cutting surface," he said.

"It looks like a hammerhead shark on legs. I have never seen anything like it. It is going to be a shocker when we eventually get this thing together. It has jaws that extend to each side of the skull. It is definitely designed to crop plants. When you look at it, you say: this is the mesozoic lawnmower."

The mesozoic era, including the triassic, jurassic and cretaceous periods, was the age of the dinosaurs, spanning from 245m to 65m years ago.

At the time of Nigersaurus grasses had not evolved. Flowering plants were just beginning to appear. Much of the foliage would have been ferns and cycad shrubs. Fossil teeth are a clue to diet. Just from teeth, researchers can reconstruct a crude picture of the vegetation of a vanished world. Duckbilled dinosaurs had as many as 250 teeth in a single jaw. Some horned dinosaurs developed a tooth battery at around the time of the first flowering plants. Nigersaurus was the third group to develop a sophisticated tooth battery. Its bones were so thin that Dr Sereno could not construct a cast of the skull from the bones he had disinterred. This raised another

pronunciation

Diplodocus	DIP-lo-DOKE-us
mesozoic	MEEZ-o-ZO-ic *(from the second, or middle geological period)*
Nigersaurus	NY-jer-SAW-rus
Sarcosuchus	SAR-co-SOOK-us

An artist's impression of Sarcosuchus, the 'supercroc' which would have been more than a match for Nigersaurus.

biomechanical puzzle: with paper thin bones, how could Nigersaurus chew?

"It was one of the smaller of the long necked dinosaurs," he said. "When we first prepared the jawbone from the rock, and we couldn't see the whole thing, I said 'this certainly doesn't belong to a dinosaur'."

The bones were found first by a French researcher. It took years, and further discoveries, to realise their significance. More remains were found in the same strata as those of the giant crocodile.

"I would not doubt for a minute that those two encountered each other, not favourably for the Nigersaurus. The crocodile would have been some-thing to watch out for along the banks of the river. It may have been a fish-eater when it was young, but when it grew up to 40ft long anything along the banks would have been fair game. Nigersaurus, a lightly built, delicate, wondrous plant eater would have been easy prey."

FLYING REPTILES OF THE LATE JURASSIC

One of the richest sources of fossil information about early flying reptiles, and the oldest birds, is the Solnhofen Limestone of southern Bavaria, dated as Portlandian (latest Jurassic, 150 million years ago). The deposits are those of a shallow marine lagoon, and the skeletons of pterosaurs, birds, and many other animals are exquisitely preserved.

The pterosaurs include the rhamphorhynchoid *Rhamphorhynchus* (left), with a long tail, and the pterodactyloids *Pterodactylus* (top right) and *Anurognathus* (middle right), both with short tails. A famous animal from this locality is the earliest bird, *Archaeopteryx* (bottom left).

How the world looked in this period

The Late Jurassic fliers were not as large as their Cretaceous relatives. Many pterosaurs, like Anurognathus (1), were tiny, Rhamphorhynchus (2) and Pterodactylus (3) were within the size spectrum of seagulls. Archaeopteryx (4) was on the scale of a pigeon.

pronunciation	
pterosaurs	TER-o-saws
Rhamphorhynchus	RAM-for-INK-us
Pterodactylus	TER-o-DAC-til-us
Anurognathus	a-NEW-rog-NATH-us
Archaeopteryx	AR-key-OP-ter-ix

WRITING TO DESCRIBE

QUEEN OF THE PREDATORS

Tim Haines

A herd of Iguanodon are idly plucking saplings from between the bare rocks. It is late afternoon and the long shadows thrown by the rocks hide danger. Just below the Iguanodon, in deep shadow, two Utahraptors make slow progress towards their quarry.

Utahraptors are truly beautiful predators. They are covered in a well-defined black and yellow pattern with a pale cream underbelly. Their sleek, well-muscled bodies are held in perfect balance by a small, highly mobile tail that constantly adjusts and readjusts as the animal slinks forward. Each Utahraptor weighs the best part of a tonne, and if they surprise an Iguanodon, it will be lucky to escape. Their heads hardly move as they walk; their eyes remain locked on the prey ahead. Their forearms are tucked up high, with their long grappling fingers held against their ribs. Each step reveals a flash of the long, black claw on the second toe, so distinctive of this group of predators.

These raptors have obviously spent some time working their way round to this position because the rest of their pack are still on the edge of the forest. They are both females, which is not surprising since female Utahraptors do most of the hunting. Somewhere nearby will be a dominant male, but he will rarely hunt. If a kill is made, he will claim his share and save his energy for the challenges that inevitably come from other males. The two stalking Utahraptors reach the edge of the outcrop unnoticed. The Iguanodon are slowly moving away from the predators and the distance the raptors will have to sprint once they are in the open is increasing. Utahraptors do not usually pursue their prey for any distance and the Iguanodon could soon outpace them, running on their long back legs. It is time to attack.

The larger female springs silently on to the outcrop and heads for the herd. She has already chosen her victim, a sturdy subadult on the edge of the group. She is spotted immediately and the Iguanodon start their screeching bellows of alarm. The rest of the Utahraptor pack appear from the forest, but the herd are already striding away towards a large meadow of white Protoanthus. Most of the Utahraptors are out of the chase before it even starts, but the lead female manages to gain on the Iguanodon before he can get into his stride. She leaps. As she travels through the air, her long fingers, tipped with hook-like claws, spread out. Her legs come forward, and as she lands on the Iguanodon's rump, she tries to drive her lethal hind claws into his flank. But the leap was mis-timed. Her feet fail to find their target and, although the Iguanodon stumbles as she lands on him, he remains on his feet. As her claws rake across his back, his bellows turn into an ear-splitting scream. He rears and bucks in a panicked frenzy. The predator loses her grip and tumbles to the ground. She springs up again instantly, but is in a very dangerous position, right in front of the Iguanodon. He rises up and knocks her back down with one forearm, then, swinging the other across, drives a thumb spike deep into her shoulder. The Utahraptor breaks free and scrabbles away, one arm dangling uselessly.

pronunciation

Iguanodon	IG-you-ARE-na-don
Utahraptor	YOU-tar-RAP-tor
Protoanthus	PRO-toe-ANTH-us *(an early flowering shrub)*

Language in context

The power of language

Key features of the texts are:

1 the language of *inform*, *explain* and *describe* texts

2 facts and figures

---

1 ## THE LANGUAGE OF WRITING TO INFORM, EXPLAIN AND DESCRIBE

Writing to **inform**, **explain** and **describe** focuses on conveying information and ideas clearly.

Writing to inform:
conveying information

The newspaper article about Nigersaurus conveys a great deal of information clearly and interestingly.

a) In order to maintain the reader's interest, the writer, Tim Radford, varies the ways in which he gets the facts across. Jot down examples of:

- three facts in paragraph 2 conveyed through Tim Radford's own description
- three facts in paragraph 4 conveyed in quotes by Dr Sereno, who discovered Nigersaurus
- three facts in the first paragraph which use comparisons (to describe the appearance and behaviour of Nigersaurus)

b) Imagine you were creating a series of dinosaur fact-cards. Write the text for a card on Nigersaurus. You could use these headings (right):

Writing to explain: using a combination of text and image

Explanatory texts will often use a combination of **text** (words) and **image** (photographs and illustrations).

c) Study the section on *Flying reptiles of the late Jurassic*. Make notes on which ideas and facts are explained:

(i) *through the* **text** *alone*

Look at the two paragraphs on the left.

(ii) *through the* **illustrations** *alone*

Look at the three illustrations and the different styles of artwork used:

- the image of the world, which uses colour and outline
- the small line-drawings
- the main picture in colour

Then write a paragraph or two commenting on the ways in which the page uses a **combination of text and image** in order to explain about flying reptiles in the late Jurassic period.

NIGERSAURUS

○ **WHEN IT LIVED** (see paragraphs 3 and 6)
How many million years ago?
In which geological period?

○ **WHERE IT LIVED** (see paragraphs 2 and 3)

○ **APPEARANCE** (see paragraphs 1, 4, 5, 7, 8 and 10)
Size? Neck? Mouth? Jaws? Teeth?
Resemblance to modern creatures? Bones?

○ **BEHAVIOUR** (see paragraphs 1, 5 and 7)
What did it feed on? How did it feed?

○ **ITS PREDATORS** (see paragraphs 2 and 10)

Writing to describe: using the present tense

> **Tense** is the name given to the form of the verb which shows when something happens: the past, the present or the future.

Tim Haines's text is based on the commentary written for the BBC television series *Walking with Dinosaurs*. It is written in the **present tense** because the commentary originally accompanied a computer-generated sequence showing the conflict between the Iguanodon and the Utahraptor:

*It **is** late afternoon…*
*the long shadows thrown by the rocks **hide** danger.*
*two Utahraptors **make** slow progress…*

d) Redraft into the past tense (a) the first four sentences of the second paragraph (*Utahraptors are truly beautiful … lucky to escape.*), and (b) the final four sentences of the last paragraph (*The predator loses … dangling uselessly*).

Then write a paragraph to explain what Tim Haines's text gains by being in the present tense. For example, it will help to remember that:

- most traditional textbooks about dinosaurs are written in the past tense
- many eyewitness accounts of dramatic events are written in the present tense

2 FACTS AND FIGURES

> Writing to inform, explain and describe will often be concerned with **facts and figures**.

One of the main purposes of these three texts about early reptiles is to provide names, dates and other key facts.

a) Draw up a table in five columns like the one below. Reread the three extracts and add:

- the name of the era which covers the age of the dinosaurs and the name of the three geological periods into which it is divided
- the names of the creatures which inhabited the Earth during those periods
- the dates of the era and how long ago the creatures lived
- anything you have learned from the text or illustrations about the creatures' appearance
- details of the creatures' habitats and the vegetation around at that time

Two entries already added to the table are not taken from the three extracts:

- *Iguanodon and Utahraptor lived about 120 million years ago.*
- *Megalosaurus also lived in the same era: you can find further facts about it in the article on page 58.*

The era which covers the age of the dinosaurs		Its dates	
The three geological periods into which it is divided	The creatures which inhabited the earth during those periods	When the creatures lived (millions of years ago)	The creatures' appearance	Their habitats and the vegetation at that time
1				
2	1 Megalosaurus			
	2			
	3			
	4			
	5			
3	1 Iguanodon	120		
	2 Utahraptor			
	3			
	4			

Compare and contrast

 1 CREATING A FACT-CARD

Read the newspaper article on the right about the discovery of some dinosaur footprints. Then use the information to create a fact-card for Megalosaurus, similar to the one you completed for Nigersaurus (see question 1b on page 56).

2 WRITING A DESCRIPTION

Write a description of a fight between two animals – a predator and its prey.

Write 200–250 words.

Planning and drafting

- Think about the various predators you could write about:
  hawks, spiders, cats large and small…

- Write your description in the present tense, as though it were an eyewitness account (see page 57).

- You could base your account on Tim Haines's description of the combat between the Iguanodon and the Utahraptor:

  paragraph 1: the prey is feeding, unaware that the predator is silently approaching

  paragraph 2: description of the predator

  paragraph 3: explanation of the predator's plan of attack

  paragraph 4: the predator attacks… What happens?

For example, you could start:
In the corner of the shed, blissfully unaware that she is being watched, a fieldmouse nibbles contentedly on a husk of corn…

National news

Stumbling with dinosaurs …
at 20mph across ancient Oxfordshire

Tim Radford
in Boston

Millions of years after the event, scientists have reconstructed the case of the dinosaur that broke into a sprint at nearly 20mph across what is now Oxfordshire.

It was a Megalosaurus, a huge hunter-killer, a relative of Tyrannosaurus rex, and made its mark in history when it went for a walk along an intertidal zone in the Jurassic era.

It left a trail of neat clear three-toed footprints which dried in the lime-rich mud of the foreshore. Sand covered them. Some freak of time and geology preserved them. Sediments buried them. Continents shifted. The landscape sank beneath the waves, and then emerged again.

And 163m years later, quarrymen at Ardley, Oxfordshire, scraped away the rock and clay above and exposed one of the most extensive dinosaur track-ways in the world, with sets of footprints that could be followed for 180 metres.

Julia Day and colleagues from Cambridge and Oxford report in *Nature* today that they used global positioning satellite measurements and close observation to tell the story of at least one stalking beast on that forgotten foreshore.

The size of its footprints, and the distance and the angles between them, were all they had to go on. The length of the foot gave a clue to the creature's height at the hip. When it walked – at an estimated 4.25mph – it had a stride of 2.7 metres. When it accelerated, its stride stretched to 5.6 metres and its speed increased fourfold.

"It was about seven metres in length, and had a hip height of about two metres. It was a bipedal dinosaur, a relative of T rex," said Dr Day.

"It is walking and the footprints vary from the midline: it is walking pigeon-toed. Then it breaks into a run or a jog for a 35-metre section of the track-way, and in that section the feet are tucked underneath the body, the way a mammal would run. It is an erect gait with the feet in line, rather than a zig-zag arrangement."

She added: "We calculated its speed at about 18mph. It fits the higher end of people's previous estimates."

"Obviously if an animal that big falls over it is more likely to break a limb at that speed. We don't know if it could sustain its run, or whether it was doing short bursts."

---

pronunciation
Megalosaurus MEGA-lo-SAW-rus

---

bipedal two-footed

HIGHER TIER TASKS

1 ANALYSING THE LANGUAGE

Read *Stumbling with dinosaurs...* on the opposite page. Explain how Tim Radford, through his content and use of language, creates an interesting and informative article.

Planning and drafting

Think about:

- the variety of ways in which facts are conveyed to the reader through:

    Tim Radford's own comments

    quotes

- the use of the past and the present tenses in the quote from Julia Day

- the inclusion of facts and figures:

    how old the footprints are

    the creature's speed, stride and body dimensions

    its running action

You could start:

Tim Radford uses a variety of different methods to inform us about the Megalosaurus. To begin with...

2 CREATING A WALL-CHART

Describe what you would include on a wall-chart entitled *The Age of the Dinosaurs*. The chart is designed for a year 6 primary school classroom.

- Write the text in full.

- Describe the illustrations that will be an important part of the chart.

- Explain how the text and images will combine to maximum effect.

Self assess

These are the main language features that you have learned about in this section. Decide how confident you feel about:

- understanding what **chronological** and **non-chronological writing** are and where and why they are used
- identifying the different uses of **parenthesis**
- distinguishing between **active** and **passive** and understanding their uses

- commenting on the effects of combining **text** and **image**
- identifying the different kinds of **nouns** and **determiners**
- understanding why writers have to be aware of **audience**

- commenting on the use of **adverbials**
- identifying **adjectives** and **adjective phrases** and discussing their uses
- understanding how **tenses** are used

What do you feel you need to revise?

Give a child a life

In this unit you will:

- study a charity leaflet which combines text and image
- examine the language of persuasion
- create one spread of a charity leaflet

This spread is one side of a leaflet published by the charity Plan International UK. Its aim is to encourage people to sponsor children in the developing world.

Every child
deserves to do more than just survive

For many children living in the developing world, every day is a struggle to survive. They often wake up hungry, work in their parents' fields for long hours just to help their families scrape by. It is no wonder there is little opportunity for them to realise their potential.

These children live in abject poverty which affects their entire lives. In Africa, Latin America and large areas of Asia poverty deprives children of growing up healthy and having an education. If they learned to read and write, they would have so many more opportunities in the future.

We don't believe this is any life for children. Every child deserves clean water, nourishing food, good health and basic education.

If you agree, please become a Plan child sponsor today. Child sponsorship gives communities and their children the chances they so desperately need to live the lives they deserve.

"I need to drink clean water"

"There is only dirty water in our village. Just one drink can give me and my friends bad stomachs and make us very sick."

Every minute 10 people die from drinking dirty water in the developing world.

Last year, Plan provided materials and training so villagers could build 20,493 water wells and helped communities to have clean, safe water. We couldn't have done it without our sponsors.

"I should be able to go to school"

"My parents can't afford to send me to school. But if I learnt to read and write then I could get a proper job when I grow up."

More than 130 million school age children in the developing world have no access to basic education.

Last year Plan helped villagers to build or improve 2,680 classrooms, we trained 20,638 teachers and distributed 287,541 school books. We couldn't have done it without our sponsors.

"I want to grow up healthy"

"If I get ill my mother and I have to walk for hours to the hospital in the nearest town nine miles away."

In some developing countries, Niger, for example, the mortality rate for children under five is over 40 times higher than in the UK.

Last year Plan provided training for villagers to build over 18,348 much-needed health clinics and trained 48,008 community health workers. We couldn't have done it without our sponsors.

Give children the life they should have

We know that children can only realise their potential by living in a thriving family and community that has skills and resources which bring self-sufficiency and dignity to everyone.

As well as providing the funds which enable projects to happen, many sponsors have a more personal relationship through the exchange of letters and photos with their sponsored child. Sponsored children look forward to receiving messages of support which boost their self-esteem. In return, sponsors hear about what's going on in the community and get a unique insight into a different culture.

Every project Plan commits to provides practical, long-term support for the whole community. For example, latrines and a clean water supply help children grow up healthy. A school gives children the chance to learn skills for the future which they can pass on to the next generation. A health centre means more children will be vaccinated against diseases.

Plan's goal is to be able to reach the point when a community doesn't need us anymore and we can move on to another community in need of our help.

Through child sponsorship we are helping ten million people in the developing world to make lasting changes to their lives.

Language in context

The power of language

Key features of the text are:

1 headings and slogans

2 repeated structures

3 abstract nouns

4 combination of text and image

1 HEADINGS AND SLOGANS

A charity or campaign leaflet needs eye-catching **headings** which are clear, direct and memorable. Some headings are similar to **slogans**: short, catchy phrases which make a point and stick in the memory.

The first heading on this spread – *Every child deserves to do more than just survive* – has all the qualities of an effective slogan. It uses straightforward language that readers will remember, and it gets its message across clearly – that children throughout the world deserve a decent quality of life.

a) Which other heading makes a powerful, eye-catching impact in this leaflet? What is its message?

b) The first heading stresses the idea that many children *deserve* a better life. Which verb phrase in the second heading picks up this idea of deserving? (A verb phrase is a group of words which acts as a verb; examples are *could be, would have, might have gone*.)

2 STRUCTURES

The **structure** of a text is the way in which it is put together in sections.

Down the middle of the page are three blocks of text, each one accompanied by a photograph. Each block follows the same structure. They are made up of:

- a quotation in two parts
- some statistics
- a brief report on work that the charity has carried out
- a concluding sentence
- a photograph

All of these combine to get across the message.

The quotation

a) The first quotation begins with a general statement – *I need to drink clean water* – and is followed up by a development of that statement which provides further details about the existing problem – *There is only dirty water in our village…*

Write down the introductory general statement and the follow-up development in the second and third blocks of text.

The statistics

b) In the first block we learn that *Every minute 10 people die from drinking dirty water in the developing world*. Statistics such as this can be extremely effective in a leaflet which is aiming to explain how bad a situation is and persuade people to take action.

Write down the statistic from these three blocks of text that you find most impressive and explain how it helps the overall argument that these children need a better quality of life.

The message

c) The message of the first block of text might be expressed as: **people need clean drinking water**. Write down in your own words the messages of the second and third blocks.

d) Imagine you were adding a fourth block of your own to this leaflet. Draft the text, based on the same structure as the three here.

- First, decide what the main message or theme will be (for example, the need for help with local farming projects).

- Then, create a quotation which begins with a simple statement in the first person (*I…*) and adds a developing point.

- Next, include a dramatic statistic (if you are not able to do any research, you will need to make this up).

- Finally, add a brief account of what the charity has so far been able to achieve.

3 ABSTRACT NOUNS

> An **abstract noun** is the label we give to something we cannot touch, such as an emotion, feeling or idea.

The writers of this leaflet use abstract nouns each time they want to refer to important concepts such as *skills* and *resources*.

a) Reread the column on the right of the spread (headed *Give children the life they should have*). It begins with some very positive abstract nouns, all to do with the idea of getting the best out of people: *potential, family, community, skills, resources*. Which two abstract nouns, central to the leaflet's message, conclude the opening paragraph?

b) Pick out the abstract nouns in the opening sentence of the second paragraph of the right-hand column (beginning *As well as providing…*). Explain in your own words what general idea links these abstract nouns and what point the writers are trying to get across.

c) Reread the text under the main slogan *Every child deserves to do more than just survive*. Pick out the abstract nouns in the first sentence of the opening paragraph (beginning *For many children…*) and the first sentence of the second paragraph (*These children live…*). There is a total of five abstract nouns in these two sentences. Explain which of them are central to the main messages of the leaflet, in your opinion, and why.

d) Write the opening paragraph of your own charity leaflet. Decide first what the aim of your charity is, think carefully about the main point you wish to convey, and select abstract nouns which will help to deliver your message effectively. (For example, a leaflet supporting an animal sanctuary might use abstract nouns such as *shelter*, *warmth* and *care*, in opposition to *cruelty*, *neglect* and *abuse*.)

4 TEXT AND IMAGE

> A successful charity leaflet will usually have an effective combination of **text** (words) and **image** (photographs and illustrations).

a) Look at each of the six photographs used in the leaflet. What do they all have in common? Why is this important?

b) Explain how the three small photographs help the points being made in the text next to them.

c) Describe the photograph in the bottom right-hand corner. Then explain the message it is trying to get across and discuss how it links up with the text above.

Writing to persuade

FOUNDATION TIER TASKS

1 SUMMARISING THE MAIN POINTS

Read the leaflet again. Summarise the information given about:

- the successful projects that have been completed by Plan International UK
- the charity's main aims

Write 200–250 words in total.
Use your own words as far as possible.

Planning and drafting

The task is in two parts. Use these points in order to make preparatory notes.

Part 1: the successful projects that have been completed

Look at:

- the final paragraphs of the three blocks of text down the middle of the page
- the second and third paragraphs of the section headed *Give children the life they should have*

Part 2: the charity's main aims

Look at:

- the four paragraphs of the section headed *Every child deserves to do more than just survive*
- the first, fourth and fifth paragraphs of the section headed *Give children the life they should have*

> You could start:
>
> *Plan International UK is an important charity organisation which has completed some successful projects. For example…*

2 EXAMINING THE WRITERS' LANGUAGE

Read the leaflet again. Explain how the content and writers' use of language encourage readers to become sponsors of a child in the developing world.

Planning and drafting

The task asks you to look at two features of the text. Use these points in order to make preparatory notes.

1: the content
Look at the use of:

- statistics (e.g. *Every minute 10 people die…*)
- accounts of the children's daily lives (e.g. *There is only dirty water…*)
- facts about the charity's projects and achievements (e.g. *Plan helped villagers to build…*)

2: the language
Look at the use of:

- headings and slogans (e.g. *Give children the life they should have*)
- the focus on what children deserve
- first-person quotations (e.g. *My parents can't afford…*)
- abstract nouns (e.g. *potential, community, self-esteem…*)
- clear structures (e.g. the three sections down the middle of the page)

> You could start:
>
> *The writers have used a number of different methods to persuade us to become sponsors. To begin with, they describe…*

HIGHER TIER TASKS

1 CREATING A CHARITY LEAFLET

Create a spread for a charity leaflet of your own choosing.

It will help to study a variety of other charity leaflets first. These appear in most newspapers and can be found in libraries or charity shops.

It will also help to collect information about particular charities from their websites. You could consult sites such as Save the Children (**www.savethechildren.org.uk**), the World Wildlife Fund (**www.wwf.org.uk**), the Fawcett Society (promoting gender equality, **www.fawcettsociety.org.uk**) or Amnesty International (fighting to stop the torture of prisoners, **www.joinamnestynow.org.uk** and **www.amnesty.org**).

Planning and drafting

Check:

- that you have taken into account the **purpose** of your leaflet and its intended **audience**
- what your main **message** is (page 63)
- that you have created striking **headings** or **slogans** (page 62)
- that each section has a clear and effective **structure** (page 62)
- that you have used **abstract nouns** to label the key concepts (page 63)
- that your design includes an effective balance of **text** and **image** (page 63)

2 WRITING TO PERSUADE

A local company has declared that it is willing to give money to charity.

Decide which charity you think ought to receive the money and make some notes on why they are deserving, in your opinion. You could consult some of the websites listed in the previous task, or select a charity which is locally based.

Then write a letter to the managing director of the company, attempting to persuade her or him to donate money to the charity you have selected. (You might like to use the Plan International UK leaflet as a model for the content and language of your persuasive letter.)

> You could start:
> *Dear ....,*
> *I am writing to you in connection with your recent announcement that you were prepared to donate money to a charity…*

A message from the president

In this unit you will:

- study two speeches
- examine the language of argument
- write a speech arguing a particular case

In 1863, at a time when America was being torn apart by a civil war between the North and South, President Abraham Lincoln made a speech. It has come to be known by the name of the battlefield on which the Confederate southern army had just been defeated – the Gettysburg Address. This is what he said.

THE GETTYSBURG ADDRESS

Fourscore and seven years ago our fathers brought forth on this continent a new nation, conceived in liberty, and dedicated to the proposition that all men are created equal.

Now we are engaged in a great civil war, testing whether that nation, or any nation so conceived, can long endure. We are met on a great battlefield of that war. We have come to dedicate a portion of that field as a final resting place for those who here gave their lives that that nation might live. It is altogether fitting and proper that we should do this.

But, in a larger sense, we cannot dedicate – we cannot consecrate – we cannot hallow – this ground. The brave men, living and dead, who struggled here have consecrated it far above our poor power to add or detract. The world will little note nor long remember what we say here, but it can never forget what they did here. It is for us, the living, rather, to be dedicated here to the unfinished work which they who fought here have thus far so nobly advanced. It is rather for us here to be dedicated to the great task remaining before us – that from these honored dead we take increased devotion to that cause for which they gave the last full measure of devotion; that we here highly resolve that these dead shall not have died in vain; that this nation, under God, shall have a new birth of freedom; and that government of the people, by the people, for the people, shall not perish from the earth.

consecrate/hallow	make holy or sacred

In December 2001, Bill Clinton, former president of the United States, delivered the annual Richard Dimbleby Lecture, named after the distinguished BBC broadcaster. The speech took place in the midst of the bombing of Afghanistan, and only three months after terrorists had flown two airliners into the World Trade Centre in New York on 11 September 2001. After a brief introduction, Bill Clinton began to talk about three issues facing the modern world, saying, 'Let me take each of these issues quickly in turn…'.

THE STRUGGLE FOR THE SOUL OF THE 21ST CENTURY

First, terror. The deliberate killing of non-combatants has a very long history. No region of the world has been spared it and very few people have clean hands. In 1095, Pope Urban II urged the Christian soldiers to embark on the first crusade to capture Jerusalem for Christ. Well, they did it, and the very first thing they did was to burn a synagogue with three hundred Jews; they then proceeded to murder every Muslim woman and child on the Temple Mount in a travesty that is still being discussed today in the Middle East. Down through the millennium, innocents continued to die, more in the twentieth century than in any previous period. In my own country, we've come a very, very long way since the days when African slaves and native Americans could be terrorised or killed with impunity, but still we have the occasional act of brutality or even death because of someone's race or religion or sexual orientation. This has a long history.

Second, no terrorist campaign apart from a conventional military strategy has ever succeeded. Indeed the purpose of terrorism is not military victory, it is to terrorise, to change your behaviour if you're the victim by making you afraid of today, afraid of tomorrow and, in diverse societies like ours, afraid of each other. Therefore, by definition, a terror campaign cannot succeed unless we become its accomplices and, out of fear, give in.

The third point I want to make is that what makes this terror at the moment particularly frightening, I think, is the combination of universal vulnerability and powerful weapons of destruction... Now, in any new area of conflict, offensive action always prevails in the beginning. Ever since the first person walked out of a cave millennia ago with a club in his hand, and began beating people into submission, offensive action prevails. Then after a time, someone figured out, well, I could put two sticks together and stretch an animal skin over it and I would have a shield, and the club wouldn't work on me any more. All the way through to the present day, that has been the history of combat – first the club, then the shield; first the offence, then defence; that's why civilisation has survived all this time even in the nuclear age. So it is frightening now because we are in the gap, and the more dangerous the weapons, the more important it is to close quickly the gap between offensive action and the construction of an effective defence...

We're gonna win this fight – then what? The reason September 11th happened – and it was shocking to Americans, because it happened on our soil – is that we have built a world where we tore down barriers, collapsed distances and spread information. And the UK and America have benefited richly – look at how our economies have performed, look at how our societies have diversified, look at the advances we have made in technology and science. This new world has been good to us; but you can't gain the benefits of a world without walls without being more vulnerable. September 11th was the dark side of this new age of global interdependence. If you don't want to put those walls back up – and I don't think you do, and we probably couldn't if we tried ... and if you don't want to live with barbed wire around your children and grandchildren for the next hundred years, then it's not enough to defeat the terrorist. We have to make a world where there are far fewer terrorists, where there are fewer potential terrorists and more partners. And that responsibility falls primarily upon the wealthy nations, to spread the benefits and shrink the burdens...

But what are the burdens of the twenty-first century? They are also formidable. Global poverty – half the people on earth are not part of that new economy I talked about. Think about this when you go home tonight. Half the people on Earth live on less than two dollars a day. A billion people, less than a dollar a day. A billion people go to bed hungry every night and a billion and a half people – one quarter of the people on Earth – never get a clean glass of water. One woman dies every minute in childbirth. So you could say 'don't tell me about the global economy; half the people aren't part of it; what kind of economy leaves half the people behind?'

...So we now live in a world without walls that we have worked hard to make. We have benefits, we have burdens; we have to spread the benefits and shrink the burdens.

non-combatants	people involved in a war who are civilians, rather than military personnel
travesty	a mockery of their original intentions
with impunity	without being punished
universal vulnerability	the fact that no country, anywhere in the world, is now safe from attack

Language in context

The power of language

Key features of the texts are:

1 structure

2 the language of speeches

3 the language of argument

---

1 **STRUCTURE**

> The **structure** of a text is the way in which it is put together in sections.

a) The most obvious way in which to structure a written speech is in **paragraphs** (see pages 88–9). Write down appropriate topic headings for each of the six paragraphs in the extract from Bill Clinton's speech. For example, the first one might be *Terrorism throughout history*.

b) What are the four or five main points that Clinton makes in the paragraph beginning *First, terror*? Write them down, in note form, in your own words. The first one might be: *There have always been civilian casualties in wars through the ages*.

c) Both Clinton and Lincoln open each of their longer paragraphs with punchy sentences. For example, Clinton opens one paragraph with *But what are the burdens of the twenty-first century?* Pick one example (from either speech) and write two or three sentences to explain why it is particularly effective. Think about the following questions:

- How does it grab the listener's attention? What is special about the language?

- What point does it make?

- How does it help to introduce the paragraph's main topic?

> **Tense** is the name given to the form of the verb which shows when something happens: the past, the present or the future.

One idea that unites both speeches is that of the violent past, the troubled present and the hoped-for future.

d) In pairs, look at the three paragraphs of Abraham Lincoln's speech. Discuss what you notice about the three different tenses of the following main verbs:

Paragraph 1: *our fathers **brought forth**…*

Paragraph 2: *Now we **are engaged**…*

Paragraph 3: *government of the people, by the people, for the people, **shall not perish** from the earth.*

Now look at these quotations from Clinton's speech. Again decide which tense each of the verbs is in and compare the arrangement of tenses with those in the Gettysburg Address:

Paragraph 1: *they **proceeded** to murder…*

Paragraph 3: *what **makes** this terror at the moment particularly frightening…*

Paragraph 4: *We're **gonna** win this fight…*

Write a short paragraph headed *Tenses in speeches by Lincoln and Clinton*. In your paragraph, explain:

- how the two speakers use tenses to give their speeches a structure

- how the arrangement of tenses in this particular structure helps us to understand the speakers' arguments

2 THE LANGUAGE OF SPEECHES

> Speakers aim for particular effects when they are composing important speeches. These effects are achieved through the use of **rhetorical language**.

Rhetorical language includes features such as **lists** and **repetition**.

Three-part lists

One structure which has been popular with public speakers for centuries is the **three-part list**.

Three-part lists are frequently used in everyday speech (*lock, stock and barrel; Tom, Dick and Harry*), but they can be very effective in formal situations such as speeches.

a) Find the three-part lists in the second and fourth paragraphs of Bill Clinton's speech. Write a sentence or two about each one, commenting on the ways in which they help to get across the important points in paragraphs two and four.

b) Abraham Lincoln's Gettysburg Address concludes with one of the most famous of all three-part lists: *government of the people, by the people, for the people*.

Find the three-part list at the opening of Lincoln's third paragraph. Write down in your own words the point that Lincoln is getting across and explain how it is developed in the sentences which follow.

Repetition

Speech-makers can achieve some very powerful effects from repetition: think of Winston Churchill's famous wartime declaration in 1940: *…we shall fight on the beaches; we shall fight on the landing grounds; we shall fight in the fields and in the streets; we shall fight in the hills; we shall never surrender.*

c) Find three examples of repetition in each speech.

In pairs, discuss which of the repetitions you find most, and least, effective, explaining why. Think about the point that the speaker is attempting to get across with each example and its purpose within the argument as a whole.

3 THE LANGUAGE OF ARGUMENT

> Speakers who hope to get across a strong **argument** or message pay close attention to language. They choose particular language features to serve different **purposes**.

a) The following grid lists some of the language and content features used by Lincoln and Clinton to get their points across. Each feature serves a particular purpose. Copy the grid and then complete it by filling in the empty boxes with examples. Two have been filled in to start you off. (You are asked to find examples from both speeches. For the first feature, for example, find two from Lincoln and two from Clinton.)

Features	Their purposes	Examples
Powerful conclusions to paragraphs	to emphasise the main point of the paragraph	AL 1 … *all men are created equal* AL 2 BC 1 BC 2
Examples from recorded history	to illustrate and add authority to the argument	BC 1 BC 2
Parallels with humankind's earlier history	to show that things have always been the same	BC
Striking images	to…	BC *walls … barbed wire*
Statistics	to…	BC

Writing to argue

FOUNDATION TIER TASKS

1 SUMMARISING THE MAIN POINTS

Read the first three paragraphs of Bill Clinton's speech again. Summarise the main points he makes about the three issues facing the modern world.

Write 200–250 words.
Use your own words as far as possible.

Planning and drafting

Use these points in order to make preparatory notes.

the three issues facing the modern world

Look at:

- the history of terrorism (paragraph 1)
- the purpose of terrorism (paragraph 2)
- terrorism at the moment (paragraph 3)

> You could start:
> *Bill Clinton begins by making the point that there is nothing new about terrorism…*

2 EXAMINING THE WRITERS' LANGUAGE

Reread Abraham Lincoln's Gettysburg Address and paragraphs 4, 5 and 6 of Bill Clinton's speech.

Explain:

- what has to be done, in each speaker's opinion, to make the world a better place
- how the writers use language to get their arguments across

Planning and drafting

The task asks you to look at two features of the texts. Use these points in order to make preparatory notes.

1: what has to be done

Look at references to:

- 'finishing the work' (Lincoln, paragraph 3)
- *a new birth of freedom…* (Lincoln, paragraph 3)
- 'closing the gap' (Clinton, paragraph 3)
- 'shrinking the burdens' (Clinton, paragraphs 4, 5 and 6)

2: the language

Look at:

- paragraphs:
    structure
    openings and conclusions
- tenses
- rhetorical language:
    three-part lists
    repetition
    striking images

> You could start:
> *Both writers address the question of what has to be done to make the world a better place. Abraham Lincoln believes that…*

HIGHER TIER TASKS

1 ANALYSING THE SPEECHES

Read both speeches again. Explain how the writers convey their arguments through the content and use of language.

Planning and drafting

The task asks you to look at two features of the texts: content and language. Use these points in order to make preparatory notes.

1: the content

Look at the use of:

- examples from recorded history (Lincoln, paragraph 1; Clinton, paragraph 1)
- parallels with humankind's earlier history (Clinton, paragraph 3)
- statistics (Clinton, paragraph 5)

2: the language

Look at:

- paragraphs:
    structure
    openings and conclusions
- tenses
- rhetorical language:
    three-part lists
    repetition
    striking images

You could start:

The two speakers use a variety of methods to get their arguments across. Both, for example, refer to events from history…

2 COMPOSING A SPEECH

Compose your own speech on an issue which interests you. This could be on a major global issue (such as the mistreatment of animals or the problem of drugs), or a question which affects your local community (such as racism or street crime). Choose your own structure or follow the example of Lincoln and Clinton: look back to a difficult past, consider a troubled present, and make recommendations for a better future.

Planning and drafting

Think about:

- the past, the present and the future
- particular examples from recent and earlier history
- paragraphs to clarify the structure of the argument

Decide whether you want to include:

- punchy openings and conclusions to paragraphs
- rhetorical language:
    three-part lists
    repetition
    striking images

You could give your speech a dramatic opening, such as:

This is a subject of the utmost importance to anybody concerned with the future of the world…

Crimestoppers

In this unit you will:

- study pages from a crime prevention booklet
- examine the language of advice texts
- create a page of an advice booklet

Many local police forces publish booklets and leaflets offering advice on how to protect yourself against crime. Here are two extracts from a publication issued by Thames Valley Police. The first extract deals with bogus callers, the second with personal safety.

Bogus Callers

1

Strangers at your door

Do not be fooled by bogus callers. When anyone calls at your home and claims to be an official of any organisation or local authority department, here's what you should do:

The Doorstep Code
Our advice is to follow these simple rules:

Be prepared. Have a door chain and spyhole fitted.
Ensure you know what to say and do when someone unexpected calls.
Secure your door chain before opening the door.
Ask all suspicious callers for identification and keep the door chain on while you check it.
Feel confident in being able to say no if someone wants to come in without showing their ID.
End up feeling safe rather than sorry. If you're suspicious don't let them in; if you're worried call the police.

DON'T BE SORRY... BE SAFE
In an emergency always dial 999

Personal Safety

The chances that you or a member of your family will be a victim of violent crime are low. However, the fear of becoming a victim is very real for many people, and if an attack does occur it can have a major impact on our lives, so it makes sense to take some simple precautions to keep ourselves and those close to us as safe as possible.

Transport

When using a taxi always sit in the back.

Only use a reputable taxi company (ask around your friends if you don't know one).

If you are being picked up by a Private Hire vehicle, ask the driver who he is there to collect. Remember! Private Hire taxi drivers are not allowed to tout for business on the street and should be pre-booked. (Don't jump in the first car that pulls up.)

If you are unhappy with the conduct of the driver make a note of the licence plate number (this should be displayed clearly inside the taxi) and report the matter.

Don't engage in conversation that lets the driver know you live alone.

When you arrive at your destination, be prepared: have your fare ready and your keys to hand.

If you are travelling a long distance, ensure you agree a fare before setting off.

On buses and trains sit near to other people or the driver.

If you are pestered by someone, report it to the driver or guard.

Never be tempted to hitch or accept a lift from someone you don't know and trust completely. If you go out for the night make sure you save enough money to get you home.

Whenever possible, share a taxi with a friend, it is safer and cheaper!!

Street Robbery

Whilst intimidation and robbery is rare, always be on your guard and don't take risks.

The following advice will help ensure your safety:

Always try to avoid carrying large amounts of cash.

When using cashpoints put the money and your card safely in your pocket or bag before walking away from the machine.

Avoid using cashpoints on your own late at night.

Don't carry your pin number with your card. Try to memorise it or write it down in code.

If someone approaches you and demands money or property, hand it over. Your safety is worth more than cash.

Do not keep cheque books and cards together.

If your credit cards are lost or stolen, tell the credit card companies immediately.

Be extra careful with your belongings in crowded places. Pickpockets operate in crowded shops and bars.

Never let your bag, purse or wallet out of your sight. Always report incidents to the Police.

Language in context

The power of language

Key features of the text are:

1. imperatives and directives
2. adverbials
3. conditional sentences

1 IMPERATIVES AND DIRECTIVES

> We use the **imperative** form of the verb when, for example, we want to give a command, issue a warning, or make a request. The imperative form is used in **directives** – sentences which ask/tell someone to do something.

a) Here are some directives of different kinds, all of which use the imperative form of the verb. Copy the grid and add at least two of your own examples in each box in the right-hand column:

Eight types of directive	Example, using the **imperative** form of the verb	Further examples
command	**Take** this.	
request	Please **be** on time tomorrow.	
warning	**Watch out**!	
offer	**Have** a sandwich.	
plea	**Help**!	
invitation	**Come out** with me this evening.	
instruction	**Take the third** on the left.	
expression of good wishes	**Have** a great birthday!	

b) Write down the imperative verbs in *The Doorstep Code*. (To start you off, there are two in the first rule: **Be** prepared and **Have** … fitted.) Which kind of directive (from the eight listed in the grid above) are the rules in *The Doorstep Code*? For example, are they commands, offers, invitations…?

c) In advice leaflets like this one, imperative sentences (directives) will be used to tell you – or strongly advise you – either *to do* something or *not to do* something.

Pick out and write down three examples of each use:

- imperative sentences telling you *to do* something
- imperative sentences telling you *not to do* something

(Avoid the examples you looked at in question b.)

d) *The Doorstep Code* is an example of an **acrostic** (a form in which the first – or sometimes the last – letter of each line goes to form a key word or phrase). The key phrase in this case is BE SAFE.

Make up your own acrostic, based on a different key word or phrase, to offer pieces of advice on an important topic. (You might opt for something to do with school, such as 'safety in the laboratory'.) Remember that each line should be an imperative sentence.

2 ADVERBIALS

> **Adverbials** are words or phrases which usually add information to a sentence. They can help us to answer questions such as When? How? and Where?

For example, the following sentence – *When using a taxi, sit safely in the back.* – contains three common types of adverbial:

- **time adverbials** answer the question **When?**
  When using a taxi,…
- **manner adverbials** answer the question **How?**
  …sit safely…
- **place adverbials** answer the question **Where?**
  …in the back.

a) In the first two columns of the following grid are the three common types of adverbials: time, manner and place. Next to each type are two examples from the *Personal Safety* page of the advice booklet. Copy the grid and write down three further examples of each type, also taken from the *Personal Safety* page.

Type of adverbial	Examples from the booklet	Three further examples from the booklet
Time adverbials (answer the question When?)	● ***When you arrive at your destination***, *be prepared* ● ***Always*** *try to avoid carrying large, amounts of cash.*	● ● ●
Manner adverbials (answer the question How?)	● *Avoid using cashpoints* ***on your own*** ● *write it down* ***in code***	● ● ●
Place adverbials (answer the question Where?)	● *always sit* ***in the back*** ● *Pickpockets operate* ***in crowded shops and bars***.	● ● ●

3 CONDITIONAL SENTENCES

A **conditional sentence** is a sentence in which one thing depends upon another. The **conditional clause** in the sentence will usually begin with the words *if* or *unless*.

Conditional clauses are **adverbials**, because they add information to the sentence: they tell us the *condition* under which something can or cannot happen.

Here are two examples of conditional sentences with the conditional clauses highlighted:

If someone calls to read the meter, *ask to see some identification.*

Do not open the door ***unless they show you some identification***.

a) Write down three conditional sentences from the *Personal Safety* page of the police booklet, underlining the conditional clauses in each one. For example:

If you are being picked up by a Private Hire vehicle, ask the driver who he is there to collect.

b) Conditional sentences are widely used in all sorts of advice texts. Invent and write down **two** examples of conditional sentences which might be found in each of the following advice texts. For each text, make up an *if…* sentence and an *unless…* sentence. Two have been completed to start you off:

Advice text	IF... sentence	UNLESS... sentence
a leaflet about healthy eating		
a booklet about safety in the home		*Never touch electrical wiring* ***unless you have switched off the power at the mains***.
a letter from school on how to revise for exams		
a book on how to care for a pet	***If your pet becomes overweight***, *ask the vet about diet and exercise.*	
a guide on getting the best out of a visit to a museum		

Writing to advise

FOUNDATION TIER TASKS

1 SUMMARISING THE MAIN POINTS

Read the two extracts from the booklet again. Summarise the main points it makes about personal safety.

Write 200–250 words.
Use your own words as far as possible.

Planning and drafting

Use these points in order to make preparatory notes.

Look at:

- the *Doorstep Code* (*Bogus Callers* section)
- what to do in taxis and buses (*Personal Safety* section, under the heading *Transport*)
- how to avoid being robbed (*Personal Safety*, under the heading *Street Robbery*)

> You could start:
>
> *The booklet makes a number of important points about personal safety. To begin with, it advises…*

2 EXAMINING THE LANGUAGE OF THE BOOKLET

Explain how the writers use language to advise readers about crime prevention.

Remember to put quotation marks round any words or phrases taken from the passage.

Planning and drafting

Use these points in order to make preparatory notes.

Look at the use of:

- imperatives and directives
    e.g. instructions such as *always sit in the back*, the *Doorstep Code* acrostic, directives advising you to do things and not to do things
- adverbials
    time adverbials: e.g. *When using cashpoints…*
    manner adverbials: e.g. *clearly*
    place adverbials: e.g. *in crowded places*
- conditional sentences
    if… sentences: e.g. *If you are travelling a long distance…*

> You could start:
>
> *The writers of this booklet have used a number of different methods to get their advice across. For example…*

HIGHER TIER TASKS

1 EXAMINING THE LANGUAGE OF THE BOOKLET

Here is a further section from the booklet, which gives advice about fire prevention.

Explain and comment on the ways in which the writers have expressed warnings and offered advice.

Fire Prevention 3

Smoke alarms save lives – have you got one? Is it working?
A fire strikes when you least expect it, often during the night. If you are asleep when a fire starts and you do not have a smoke alarm to wake you, the chances of you and your family surviving are zero. Smoke suffocates quickly, and you'll be dead before the flames reach you.

ACTION
- If you do not have a smoke alarm **FIT ONE**.
- If you do have a smoke alarm **TEST IT**.

Smoke alarms are not an early warning they are your ONLY warning!

Escape Plan
Fitting a smoke alarm will give you the vital moments to alert everybody in the house and escape. The next step is to have a FIRE ACTION PLAN so everyone knows exactly what to do if there's a fire. Key points of the plan should be:

- Take all persons in your home into account including children and elderly or disabled people.
- Choose the best escape route and another way out just in case the normal way is blocked. Keep all routes clear.
- Tell every member of the household the plan including the location of door and window keys.

Remember – If a fire should start in your home.

GET OUT – and get others out, but don't risk your own life.

GET THE FIRE BRIGADE OUT – Go to the nearest phone and dial 999.

STAY OUT – do not go back inside for anything.

For free advice on any fire safety matter please contact your Community Fire Safety Team – please see our advertisement opposite.

Planning and drafting

Use these points in order to make preparatory notes.

Consider the points about:
- smoke alarms
- escape plans
- what to do after leaving the building

Look at the use of:
- imperatives and directives
- conditional sentences (the two bullets under ACTION are examples of both)
- adverbials (such as *when you least expect it*)

You could start:
The Fire Prevention page covers a number of different areas. The first…

2 CREATING YOUR OWN ADVICE LEAFLET

Use the police booklet as a model to create a page from an advice leaflet of your choice. For example, it could be on *How to survive your first day of work experience*, or *Things you should and should not do at a party*. It will help to study other advice booklets.

Planning and drafting

Use these points in order to make preparatory notes.

Decide on a clear structure. For example, the *Fire Prevention* extract on the left was made up of three sections: smoke alarms, escape plans and what to do after leaving the building.

Consider the use of:
- imperatives and directives (possibly used in an acrostic)
- adverbials
- conditional sentences

If you were writing a leaflet about work experience, you could start:
Preparing for your first visit
As soon as the experience has been arranged…

Save the rainforest!

In this unit you will:

- compare three texts, all to do with rainforests
- examine the language appropriate for writing to persuade, to argue and to advise
- create a page of a leaflet or brochure

WRITING TO PERSUADE

This text, an example of writing to persuade, is one side of a leaflet encouraging people to visit The Living Rainforest, near Newbury in Berkshire.

THE LIVING RAINFOREST

Our mission

Bringing the Rainforest to Life

The Living Rainforest's mission is to explore the relationship between humanity and the world's rainforests through education and research. The Living Rainforest provides a hands-on rainforest experience to many thousands of visitors. Throughout its work, an emphasis is placed on being engaging, down-to-earth and innovative.

A visit to the Living Rainforest is a rare and valuable opportunity to see some of the wonderful plants and wildlife that the world is losing as rainforests disappear.

The Living Rainforest is committed to providing an opportunity for as many people as possible to experience an authentic rainforest environment, without having to travel thousands of miles for the privilege.

A Living Learning experience

To walk in a rainforest is to experience a different world. Every year, thousands of visitors are delighted by the sights, sounds and smells of a living rainforest environment – without leaving England.

Over 10,000 school children visit The Living Rainforest each year. School tours are linked to the National Curriculum.

Special workshops aim to enhance and expand the visitor experience. Day, night and school tours give different perspectives on the rainforest world. Please call (01635) 202444 for a programme of events geared to all ages.

NATIONAL LOTTERY CHARITIES BOARD

In 1998 the National Lottery Charities Board granted over £108,000 for a Special Needs Education Project to improve access and learning opportunities at the rainforest. Come and see the difference this money is making, particularly for people with physical, mental or sensory difficulties.

WRITING TO ARGUE

This advertisement, which includes examples of writing to argue, encourages people to sponsor acres of threatened rainforest in Ecuador, South America.

DON'T LET IT GO TO PIECES

Frustrated and tired of hearing about the disappearing rainforests? Well here's your chance to do something positive about it – by protecting areas of rainforest forever.

The world's rainforests represent a vast reservoir of knowledge and hold potential for the discovery of new medicines and foods. There is no doubt that large-scale deforestation alters the climate – intensifying droughts in the dry season and floods in the rainy season. The result being fewer animal and plant species, soil erosion, an unreliable water supply and poorer health for the local people.

Photograph: ARDEA London Ltd

direction of Corridor

protected areas

What can you do to help?
By joining Rainforest Concern and sponsoring acres of threatened rainforest for the Choco-Andean Rainforest Corridor in Ecuador, South America, you will be protecting one of the world's most important ecological areas.

Within these forests live an amazingly high number of endangered species, many of which are found nowhere else on earth. This is why the region has been classified as one of the world's "biodiversity hotspots".

You will be helping to secure the survival and culture of the Awa and Cayapas indigenous people who still live in harmony with their natural environment. These forests are also home to exotic animals such as jaguars, pumas, tapirs, sloths and monkeys, hundreds of species of birds and thousands of species of plants.

We are two thirds of the way to achieving our objective of completing the Choco-Andean Corridor, so please help this dynamic conservation project by completing the coupon now or, if you prefer, telephone us. All currencies will be accepted when paying by credit card.

Your sponsorship will be a wonderful gift for your children, their children and the Earth itself.

YOU CAN MAKE A DIFFERENCE – THERE IS STILL TIME IF WE ACT QUICKLY!

From the *Big Issue*, 1–7 October 2001

WRITING TO ADVISE

Many students decide to spend a year working and travelling abroad between leaving school and starting higher education. This has become known as a 'gap' year. The page below is from a magazine called *Go Global!*, published by Gap Activity Projects, which organises gap year placements.

conservation

GAPpers (left to right) Chris Palmer from Stocksfield and Charlotte Berry from Abingdon in the Northern Territories, Australia

Getting involved in conservation with GAP means getting out there with groups of like-minded people. You'll see the real difference you can make to the environment, as you work on ongoing projects. It's a great way to appreciate the natural world and the mod cons which you'll have to do without!

The work in Australia and the rainforests of Latin America is more land management and heritage refurbishment than the protection of endangered species, although there is often the scope for surveys of flora and fauna, which will be of ecological value. Conservation can be hard physical work, so you'll need to be prepared to get stuck in. You could be working alongside volunteers from all over the world and you'll be able to see the results of all that hard work! As your project develops, you'll be looked upon as an experienced volunteer, having been trained for each particular job, be it coppicing, laying tracks or restoring old buildings. You'll come home with skills you never thought yourself capable of, and a new group of international friends. Steve Chapman from Leeds describes settling in at Iracambi Rainforest & Research Centre in Brazil.

Kerry Dinsmore from County Antrim, Northern Ireland, volunteered on a conservation project in Australia:

"We soon learned the way our project operated. Rocklea was our home, our base that we came back to each weekend, and during the week we got sent off in a team of usually about six to pretty much anywhere in South Queensland that needed help in protecting the environment. We built fences to protect Bilbys — strange-looking marsupials that were like overgrown mice with rabbit ears and baby pouches — in Currawinga. We built paths through Brisbane Forest Park, and planted hundreds of thousands of trees just about everywhere."

"The work is hard and physical, in temperatures of above 35°C and in hot sun, and the diet is very healthy. Tonight I hope to catch some fish from our lake, it's small yet there are 8000 fish in it apparently! Our diet consists of fish, veg, rice and pasta. But the lack of a TV, shower, or anything hi-tech merely stands to make them seem insignificant. The river is far more fun than any shower and without TV, people actually talk — the people here are great.

"The interaction is fantastic, and the general experience is life changing. My views on the world have changed already! The most fun part is the improvisation. Using a foam box as a freezer (with ice packs), using the river as a fridge. It brings a new meaning and diversifies your thoughts. Also, the little things like waking up to a humming bird at 7:30 and the noise of crickets as you go to sleep."

"the general experience is life changing"

Other Opportunities . . .

GAP has some projects that don't fall easily into the previous categories.

Currently these other opportunities include things like research posts in the Falkland Islands and Community Centre work in Fiji. These options can be discussed at your interview.

VSO welcomes the contribution of GAPpers to building a more equitable world.

A Duke of Edinburgh's Award is always good preparation for your GAP project. Furthermore, your experiences with GAP can count towards the service or residential sections of the award, through the Award's Access Scheme. It doesn't matter if you haven't started the Award Scheme before — it's open to everyone. For more information, contact GAP House.

medical

This is a great opportunity to get real experience of living and working in a hospital, and will be useful if you intend to study medicine or nursing. There will be different tasks and challenges to adapt to as you move around different wards with patients with different conditions, you will also gain administrative experience as well as a good range of general skills. You don't have to be planning a career in medicine, but a GAP medical project will certainly help if you are. GAPpers work with the Red Cross or local organisations.

Clare Bradley from Hertfordshire volunteered at Kitami Red Cross Hospital, Hokkaido, Japan:

Amy Done, GAPper from Wolverhampton, on her project at Wakayama Red Cross Hospital, Japan

"My work included basic stuff like making beds, cleaning wheelchairs and collecting supplies. At mealtimes we would feed the patients and we'd have to wheel patients around the hospital for X-rays, appointments in other departments, and to collect lab results.

"Kitami is a well-supplied modern hospital, and we had a four-day induction touring both the town and the hospital. We met the hospital Director and had lessons in calligraphy and ikebana. I did actually learn to speak a bit of Japanese although it was necessary to learn not to care if you sounded silly or made mistakes!"

"team building, climbing towers, water sports, high ropes and archery"

Outdoor Activities

There are a variety of outdoor activities – you could be farming in the Falklands or orienteering in Ohio. You will need to enjoy being out in all weathers and working with other people towards a shared aim. Outdoor work can seem repetitive and physically draining, but the rewards will be obvious and you'll know you've achieved something as you learn new skills. Think about the climate that appeals to you.

GAPper Jessica Apps from Kent on her outdoor activities project. Photo: Jessica's GAP partner, Amy McPhedran from Wiltshire

Jessica Apps from Kent describes her outdoor project at the Therapeutic Riding School, Israel:

"Our work was divided into three main areas – Hippo therapy uses the horse's movement to physically help the riders' healing process, and gives vital movement to muscles that are not generally worked daily. The horses also provide the ideal opportunity to help autistic children or those with behavioural problems, as they learn discipline and concentration. The final therapy is recreational – sports riding is undertaken by riders with many different problems, and can provide confidence, exercise and independence from the confines of a wheelchair or crutches."

Craig Argent from Stafford volunteered at YMCA Camp Becket, Massachusetts, USA:

"During the busy season we led, instructed and assisted in team building, climbing towers, water sports, high ropes and archery. Evenings included campfire songs and skits, night hikes and square dances, plus quieter moments for office and admin work. When the snow arrived, programmes switched to snow sports, tracking, hibernation and survival studies, and indoor activities like arts and crafts.

"All groups on camp have to be prepared for, fed, cared for and cleaned up after. GAPpers take part in nearly every part of running the camp."

check it out

www.gap.org.uk

Language in context

The power of language

Key features of the texts are:

1 the language of *persuade*, *argue* and *advise* texts

2 writing for a purpose

3 the combination of text and image

---

1 **THE LANGUAGE OF WRITING TO PERSUADE, ARGUE AND ADVISE**

Writing to **persuade**, writing to **argue** and writing to **advise** all focus on presenting a case and influencing the reader. This kind of writing is found, for example, in leaflets (e.g. for places to visit), advertisements (including those for charities and campaigns) and brochures (e.g. for organisations).

Writing to persuade: the use of adjectives and adjective phrases

An **adjective** is a word which gives us information about a noun or pronoun. A group of words which does this is called an **adjective phrase**.

The leaflet advertising The Living Rainforest depends upon adjectives and adjective phrases to explain the centre's attractions.

a) Below are a number of quotations taken from the leaflet. They all contain adjectives and adjective phrases:

Living Rainforest | **hands-on rainforest** experience | being **engaging, down-to-earth** and **innovative** | **rare** and **valuable** opportunity | **wonderful** plants and wildlife | an **authentic rainforest** environment | to experience a **different** world | **Special** workshops | **different** perspectives | **physical, mental** or **sensory** difficulties

Write three short paragraphs to show how these adjectives and adjective phrases help to get across the main themes of the text, that:

- a visit to The Living Rainforest is an *active* experience
- this particular conservation centre offers a chance to see first hand some of the remarkable vegetation that is under threat
- the experience is geared to the needs of schools and also to people with particular difficulties

Writing to argue: the use of abstract nouns

An **abstract noun** is the label we give to something we cannot touch, such as an emotion, feeling or idea.

b) The writers of the Rainforest Concern advertisement have used abstract nouns to label key concepts – starting with the idea of *concern* itself. They include the following (in the order in which they appear):

areas, knowledge, potential, discovery, deforestation, climate, season, result, species, erosion, supply, health, number, hotspots, survival, culture, harmony, environment, objective, project, sponsorship, difference, time

Find where these abstract nouns appear in the text. Then copy out the grid below and place the abstract nouns into four groups, according to the message they are helping to convey. Some have been inserted to start you off:

Message	Abstract nouns
Rainforests are a source of very important scientific information and future discoveries.	*knowledge*
They are home to a huge variety of plants and animals.	*species*
Cutting down the rainforests is therefore doing great damage.	*climate*
Your money is needed to help protect rainforest in Ecuador and support the Awa and Cayapas people who live there.	*sponsorship*

Writing to advise:
the use of the second person

> **Verbs** can be in the **first person** (*I hope to… We soon learned…*), the **second person** (*You'll see…*) or the **third person** (*It's a great way… She enjoyed herself… Conservation can be hard work…*).

A successful brochure or leaflet offering advice and information will vary the ways in which it addresses the reader. We can see this by looking at the person of the verb.

c) Write down the two persons of the verb which are used in:

- the introductory paragraphs (*Getting involved … in Brazil*).
- Steve Chapman's account of his work in Brazil (*The work is … people here are great*)

d) Write three or four sentences to explain how different viewpoints (using different persons of the verb) help to add variety and interest to this page. For example, how important is the use of the second person in the opening paragraph? What would be lost if the accounts by Steve Chapman and Kerry Dinsmore were wholly in the third person?

2 PURPOSE

> Whatever we write – whether it is a shopping list or a short story – we should always have a **purpose** in mind.

In all three of these texts the writers have had three linked purposes: *to persuade*, *to argue* and *to advise*. These three purposes overlap – the writers might be aiming to persuade while they are offering advice, for example, or they might be arguing in order to persuade you.

a) Copy the grid below and fill it in with examples of the different kinds of writing: to persuade, to argue and to advise. A short quotation will do for each example. Three have been filled in to start you off. Remember that purposes overlap, so, when you have completed the grid, compare your entries with other people and talk about your decisions.

Text and purpose for writing	Example
The Living Rainforest	
Writing to persuade	
Writing to argue	*…the difference this money is making, particularly for people with physical, mental or sensory difficulties.*
Writing to advise	
Rainforest Concern	
Writing to persuade	*Your sponsorship will be a wonderful gift…*
Writing to argue	
Writing to advise	
GAP: Go Global!	
Writing to persuade	
Writing to argue	
Writing to advise	*It doesn't matter if you haven't started the Award Scheme before…*

3 TEXT AND IMAGE

> A successful leaflet or brochure will usually have an effective combination of **text** (words) and **image** (photographs and illustrations).

a) Write three paragraphs to show how the designers of each extract have effectively combined text and image. In the Rainforest Concern advert, for example, think about the effect of combining:

- the two photographs at the top, juxtaposed (placed next to each other) with the text beneath
- the jigsaw puzzle shape with its slogan

Compare and contrast

FOUNDATION TIER TASKS

1 SUMMARISING THE INFORMATION

Reread the advertisement for Rainforest Concern. Then summarise what it says about:

- the threats to the rainforest environment
- the steps that are being taken to protect rainforests

Write 200–250 words in total.
Use your own words as far as possible.

> ### Planning and drafting
>
> The task is in two parts. Use these points in order to make preparatory notes.
>
> *Part 1: the threats to the rainforest environment*
>
> Look at:
>
> - the paragraphs which begin *The world's rainforests…* and *Within these forests…*
>
> *Part 2: the steps that are being taken to protect rainforests*
>
> Look at:
>
> - the paragraphs which begin *What can you do to help?*, *You will be helping…* and *We are two thirds…*
>
> ....
> You could start:
>
> *The advertisement begins by listing some of the threats to the rainforest environment. It says that…*
> ....

2 WRITING TO ARGUE

Write a letter to a newspaper arguing that we should care about what happens to the rainforest and should support attempts to protect it.

....
You could start:

I am writing to urge people to wake up to the fact that…
....

HIGHER TIER TASKS

1 EXAMINING THE LANGUAGE OF PERSUASION

On the next page is part of a leaflet advertising an exhibition at the Natural History Museum, London, called *Predators*.

Explain how the creators of the leaflet, through their choice of content and use of language, persuade us to visit the exhibition.

> ### Planning and drafting
>
> Look, for example, at the use of:
>
> - persuasive language to do with (a) the creatures represented (e.g. *sophisticated killers, amazing range of weapons, fight for survival, far from helpless, the drama behind the 'evolutionary arms race'*) and (b) the ways of exhibiting them (e.g. *major new exhibition, ideal for families, Dynamic displays, stunning photography…*)
> - slogans and catchphrases (e.g. *Eat or be eaten, hunter and hunted…*)
> - powerful ends of paragraphs
> - imperatives (e.g. *Operate its eyes…*)
> - questions (e.g. *dare you…?*)
> - abstract nouns (e.g. *strategies, survival, defences, camouflage, armour…*)
> - adjectives and adjective phrases (e.g. *tiny but lethal, sophisticated, amazing, helpless, cunning, lightning…*)
> - combination of text and image

2 CREATING YOUR OWN LEAFLET

Create a leaflet, an advertisement or a page from a brochure which has something to do with the protection of the environment. You might want to base your work on the examples in this unit, using some of the language features listed in the *Planning and drafting* section of the previous question.

Predators try to eat ...
Prey try to escape ...
Every meeting is
a battle of life
and death ...

Survival is the aim

Predators, a major new exhibition at the Natural History Museum, is ideal for families with children aged 7–12. Dynamic displays include three huge moving models: a life-size shark, a man-size spider and a chameleon you can control. Operate its eyes and sticky tongue to see if you could eat enough to survive – or test your skills against others in a high-speed interactive game. Before you leave, dare you touch the giant spider's sprung steel web?

Museum specimens and stunning photography give a powerful insight into the drama behind the 'evolutionary arms race', and show the delicate balance that exists between hunter and hunted.

From great white sharks to tiny but lethal spiders, the natural world is full of sophisticated killers. They use an amazing range of weapons and strategies to hunt and kill. But their prey are far from helpless. They too fight for survival using cunning defences, from lightning speed to camouflage and armour. The outcome of each battle for life is never certain.

Eat or be eaten

Self assess

These are the main language features that you have learned about in this section.
Decide how confident you feel about:

- understanding the effects of **headings** and **slogans**
- identifying **abstract nouns** and explaining their uses
- commenting on the effects of combining **text** and **image**

- understanding the part played by **paragraphs** in a text's structure
- understanding how **tenses** are used
- giving examples of **rhetorical language** in speeches

- understanding the uses of **imperatives** and **directives**
- commenting on the use of **adverbials**
- explaining the uses of **conditional sentences**

- identifying **adjectives** and **adjective phrases** and discussing their uses
- explaining the different uses of **first**, **second** and **third person**
- understanding the different **purposes** for writing

What do you feel you need to revise?

The big question

In this unit you will:

- study an analysis of an important question
- examine the way in which the writer has structured her article
- write an analysis of an issue

The article from which this extract is taken appeared in the *Daily Express* on 3 November 2001.

Has the time now come for London Zoo to free its captives?

Cheryl Stonehouse

It's hard to be critical of London Zoo after a weekday spent there watching hosts of schoolchildren wandering through its 36 acres on the edge of Regent's Park on a crisp and sunny autumn day, their faces lighting up with delight, wonder and enthusiasm as each turn brings yet another exotic animal into view.

Then there are the mothers and nannies with toddlers who appreciate everything about the place – something to fascinate the children, something to get them all out in the fresh air, and a very pretty and efficient café set by a fountain where the grown-ups can get some respite.

And there's Alan a retired local government worker who has paid his annual £30 membership fee and comes almost every day. There is, he says, a small battalion of pensioners like him, all regular visitors to the world's oldest zoo. "But we come to watch the people," he

vital dispensation	essential special treatment (in this case, allowing the rhinos the same privilege as the elephants: to be kept in a more spacious environment)

says, chuckling.

The elephants, however, have given up watching the people. Some time before this week's announcement that the three of them, Dilberta, Mya and Layang-Layang, will shortly be sent off to the zoo's country estate at Whipsnade, visitors had begun asking questions about the way they stand at the closed door to their pavilion for hours on end, their bottoms firmly turned towards the gawping visitors. Layang-Layang, a Sri Lankan orphan "rescued" from a logging camp more than a decade ago, sometimes stands at the back of the queue swaying compulsively from side to side in a way which looks weird to even the most elephant-ignorant of observers.

On Thursday, this went on for hours; after a brief wander around their tedious and rather small enclosure, the three elephants began to line up at their pavilion door at midday, seemingly entertaining a vain hope that someone might open it. Although no one did, they went on hoping until the zoo closed at 4.30 pm.

…Still, these problems will be solved won't they, when the three of them go to join the bull and two females, one of them pregnant, at Whipsnade?

Well, perhaps not. Not only does it turn out to be difficult to find well-known figures with an interest or expertise in animal welfare who will support London Zoo without hesitation, but it becomes clear that, for some, the removal of the elephants should really be only the beginning of a determined dismantling of the zoo as it stands.

"Despite all the fine words about education and conservation that we've heard over the past few years, it is what it always has been since it opened in 1827 – a living gallery of imprisoned beasts for people to gawp at," is the uncompromising verdict of Andrew Tyler, director of campaigning charity Animal Aid.

And celebration is the last thing on the mind of Virginia McKenna, the *Born Free* actress who has campaigned for an end to the 170-year tradition of keeping elephants at London Zoo for 18 years. Her immediate reaction to the elephants' release from Regent's Park was to ask when the rhinos would get what she sees as the same, vital, dispensation.

Even the zoo's management has admitted recently that the most frequent question asked by worried visitors was whether the rhino enclosure, a muddy, barren strip of land behind the elephant house, was really big enough. Only one rhino now remains, the others having been shipped out to Whipsnade over recent months. But there's more, much more. Visitors are surely charmed and worried in equal parts by the two lions who live on a strip of land which would make you or I laugh with disbelief if we were offered it as a suitably-sized garden for a semi-detached house; the amur leopard next door has worn a groove in the ground alongside the glass wall which allows children to stand inches away from this magnificent creature and – now here's an experience – watch as it turns its bottom to them and squats to defecate; the maned wolves do regular, apparently mind-numbing, circuits of their pen while, it is easy to imagine, being tormented by the freedom of the joggers who regularly pass them on the other side of the park railings.

…There's no doubt at all that the zoo and its staff work hard to give their animals the best care possible, and the reduction of the number of animals housed there from more than 5,000 in 1990 to the present population of under 2,000 has vastly improved conditions.

"We keep the welfare of all our animals under constant review and we act promptly on all expert advice," said a spokesman for London Zoo. "We are confident we are doing the best we possibly can for our animals."

But critics argue that while the efforts and intentions of the zoo's management can't be faulted, the very concept of a city zoo is faulty and can never provide more than a handful of animals with a satisfactory environment.

Language in context

The power of language

Key features of the text are:

1 emotive vocabulary

2 paragraphs which help to structure the analysis

3 the presentation of both sides of the argument

---

1 EMOTIVE VOCABULARY

> **Vocabulary** is the term given to a writer's choice of words. **Emotive vocabulary** is designed to have a particular effect on our feelings.

The issue of how we treat animals in zoos is one which raises high emotions. The writer of this article, Cheryl Stonehouse, has chosen emotive vocabulary which reflects the strong feelings on both sides of the argument.

a) In the opening three paragraphs the writer uses **positive emotive vocabulary** to present all the favourable aspects of the zoo, things that people enjoy. For example, she describes the children's faces *lighting up with delight, wonder and enthusiasm*. Pick out the emotive words used to describe:

- the autumn day
- the air
- the café

b) In the fourth paragraph the mood changes as Cheryl Stonehouse describes the behaviour of the elephants, who *stand at the closed door to their pavilion for hours on end.*

Pick out the **negative emotive vocabulary** used to describe:

- the visitors
- the elephants' movements
- the elephant enclosure

c) Look again at the emotive language in the article's headline. Explain its use and comment on its effect.

d) Reread lines 103–36 (*Even the zoo's...*). Pick out and write down the emotive words used to describe:

- the visitors
- the rhinos' enclosure
- the wolves' circuits of their pen

Explain whether this vocabulary is negative or positive, giving your reasons.

e) The emotive words in lines 103–36 play a major part in the description of the animals' living conditions. In your own words, summarise the writer's main points in that paragraph (from *Even the zoo's...* to *...the park railings*).

2 PARAGRAPHS AND STRUCTURE

> A **paragraph** is a block of sentences linked together by one main idea or subject.

Paragraphs in newspaper articles tend to be shorter than paragraphs in most other kinds of writing (see the unit on newspapers, pages 112–19). There are thirteen paragraphs in this extract. Each one can be given a **topic heading**: a brief title which summarises the content. For example, the first paragraph might be headed *Introducing the pleasures of the zoo*.

a) Write a topic heading for each of the other twelve paragraphs.

b) The article as a whole can be divided into five larger sections, each one made up of one or more paragraphs. Each section plays a part in analysing the problems facing London Zoo. The fifth section, for example, is a conclusion in which the writer sums up the progress that has been made and offers her own viewpoint.

- Copy out the chart on the following page. In the left-hand column add the topic heading that you have devised for each paragraph.

Paragraphs and topic headings	Sections of the analysis
1 *Introducing the pleasures of the zoo*	
2	
3	
4	
5	
6	
7	
8	
9	
10	
11	Section 5: *a conclusion in which the writer sums up the progress that has been made and offers her own viewpoint.*
12	
13	

- Now reread the article and draw lines across the right-hand column to show where the divisions between the five sections should come. In the four remaining spaces, add a brief explanation of what is included in each section.

3   PRESENTING AN ARGUMENT

An **analysis** of an issue presents **both sides of the argument** and considers the **evidence**.

Cheryl Stonehouse's analysis of the problems facing London Zoo includes favourable comments about the zoo as well as criticisms. Her points throughout the article are supported and illustrated by evidence.

a) Points in favour of the zoo
List the evidence from the first three paragraphs which shows what an enjoyable place London Zoo can be. Explain in your own words which features of the zoo are being presented in a positive light. Summarise the attempts being made by the zoo authorities to improve conditions (lines 137–53).

b) Points against the zoo
Explain, referring closely to the text, how the writer uses particular examples to demonstrate how bad the animals' living conditions are.

c) Presenting the evidence

The final three paragraphs of the article (from *There's no doubt...*) are a good example of a method known as **point–evidence–comment**.

When you employ this method, you:
- make your **point**
  (any general point, or a specific one)
- cite your **evidence**
  (such as a quote from an expert or some statistics)
- make your follow-up **comment**
  (this might be in support of the evidence; or it might query or challenge it)

Reread the final three paragraphs. Write down in your own words the point being made (lines 137–45), the evidence cited (146–53) and the follow-up comment (154–61).

Writing to analyse

FOUNDATION TIER TASKS

1 SUMMARISING THE MAIN POINTS

Reread the article *Has the time now come for London Zoo to free its captives?* and then summarise:

- the conditions in which the animals are living
- the views of people who are against keeping animals in this way

Use your own words as far as possible.
Write 200–250 words in total.

Planning and drafting

The task is in two parts. Use these points in order to make preparatory notes.

Part 1: the conditions in which the animals are living

Look at the writer's points about:

- the elephants (lines 31–63)
- the rhinos, lions, leopard and wolves (91–136)

Part 2: the views of people who are against keeping animals in this way

Look at the views of:

- Andrew Tyler and others (69–90)
- Virginia McKenna (91–102)

You could start:

The animals are living in cramped and depressing conditions. The elephants, for example…

2 ANALYSING THE ARGUMENTS

Is it right to keep large animals in traditional zoos?
Your class is about to discuss this topic.

Write two short speeches (about 150 words each): one summarising the arguments in favour of keeping large animals in traditional zoos, and one against.

Remember that:

- **positive** and **negative emotive words** can help you to express points effectively
- **paragraphs** will help you to structure your ideas
- you are presenting **both sides** of the argument

Planning and drafting

Use the article to help you make preparatory notes.

1: in favour
Look at paragraphs 1, 2, 3, 11 and 12.

2: against
Look at paragraphs 4 to 10 and paragraph 13.

You could start:

There are clear and convincing arguments in favour of (or: against…) keeping animals in zoos. To begin with…

HIGHER TIER TASKS

 1 **EXAMINING THE CONTENT AND LANGUAGE**

Explain how the writer, through content and use of language, helps us to understand the issues involved in keeping larger animals at London Zoo.

Refer among other things to the structure of the article, the presentation of evidence and the use of emotive language.

> You could start:
>
> *Cheryl Stonehouse creates a clear structure in order to present the arguments. The paragraphs…*

2 **WRITING YOUR OWN ANALYSIS**

Write your own analysis of an issue which interests you. Choose an issue about which there are strong arguments on both sides, such as whether or not animals (or even humans) should be cloned, or whether vivisection (experiments on living animals) should be banned.

The internet is a good source of information; look at the collection of articles for GCSE students published weekly in *Guardian Education* (available on **www.guardian.co.uk**).

Planning and drafting

Think about:

- presenting both sides of the argument
- the point-evidence-comment method
- paragraphs and structure
- emotive language

> You could model your opening on the introductory sentence of the London Zoo article:
>
> *It is hard to be critical of the idea of cloning, when we think of the medical advances that…*

Blockbuster

In this unit you will:

- compare two film reviews
- examine the language of criticism
- write a review for a newspaper, magazine or website

The first of these film reviews appeared in the *Mirror* on 16 November 2001. Jonathan Ross begins by referring to two films; in this extract he writes about the first, *Harry Potter and the Philosopher's Stone*. (His comments on the second film, *Ghost World*, do not appear here.)

A magical mythical tour de force

By JONATHAN ROSS

SOMETIMES I really love this job. This week sees the release of two wildly different movies that I've been looking forward to all year and, remarkably, both manage to live up to my very high expectations.

Let's get the biggest one out of the way first. **Harry Potter And The Philosopher's Stone** is finally out, and there can't be a parent in the land who isn't delighted at the prospect of having to take their kids to see it. In fact, I suspect that just about everyone, with or without offspring in tow, will be rushing to cinemas to join in what's going to be the movie event of the year. It will be a smash whatever happens, but the big question is, will it be as good as the book?

It seems almost pointless to recount the plot, seeing as most of you will have read volume one in young Harry's story. He is raised by non-magical relatives – muggles of the worst sort – and then discovers to his delight that he's from wizarding stock and will be journeying to Hogwarts School Of Witchcraft And Wizardry to study.

Once there, he makes friends and a few enemies, and discovers that he's a celebrity thanks to a run-in with the most evil wizard of all, Voldemort. He also turns out to be a whiz on the broomstick and ends up on his house's Quidditch team.

If none of this makes sense you might want to give the film a miss, because one of the few criticisms I have of the movie is that it relies rather too heavily on us having a working knowledge of the book. The early scenes in which Harry is living a miserable existence with his cold-hearted uncle and aunt – the dire Dursleys – are sketched in with such haste and brevity that they might as well not have been included.

The same might be said of the background story which details the pivotal role Harry's parents had in defeating Voldemort, and how the infant Harry was the means by which Good triumphed over Evil. Of course, most of us have read the books, so maybe it doesn't matter that much, but it's lazy all the same.

I guess we can forgive screenwriter Steve Kloves and director Chris Columbus for wanting to get us to Hogwarts quickly, as that's where the real fun is to be found. The sets and the design are flawless, beautifully bringing to life the school and the grounds that were so brilliantly realised by author JK Rowling.

85 The cast is impeccable. Richard Harris brings just the right amount of benevolent gravitas to his role of Headmaster Dumbledore. 90 Maggie Smith is a sheer delight to watch as the crotchety but lovable Deputy Head Miss McGonagall. And Alan Rickman almost manages 95 the impossible by nearly stealing the film as Snape.

Most importantly, the key roles of Harry (Daniel Radcliffe), Ron (Rupert Grint), 100 Hermione (Emma Watson) and Draco (Tom Felton) are perf- 120 ormed by smart, intelligent and likable youngsters who do not put a foot wrong. Bravo 105 to the lot of 'em.

Robbie Coltrane is also terrific as Hagrid, the giant groundskeeper. It's impossible to think of anyone else filling 110 the role as comfortably.

At more than two and a half hours, it's a long film, but it never drags – even my youngest daughter, who is 115 not yet five, found it thrilling from beginning to end. The Quidditch match is astounding, exciting cinema at its best, and though it's not 120 quite up there with the chariot race from Ben Hur it's more than a match for the pod-racing sequence in the last Star Wars flick.

125 The final few scenes felt less gripping and tense than they should have, but I'm not sure if that's because we all know the outcome or because 130 it's impossible to top what's gone before. Either way, the film is a fantastic blast of unforgettable, thrilling, magical entertainment. My 135 kids were begging me to take them to see it again the very moment it ended. And you know what? I can't wait either!

Anabel Inge's review appeared in the *Daily Telegraph* on the same day.

Not so wild about Harry

ANABEL INGE

BEFORE Harry Potter, I can honestly say I had never read a book for pleasure. JK Rowling changed all that for me. I am dyslexic but have read all the Harry Potter books twice and listened to Stephen Fry's 5 audiotapes more times than I can remember – so, as you might expect, the words are precious to me. I was desperate to see the film.

It was always going to be hard for me to appreciate it for what it is, however, because I was bound to be 10 disappointed at what was left out. Even so, I felt let down.

Many of the child actors were clearly not experienced. Ron looked right, but I never quite stopped thinking that he was an actor saying his 15 lines. The same applied, though to a lesser degree, to Hermione and Harry.

My main criticism, though, is that the film has reduced a story that has a lot to say about childhood and loneliness into a detective action-thriller. The 20 beginning was skimpy and failed to give us a sense of what Harry was feeling. I think every child has at some point felt like a misfit, and I didn't think the film brought that out.

There wasn't enough on Harry's childhood of 25 misery with the Dursleys, which would have made us care more about what happened to him. I also thought it was a mistake to dive straight in with a magical scene, instead of giving us more of a chance to identify with Harry.

30 After Harry met Hagrid, everything seemed to happen in one day: his shopping trip in Diagon Alley, his train journey, his first day at Hogwarts. All the way through these events, Harry said little, just reacting with his mouth open, looking stunned and 35 happy. Far from identifying with him, I grew slightly bored.

There were some parts I loved: the troll, the Mirror of Erised, the giant chess game, every scene with Robbie Coltrane as Hagrid, the lessons, and 40 Hogwarts itself.

The Quidditch game was exciting, though the match commentator, Lee Jordan, wasn't as funny as the one in the book. Perhaps the film-makers thought the original Lee Jordan was too sexist, 45 because he said things like: "What an excellent chaser that girl is, and rather attractive, too."

The end was pure *Indiana Jones*, and its duration was disproportionate to the rest of the film. Maybe that's the problem: they made this film for boys.

Language in context

The power of language

Key features of the texts are:

1. appropriate register
2. personal perspective
3. first and third person
4. the language of criticism

1 APPROPRIATE REGISTER

A reviewer for a newspaper or magazine has to make decisions about which **register** to use. Register is the term given to the style of language which suits a certain kind of subject matter, or is appropriate to a particular situation or social context.

The author's choice of register will be influenced by the **purpose** of the writing and the **audience** it is aimed at. An informal register will tend to include examples of colloquial language (closer to everyday speech); a formal one will usually be closer to standard written English.

a) Jonathan Ross's review contains many elements of informal register.

Find, and note down, examples of each of the following:

- a chatty, 'matey' relationship with the reader (see lines 1–8 and 134–9)
- slang or colloquial expressions (see 9–24 and 119–39)
- a mock familiarity with the characters in the novel (see 25–9)
- abbreviations more commonly found in speech (see 104–5)
- jokes (see 108–10)

b) Anabel Inge's review is in a more formal register, but retains a direct address to the reader. (*I can honestly say… as you might expect…*)

Redraft her opening paragraph and concluding paragraph as Jonathan Ross might have written them, in a more informal register. Include examples of the five features of informal register that you found in his review.

2 PERSONAL PERSPECTIVE

Reviewers often like to open their reviews with a statement about themselves which helps the reader to understand the **context** in which they are writing.

a) Reread the opening of each review (paragraph 1 of Jonathan Ross's review, the first two paragraphs of Anabel Inge's). Briefly note down the main facts that each writer gives us in order to set the context for their review and help us to understand their personal perspective.

b) Write a short paragraph to explain how each reviewer's context-setting helps us to understand and respond to the opinions they each set out in their review.

3 FIRST AND THIRD PERSON

> Reviewers can express their opinions in either the **first person** or the **third person**.

When writers want to express clear-cut personal opinions, they often use the first person: *I enjoyed the scene in which… We were not expecting… I was amazed by…* The subjects of the verbs are the first person pronouns *I* or *we*.

But in reviews of this kind, opinions are much more frequently expressed in the third person: *There were some powerful effects… The ending was less successful… The opening scenes are brilliantly filmed…* Here, the subjects are: *some powerful effects, The ending, The opening scenes.*

a) Look back at the two reviews and write down three statements from each in which the writer expresses an opinion using the third person. Look, for example, at:

- lines 47–61 of Jonathan Ross's review (beginning *If none of this…*)
- lines 12–16 of Anabel Inge's review (beginning *Many of the…*)

> The most interesting reviews to read are often those in which the writer uses **both** the first and the third person. This can add variety to the writing and help to avoid repetitiveness.

b) Find a paragraph in Anabel Inge's review which begins with an opinion expressed in the third person, and concludes with one expressed in the first.

c) Now write a short paragraph of your own, reviewing a new film or television series. Make it similar in structure to the one you have just found: one sentence expressing an opinion in the third person; one sentence in the first person.

4 THE LANGUAGE OF CRITICISM

> A typical review will include both **positive** and **negative** criticism.

Many people find it much easier to express their enjoyment of a film or book than to explain why they did not like it. Review writers need to develop a language which can effectively express both approval and disapproval.

a) Find some examples of the phrases Jonathan Ross uses to express his enjoyment and approval of:

- the scenes in Hogwarts
- the cast and their performances

b) How effectively does he express his disappointment with certain features of the film? Reread lines 47–72 of his review. Note down:

- a general, overriding reservation he has about the film
- particular examples of this weakness

c) Write a sentence commenting on each of the following:

- the way in which Anabel Inge helps us to understand why she was disappointed with the film (see lines 1–11)
- the clear and economical way in which she expresses an initial criticism and supports it with brief examples (12–23)
- her ability to distinguish between what she liked and disliked (her references to the Quidditch game in lines 41–6)
- her very direct and unambiguous first-person statements (lines 6–7, 10–11, 22–3 and 35–6)

d) In pairs talk about the extent to which – and the ways in which – the two reviewers have expressed approval and disapproval.

Which of these reviews do you find more interesting to read (if you haven't seen the Harry Potter film), or more useful in helping you to examine your own views (if you have seen it)?

Writing to review

FOUNDATION TIER TASKS

1 SUMMARISING OPINIONS

Reread Jonathan Ross's review *A magical mythical tour de force* and then summarise:

● why he likes the film *Harry Potter and the Philosopher's Stone*
● what he dislikes about it

Use your own words as far as possible. Write 200–250 words in total.

Planning and drafting

The task is in two parts. Use these points in order to make preparatory notes.

Part 1: why Jonathan Ross likes the film
Look at his comments on:
● the Hogwarts scenes (lines 73–84)
● the cast (85–110)
● the excitement (111–24)
● the overall entertainment (131–39)

Part 2: what he dislikes
Look at his comments on:
● the early scenes (47–61)
● the background story (62–72)
● the final few scenes (125–31)

You could start:
Jonathan Ross likes the Harry Potter film for a number of reasons. To begin with…

2 LOOKING AT A WRITER'S LANGUAGE

Reread again Anabel Inge's review *Not so wild about Harry* and then explain:

● what she does not like about the film
● how she uses language to get her opinions across clearly and interestingly

Remember to put quotation marks round any words or phrases taken from the passage.

Planning and drafting

The task is in two parts. Use these points in order to make preparatory notes.

Part 1: what Anabel Inge does not like about the film
Look at her comments on:
● the child actors (lines 12–16)
● what has happened to a story about childhood and loneliness (17–26)
● the opening scene (26–9)
● the timing (30–2)
● Harry's behaviour through the film (32–6)
● the Quidditch match-commentator (41–6)
● the ending (47–9)

Part 2: how she uses language to get her opinions across clearly and interestingly
Look at the way she:
● introduces her review (1–11)
● gives particular examples (12–16 and 24–9)
● chooses words carefully (17–23)
● adds variety by expressing opinions in the first and third persons (30–6)
● uses lists (37–40)

You could start:
There are several things that Anabel Inge does not like about the Harry Potter film…

HIGHER TIER TASKS

1 WRITING YOUR OWN REVIEW

Write your own review of any new film, television programme (or series) or music album. The audience can be fairly narrow (e.g. other interested people in your year at school) or broad (for example, if the review is to be posted on a website).

It will help to read a variety of other reviews first. You can read the latest film reviews on sites such as **www.movies.yahoo.com** or **www.mrqe.com** (the Movie Review Query Engine).

Planning and drafting

Check:

- which **register** to write in (page 94)
- how much **personal perspective** to include in your introduction (page 94)
- take into account the **purpose** of your review and its intended **audience**
- vary the way you express your opinions, for example by using both the **first** and **third person** (page 95)
- find interesting and effective ways in which to express **approval** and **disapproval** (page 95)

> You could start with a sentence based on one of Jonathan Ross's:
>
> *This week sees the release of a (film/album...) that I have been looking forward to all year...*

2 ANALYSING THE TWO REVIEWS

Jonathan Ross and Anabel Inge both express their opinions about the Harry Potter film in newspaper reviews.

Explain and comment upon the choices that each writer has made and the different ways in which each one has expressed his or her opinions.

Support your answer by referring to the content, style and language of both reviews.

Planning and drafting

The task is in two parts. Use these questions in order to make preparatory notes.

Part 1: content
why Jonathan Ross likes the film
Refer to at his comments in lines 73–139

what he dislikes
Refer to his comments in lines 47–72 and 125–31

why Anabel Inge dislikes the film
Refer to her comments in lines 12–49

Part 2: style and language
Look at the register of Jonathan Ross's article
Look at the way Anabel Inge:

- introduces her review (1–11)
- gives particular examples (12–16 and 24–9)
- chooses words carefully (17–23)
- adds variety by expressing opinions in the first and third persons (24–9)
- uses lists (30–6)

> You could start:
>
> *The two reviewers have responded quite differently to the film...*

Harry and the press

In this unit you will:

- compare two opinions
- examine the language of newspaper comment
- write an article commenting on a news item

In January 2002, stories appeared in the newspapers about Harry, the 17-year-old younger son of Prince Charles. Harry had been caught drinking alcohol and smoking cannabis, and his father had responded by sending him on a day's visit to a drugs rehabilitation centre in south London to speak to addicts.

All daily newspapers carried the story when it broke, and all had articles in their comment pages. Here are two examples of newspaper comment, taken from the *Mirror* and the *Daily Mail*, 14 January 2002.

A father's love helps Harry to weed out problem

Tony Parsons

Drug shame? What drug shame? Prince Harry's brief flirtation with cannabis is only the modern equivalent of drinking cider 5 behind the bike sheds – equal parts curiosity, experimentation and healthy rebellion.

Harry is the teenage child of 10 a single parent in the 21st century – of course he can tell one end of a spliff from the other.

When Prince Charles was a teenager – and I know that's a 15 difficult concept to imagine – he was famously caught knocking back one cherry brandy over the odds.

Times change, and become 20 more dangerous. Once you had to hang out with bands, students and men with beards to be around drugs.

Now they are in every school, 25 in every playground, as much a part of life in certain pubs as darts and Scotch eggs.

There are, of course, a few subtle differences between cider 30 and cannabis.

Dope can get you kicked out of Eton, for a start. And if you are dumb enough to develop a real taste for spliff, you will 35 eventually find yourself in far dodgier surroundings than the local off-licence.

You can't score cannabis in the supermarket. It's illegal. For 40 now. Although the fact that the Queen's youngest grandson has been revealed as a user brings complete legalisation of puff a lot closer than it was a week ago. 45

Prince Harry has been outed as a lawbreaker, a drug user – and a boy who is gloriously human.

For all the polo, privilege and slaughter of small animals, 50 Harry's brush with pot shows that the Royal family sometimes have to face exactly the same problems as an ordinary family.

Clever kid. He has probably 55 ensured the survival of the monarchy for at least another hundred years.

It is impossible to feel anything but sympathy for both 60 Prince Harry – a good-natured

What Harry needs is a firm hand

PETER MCKAY

Prince Charles's method of dealing with the errant Prince Harry is agonisingly correct – but was it sensible? After it emerged that Harry had been drinking alcohol and smoking cannabis, Charles arranged for Prince William to have a word with him and for his younger son to visit a rehabilitation clinic which deals with heroin addicts.

No doubt the theory was that Harry would pay more attention to William than he would do to his father. Visiting a rehab clinic would also serve to remind him that many other young people have problems with drugs.

But William can't be a substitute father for Harry; and Harry, whatever he said at the time, is bound to have seen the south London clinic visit as an embarrassingly symbolic gesture.

Most parents of teenage children will sympathise with Charles; how can they be kept under surveillance at all times? But Prince Charles has a better chance of doing that than most of us.

For reasons of security, Harry and William enjoy (or otherwise) round-the-clock police protection; besides (as Richard Kay discussed in Saturday's *Mail*) Charles has a staff of 85.

Personally I'd have been happier to read that he'd given Harry a right royal roasting, reminded him of his privileged position and then taken strong measures to tighten up his son's private life and friendships. Futile, maybe, but better than the New Agey concept of visiting Featherstone Lodge rehabilitation unit in Peckham.

Was Charles over-concerned about how *he* would be seen in the light of Harry's misbehaviour? Perhaps so.

rehab centre/ rehabilitation clinic	centre attended by people who are hoping to be cured of drug or alcohol addiction

but curious teenager, much like any other – and for his father.

It is never easy to discover that your child is not as innocent as you would wish and hope. Charles responded to Harry's dope smoking with exactly the right measure of firmness and understanding. No screaming, no shouting and no ultimatums. [70]

[65]

Just a trip to see what drugs can do to young lives at a clinic for heroin addicts. As Harry knows, people who smoke the odd spliff [75] are not quite the same as people who jack up smack with dirty needles in abandoned buildings.

Even if he had continued smoking dope, the chances of [80] Harry ending up as a heroin addict are pretty much non-existent.

But the trip to the rehab centre would have been an education for Harry. It would have taught [85] him what every drug user needs to learn – that drugs are a dead end. The best thing you can do with drugs is grow out of them.

the New Agey concept	the idea associated with progressive 'New Age' thinkers

Language in context

The power of language

Key features of the text are:

1 colloquial language

2 slang and neologisms

3 language to express opinions

1 COLLOQUIAL LANGUAGE

> **Colloquial language** is the term given to vocabulary and expressions which are more commonly heard in everyday informal speech. Particular examples are called **colloquialisms**.

Journalists often use colloquialisms to give their writing an informal style which speaks directly to the reader.

a) Tony Parsons writes about the young Prince Charles *knocking back one cherry brandy over the odds*. In more formal writing this might appear as *drinking one too many cherry brandies*. Redraft these colloquialisms used by Tony Parsons as they might appear in formal standard English:

hang out with bands
kicked out of Eton
if you are dumb enough
far dodgier surroundings
Clever kid

b) Peter McKay uses the colloquial expression *a right royal roasting*. Write an explanation of what this phrase means and how effective it is in the context of the article. Include comments on McKay's use of alliteration and wordplay.

2 SLANG AND NEOLOGISMS

> Colloquial language often makes use of slang and neologisms. **Slang** is a form of language used by particular groups in informal situations, often to add vividness and immediacy. A **neologism** is a newly invented word or phrase.

Slang

a) Tony Parsons employs a number of slang terms to do with drugs and their use. They are: *spliff, dope, score, puff, pot, jack up smack.*

Give your opinions on his use of drugs slang in this article. Is it appropriate? Think about Tony Parsons' **audience** (readers of a popular, wide-circulation, national daily newspaper) and the **purpose** of the article (to express opinions). In your discussion consider the following points:

Slang is inappropriate here because it:

- alienates older readers (i.e. makes them feel outsiders because they might not understand the terms)
- risks trivialising a serious subject (i.e. suggesting that drugs are something we don't have to take too seriously)

Slang is appropriate here because it:

- helps ordinary readers to identify with the issues
- adds a helpful feeling of commonsense normality to a difficult subject

Neologisms

b) Neologisms arise when there is a need for a word or phrase to describe a new concept. For example, the term *couch-potato* was coined in the late 1980s to describe people who spend all day in front of the television. Explain the origin and meaning of the term *outed* in paragraph nine of Tony Parsons' article. How appropriate is it in this context?

c) Write a short paragraph to explain what the use of colloquial language adds to these two articles (include comments on slang and neologisms). How effective is it in this context, in your opinion? Before you write, think about audience and purpose.

3 LANGUAGE TO EXPRESS OPINIONS

> Comment texts usually include an expression of the writer's **opinions**.

a) The incident involving Prince Harry and his father Prince Charles opened up more than one debate in the newspapers. Find the places where the two writers address the question:

Did Charles do the right thing in sending Harry to visit the rehabilitation centre?

Write a paragraph in which you compare the different responses of the two writers to this question. Refer in particular to phrases such as: *No screaming, no shouting and no ultimatums* (Parsons), and *an embarrassingly symbolic gesture* (McKay).

b) Personal opinions do not have to be expressed in the first person (see page 95). Reread the extracts and write a paragraph in which you compare the writers' use of **first** and **third person** to express opinions. Look, for example, at:

- Tony Parsons' occasional first-person comments within a largely third-person article
- Peter McKay's use of the third person (but see paragraph 6)

c) What can you tell, from the articles' content and the writers' use of language, about:

- Tony Parsons' attitude to smoking cannabis
- Peter McKay's attitude to Prince Charles?

Writing to comment

FOUNDATION TIER TASKS

1 SUMMARISING OPINIONS

Reread Peter McKay's article, *What Harry needs is a firm hand*, and then summarise:

- how Prince Charles responded to the discovery that his son Harry was smoking cannabis and drinking, and why he chose to take the action he did
- Peter McKay's opinion of Prince Charles's actions

Use your own words as far as possible. Write 200–250 words in total.

Planning and drafting

The task is in two parts. Use these points in order to make preparatory notes.

Part 1: how Charles responded and why

Look at the writer's points about:

- Charles's response (paragraph 1)
- his reasons for taking the action (paragraph 2)

Part 2: McKay's opinions of Charles's response

Look at the comments on:

- the action taken by Charles (paragraph 3)
- the methods Charles has for keeping an eye on his sons' behaviour (paragraphs 4 and 5)
- the action that McKay would have preferred (paragraph 6)
- McKay's interpretation of Charles's actions (paragraph 7)

You could start:

When Prince Charles discovered that his son Harry was smoking cannabis and drinking, he…

2 GIVING YOUR OWN COMMENTS

Did Prince Charles do the right thing? What would you have done in his place?

Write two paragraphs: one giving your opinions on the actions taken by Prince Charles, the other explaining what you would do in similar circumstances and why.

Remember that you are expressing a personal opinion; you do not have to agree with either of the writers.

Planning and drafting

Use the articles to help you make preparatory notes. They will also give you ideas and remind you of the different ways in which people express their contrasting opinions.

1: your opinions on Prince Charles's actions

Look at:

- Tony Parsons (lines 59–78 and 83–89)
- Peter McKay (the whole article)

2: what would you have done in his place?

Look at:

- Peter McKay (paragraph 6)

You could start:

In my opinion, Prince Charles did (or: did not) take the right action with his son. Firstly,…

HIGHER TIER TASKS

1 COMPARING THE ARTICLES

The following extract is taken from an article which appeared in the *Independent* on the same day as the other articles that you have read.

Explain and comment on the different ways in which each of the three writers has tried to make you share their feelings and point of view.

Support your answer by referring to the content, style and language of all three extracts.

> You could start:
>
> *Each of the three writers views the question from his or her own perspective…*

2 WRITING YOUR OWN COMMENT ARTICLE

Write your own comment article based upon any current item of news. Decide which issues have been raised by the news item and give your opinions on them.

For example, news about a new government policy to combat bullying in schools might lead you to (a) express your opinions on the details of the proposed policy, (b) discuss bullying as a problem more generally and (c) offer suggestions on what you think ought to be done.

It will help to read a selection of newspaper comment articles. These are often the 'leader' or the daily 'opinion' column.

Planning and drafting

Decide whether you want to include:

- colloquial language
- slang and neologisms
- opinions expressed in both the first and third person

Reread the three extracts as examples of the ways in which writers:

- can take very different approaches to the same subject
- convey attitudes through their use of language

> You could start:
>
> *Bullying in schools has now become such a serious issue that something has to be done urgently. But what?…*

Another media feeding frenzy

DEBORAH ORR

'Prince Harry has certainly had quite a punishment meted out to him for what in this day and age is a common misdemeanour'

In my world, there would be no princes, no thirds-in-line, no monarchy. I snigger when those who claim to support the crown – such as the *News Of The World* – do more than any republican to smear the institution. I'd enjoy letting rip myself, and putting my tuppence-worth in. Yes, I smile wryly at Prince Charles sending Prince Harry to look at a rehab in south London. Because I believe drugs education in this country is too much based on the apocalyptic one-puff-and-you're-dead-in-a-gutter approach. Any young person knows from his own experience and that of his friends that this is simply not true.

Anyway, the whole country knows that if the worst comes to the worst, Prince Harry's sort go to that joint in Arizona, or at the very least the Priory. Maybe the punishment was the trip to Peckham. After all, Prince Harry must have found his visit to the real world frightening. It's so scary that even papers don't go there any more.

---

apocalyptic	earth-shattering, signifying the end of the world
that joint in Arizona … the Priory	expensive private rehabilitation centres used by the rich and famous

The Lord of the Rings

In this unit you will:

- compare three pieces of writing about the film
  The Fellowship of the Ring
- examine the language appropriate for writing
  to analyse, to review and to comment
- write an introductory analysis of a new film

WRITING TO ANALYSE

This extract, an example of writing to analyse, is from an article on *The Fellowship of the Ring*, the first film of a trilogy based upon JRR Tolkien's epic, *The Lord of the Rings*. It appeared in *Unreel*, the movie magazine distributed in Odeon cinemas.

The many cultures of the Ring

At the core of the story in 'The Fellowship of the Ring' are the cultures that make up Middle-earth: hobbits, dwarves, humans, elves, wizards, trolls, ents, orcs, ringwraiths and Uruk-Hai.

Each culture has its own rich way of life, its own customs, myths, ways of dress and even style of fighting. Each is fully developed in 'The Fellowship of the Ring', creating the essence of a living, breathing world just beyond our own history.

For example, hobbits are gentle and close to nature, an almost child-like group who live off the land. With an average height of 3'6", the furry-footed creatures dwell deep in furnished holes on the sides of hills. They love the simple things in life: smoking pipes, eating, and, of course, storytelling. They live to around 100 years old, with the age of 33 marking the start of adulthood.

Elves, on the other hand, are noble, elegant, magical beings whose time is running out and who seem to possess a bittersweet sense that they are now about to pass into myth. Although they could be slain or die of grief, elves are immortal in that they are not subject to age or disease.

Dwarves are short but very tough, with a strong, ancient sense of justice and an abiding love of all things beautiful. Small in stature, they live to be about 250 years old.

Wizards are supremely powerful but can use that power for good or for evil, depending on where their hearts lie.

Men in 'The Fellowship of the Ring' are a fledgling race just coming into their own.

Other creatures are even more fantastical: the leaf-covered ents try to protect their brethren, the trees; the misshapen orcs fight for Saruman; and the sinister, black-cloaked ringwraiths are neither living nor dead but cursed to live in the twilight world of Sauron.

To bring these remarkably diverse beings to life would require a cast of true versatility – and also a cast willing to spend months in the deep heartland of New Zealand bringing life to a literary legend. It would require a group of actors who could carry their characters through three chapters of climactic changes.

In the first instalment, 'The Fellowship of the Ring', the actors get a chance to introduce their characters and their individual quests. At the centre of it all is the story's 3'6" hero – Frodo Baggins, the shy but forthright hobbit who assumes the responsibility for destroying The Ring. Despite the help of the Fellowship, it is Frodo who must bear the burden of

prosthetic ears and feet   artificial ears and feet (here made to look hobbit-like)

The Ring and resist its constant temptations of evil. For the actor to play Frodo, the filmmakers chose 20-year-old Elijah Wood for his energy, innocence and charisma. 75

"Elijah has a sincerity of purpose that just makes him a natural in the role," observes Barrie M Osborne. "He is capable of taking the character through a real transformation, which begins with 'The Fellowship of the Ring'." 80

Wood describes Frodo as "a very curious adventurer. Frodo lives in a time when most of his fellow hobbits want to stay with their own kind, but Frodo is very different in that he wants to leave and see the rest of the world and all its wonders." 85 90

Which is exactly what he does in 'The Fellowship of the Ring'. As Frodo begins his journey, Wood was struck by how much like a person, rather than a fantasy character, the hobbit began 95

to seem "He became alive for me," he admits. "The way we shot the movie, everything was so real that we all believed that Frodo and the others really existed in history. Once I had on my prosthetic ears and feet for the first time, I knew what it was to feel like a hobbit. It sounds bizarre, but it felt the same as playing a historical character, as if hobbits had actually once been alive." 100 105

This review of the film by Christopher Tookey is from the *Daily Mail*, 2 January 2002.

THE LORD OF THE RINGS:
The Fellowship of the Ring (Cert PG)

by CHRISTOPHER TOOKEY

The biggest gamble in cinema is about to pay off. This is just the first part of a hideously expensive trilogy – it is rumoured to have cost upwards of £190million – that is already filmed and scheduled for release over the next two years.

The good news is that these first three hours are a landmark in cinema, an awesome feat of imagination and daring.

Critics who gave five-star ratings to Chris Columbus's competent but uninspired Harry Potter movie are going to have to find ten if they are to do justice to *The Fellowship of the Ring*. Peter Jackson's adaptation of JRR Tolkien's fantasy classic is as near to perfection as makes no difference.

…This first third of Tolkien's saga shows how a young, distinctly unheroic hobbit called Frodo Baggins (wonderfully played, with a near-perfect English accent, by the young American star Elijah Wood) comes into possession of a ring, reluctantly passed on to him by his uncle Bilbo (Ian Holm).

The ring can make its wearer invisible, but also has the potential to wreak universal havoc (it has been likened by some commentators to the nuclear bomb).

It attracts the interest of a good wizard gone to the bad, Saruman (Christopher Lee), as well as the ring's original maker, the satanic figure Sauron, who dispatches nine Ringwraiths to hunt it down.

Frodo is warned by a friendly, Merlin-like wizard, Gandalf (Ian McKellen), to carry the ring to safety in the elves' land, Rivendell. He and his three hobbit friends (Sean Astin, Billy Boyd and Dominic Monaghan) escape the Ringwraiths, with the help of a mysterious human called Strider (Viggo Mortensen) and a beautiful elfmaiden, Arwen (Liv Tyler).

But they soon discover from the elf lord Elrond (Hugo Weaving) that the ring is not safe even in Rivendell. It must be carried to the very centre of Sauron's empire, Mount Doom, and destroyed.

A fellowship to achieve this is formed of the six original travellers, plus Legolas the elf (Orlando Bloom), Gimli the dwarf (John Rhys-Davies) and Boromir, a nobleman (Sean Bean).

Peter Jackson's direction shows wonderful flair. It is his skill at moving the camera that makes a classic action sequence of the Ringwraiths' chasing on horseback of Arwen and Frodo.

Cate Blanchett as the elfwitch Galadriel is photographed with an ethereal glow that perfectly complements her finely judged, slightly threatening performance.

Even smaller moments of awe, such as Gandalf's firework display at Bilbo's birthday party, are richly imagined and superbly realised.

There are frightening, even horrific moments here, that will certainly make most adults jump – and will probably be too much in the cinema for the average eight year old.

I have no serious criticisms. The film does full justice to Tolkien, who has often – and erroneously – been accused of escapism.

As this movie demonstrates, he made inspired use of fantasy to grapple with the greatest trauma of the twentieth century – the degree of human corruptibility revealed by two world wars and the curse of totalitarianism.

WRITING TO COMMENT

This comment is part of an article about the actor Ian McKellen, who plays the wizard Gandalf in *The Fellowship of the Ring*. It is by Adam Macqueen, and appeared in the *Big Issue*, 10–16 December 2001.

MAGIC TOUCH

Sir Ian McKellen has, at different points in his career, played Adolf Hitler, Tsar Nicholas, DH Lawrence, Death, Macbeth, John Profumo and Kings Richard the second and third, all to general acclaim. But if he gets this role wrong, he'll really be in trouble. If so much as a whisker is out of place when he hits cinema screens later this month as Gandalf, the definitive wizard in what the film-makers hope will be the definitive film of the definitive classic of fantasy literature, an awful lot of people will get disproportionately angry.

"Tolkien fans amaze me," he says, picking his words carefully. "I've only met them through my website and they send emails there. Not to put anyone off, but *Lord of the Rings* and *The Hobbit* are just part of his attempt to present a mythology, so there are other books as well, and if you've read them and you're interested, you are likely to get a bit ... obsessed."

McKellen plays several scenes opposite Elijah Wood and Ian Holm as the hobbits, Frodo and Bilbo, in their house, Bag End. All three actors are around the same height, but Gandalf is meant to be normal-sized, whereas the hobbits are supposed to be about three-foot six. McKellen details the mechanics of such scenes in *The Grey Book*, the online journal he kept during the film-making at www.mckellen.com.

"There is a small Bag End with small props," he relates. "Ian Holm and Elijah Wood would be too big, so they have 'scale doubles' who are of a matching size with the miniature furniture."

With us so far? That's not all. "There's also a big Bag End, where all the objects are duplicated bigger. There the camera gets a gigantic Gandalf played by Paul Webster, who's seven-foot four. It's not easy acting, as you try to feed off your colleagues' reactions; but we manage."

There are also special effects to contend with; having reacted to tennis balls and brooms as if they were trolls and goblins, McKellen is relieved to have viewed the final product and seen that they are all present for the audience. After his FX-heavy turn as Magneto in last year's X-Men, has he got used to this sort of thing? "Bluescreen acting can be overrated as a problem," he tuts. "When you're on stage, you're not in the room you appear to be, you're in the theatre, with the audience in the fourth wall. Actors are quite used to not being where they appear, so it's not that difficult. I only saw the Balrog (the nastiest of several nasty beasties) for the first time when I saw the film, so yes, that was acting into space, but if you've played with a ghost in Shakespeare, it's not an unusual problem! It's just part of the job."

FX-heavy turn	role involving a lot of special effects
Bluescreen acting	In many fantasy, horror and science-fiction films which involve special effects (such as *Star Wars*), the actors are filmed against a plain blue screen, and the computerised monsters or aliens added later.

Language in context

The power of language

Key features of the texts are:

1 the language and content of *analyse*, *review* and *comment* texts

2 plot summaries

3 quotations

1 THE LANGUAGE OF ANALYSIS, REVIEW AND COMMENT

- Writing to *analyse* uses **facts** and provides **explanations**. This kind of writing helps to answer questions such as: Why are things as they are, or were?

- Writing to *review* uses people's **viewpoints** and **perspectives**, and offers **opinions**. It answers questions such as: What is my (or her, his, their...) opinion of things?

- Writing to *comment* uses **examples** and **details** to think through ideas and make **observations**. It answers questions such as: What do I want to say about this?

Writing to analyse

a) Use of facts

Look back at the analyse article, *The many cultures of the Ring*. It offers a helpful account of the different 'cultures' that make up the population of Middle-earth. List the eight types of creature described and write down one fact given about each one.

b) Explanations

In your own words as far as possible, list the main qualities of the actor Elijah Wood which, according to the article, make him ideal for the part of Frodo.

Writing to review

c) Viewpoints and perspectives

Reread the review article from the *Daily Mail* by film critic Christopher Tookey. The opening paragraphs contain the following phrases:

a landmark in cinema
an awesome feat of imagination
competent but uninspired
as near to perfection as makes no difference

Use these quotations to explain in your own words the comparison that Christopher Tookey is drawing between *The Fellowship of the Ring* and the Harry Potter film.

d) Opinions

Each of the quotes below is an opinion expressed by the reviewer. Copy out the chart and add in the right-hand column the subject of each comment. The first one has been completed to start you off. (The quotes are in the order in which they appear.)

Opinion	Subject
as near to perfection as makes no difference	*Peter Jackson's adaptation of JRR Tolkien's fantasy classic*
wonderfully played	
shows wonderful flair	
finely judged, slightly threatening	
richly imagined and superbly realised	

Writing to comment

e) Examples and details

Reread Adam Macqueen's comment article *Magic touch*. Summarise in your own words Ian McKellen's comments on Tolkien fans.

f) Observations

Reread the final paragraph and explain why some actors might find bluescreen acting difficult, using facts from the article. Then summarise Ian McKellen's comments on bluescreen acting.

2 PLOT SUMMARIES

An *analysis* or *review* of a film, or a *comment* upon it, will often include a brief **plot summary** or **introduction** to the story.

The kind of summary chosen by the writer will be influenced by the **purpose** of the writing and the **audience** it is aimed at.

Writing to review: plot summary

a) Reread the extract from the *Daily Mail* review. One purpose of a film review is to give the reader an idea of the story. Note down the main facts we are told about the plot of this film. Look in particular for facts concerning:

- the hero
- the importance of the ring
- the actions of Saruman, Sauron and Gandalf
- things that happen when Frodo tries to carry the ring to safety
- the formation of the fellowship

Writing to analyse: introduction

b) The article in the movie magazine *Unreel* does not recount much of the plot itself, but includes an introduction which lists the main 'cultures' that are featured, such as hobbits and elves. If you did not know *The Lord of the Rings*, what would the article tell you about the kind of story you could expect? Write down five things that you have learned about the film's story from this article (not counting the descriptions of the different 'cultures').

c) **Comparing audiences and purposes**
The *Daily Mail* is a major national newspaper bought in the high street; *Unreel* is a free magazine available in the cinema foyer.

- Write down what you think might be the main differences between the audiences of these two publications.
- Because the audiences are different, the two articles serve different purposes. Explain in what ways the different audiences have influenced the kind of introductory information each writer has chosen to provide.

3 QUOTATIONS

Journalists often use quotations (commonly called **quotes**): word-for-word comments from people closely involved with the story.

Quotes in an article serve a variety of purposes, for example:

- they help the reader to become interested in the people featured in the article
- they add 'authority', especially if they are spoken by someone closely involved with the story

a) **Quotes to add interest**
Look at the quotes from Ian McKellen in the *Big Issue* article, *Magic touch*. Some of them are facts about the filming (for example, *There is a small Bag End with small props*), others are opinions or responses which give us an insight into the speaker's personality.

In two columns, write down:

- the quotes which are facts about the filming
- the quotes which show the actor's personal viewpoint

b) **Quotes to add authority**
There are two quotes in the *Unreel* article. The first is by Barrie M Osborne, the film's producer; the second is by Elijah Wood, the young actor who plays Frodo.

Write down in your own words:

- what Barrie M Osborne says about Elijah Wood's character and personality which makes him ideal for the role of Frodo (reread lines 77–83)
- what Elijah Wood says about the experience of playing a hobbit (lines 96–106)

c) **The purposes of quotes**
Reread the quotes from Barrie M Osborne and Elijah Wood. Each one serves a particular purpose.

Select and write down:

- one quote which adds authority, because it is spoken by someone closely involved with the production of the film
- one quote which could only be spoken by an actor who knows exactly what it felt like to play that part
- one highly complimentary quote which would be inappropriate for the actor to make about himself

Compare and contrast

FOUNDATION TIER TASKS

1 SUMMARISING THE INFORMATION

Reread the article from *Unreel*, *The many cultures of the Ring* and then summarise:

- the information given about the different 'cultures' of Middle-earth
- the account of the main character, Frodo, and the actor who plays him, Elijah Wood

Write 200–250 words in total.
Use your own words as far as possible.

Planning and drafting

The task is in two parts. Use these points in order to make preparatory notes.

Part 1: the different cultures of Middle-earth
Look at what the article says about:

- the names of the cultures (lines 1–6)
- the details given about each culture (14–52)

Part 2: Frodo and Elijah Wood
Look at the comments on:

- the role of Frodo in the story (62–73)
- the actor, Elijah Wood (77–106)

You could start:
The cultures of Middle-earth listed in the article are…

2 ANALYSING A WRITER'S LANGUAGE

Reread Christopher Tookey's review from the *Daily Mail* and then explain:

- what he likes about the film
- how he uses language to get his opinions across clearly and interestingly

Remember to put quotation marks round any words or phrases taken from the passage.

Planning and drafting

The task is in two parts. Use these points in order to make preparatory notes.

Part 1: what Christopher Tookey likes about the film
Look at his comments on:

- the qualities of the film and the direction (lines 6–8 and 45–55)
- the actors' performances (15–20 and 49–52)
- Tolkien's original story (60–7)

Part 2: how he uses language to get his opinions across clearly and interestingly
Look at the way he:

- introduces his review (1–14; see question 1c, page 108)
- summarises the plot (15–44; see questions 2a and 2c, page 109)
- expresses opinions clearly (15–20, 45–8 and 53–9; see question 1d, page 108)

You could start:
There are a number of things that Christopher Tookey admires about the film. Firstly,…

HIGHER TIER TASKS

1 WRITING AN ANALYSIS

Write your own introductory analysis of a new film of your choice. The audience is other movie-goers of your own age and the article will appear in a cinema magazine such as *Unreel*.

It will help to read a variety of other articles first. These can be found in the free magazines published by all cinema chains, as well as other high-street magazines and newspapers. Articles such as *The many cultures of the Ring* can be found on the *Unreel* website, **www.unreel.co.uk**

Planning and drafting

Check that you have:

- taken into account the purpose of your article and its intended audience (page 109, question 2c)
- included an appropriate plot summary (page 109, question 2a)
- used quotes effectively (page 109)
- discussed the main features of the film and the qualities of the actors which make them suitable for the roles they play

You could start:

The story of .... centres upon…

 2 COMPARING THE THREE KINDS OF WRITING

The three articles, from *Unreel*, the *Daily Mail* and the *Big Issue*, are examples of three different kinds of writing: writing to analyse, to review and to comment.

Explain and comment upon the choices that each writer has made in approaching their particular kind of writing.

Support your answer by referring to the content, style and language of all three articles. (It will help to look through the work that you have done earlier.)

You could start:

Although the three writers are dealing with the same topic – the Lord of the Rings film – their purposes are different. The article from Unreel, *for example, is an analysis of the film, and therefore…*

Self assess

These are the main language features that you have learned about in this section. Decide how confident you feel about:

- commenting on the effects of **emotive vocabulary**
- understanding the part played by **paragraphs** in a text's structure
- being able to use the **point-evidence-comment** method in presenting an argument

- understanding the idea of **register** and how it relates to **purpose** and **audience**
- explaining the different uses of **first person** and **third person**
- using the **language of criticism**

- identifying **colloquial language** and being aware of its uses
- giving examples of **slang** and **neologisms**

- commenting on the uses of **quotes**

What do you feel you need to revise?

Mysteries of the dead

In this unit you will:

- read two newspaper articles
- examine the language of journalism
- write a news article

The following article appeared in the *Guardian* on 21 March 2002.

How Oetzi the Iceman was stabbed in the back and lost his fight for life

Rory Carroll in Rome

Scientists have discovered that Oetzi the Iceman, the world's oldest and best preserved mummy, was engaged in hand-to-hand combat shortly before perishing in the Alps 5,300 years ago.

Two wounds to his right hand and wrist show he was stabbed while trying to defend himself with a dagger against an attacker, bolstering theories that bronze age tribes waged war on mountain peaks. The discovery scotches claims that Oetzi was a human sacrifice and suggests instead that he was a warrior or the victim of an ambush who fought hard to save his life.

Researchers revealed the findings last night from the archaeological museum in the northern Italian town of Bolzano which keeps the mummy in a refrigerated room.

"This is very exciting. It tells us that Oetzi was involved in a battle, or at least in hand-to-hand combat of some kind," Eduard Egarter Vigl, the main caretaker for the corpse, told the *Guardian*.

A sharp object, possibly a flint-tipped spear or dagger, punctured the base of his thumb, shredding skin and muscle right to the bone, and a second blow damaged a bone on his wrist. The thumb wound had no scar, meaning it was fresh when the Iceman died.

It is the latest piece of a jigsaw which started in 1991 when two German hikers found a corpse in an Alpine glacier bordering Italy and Austria. Eleven thousand feet above sea level, it caused a sensation as the astonishing state of preservation held secrets about pre-history.

It is known that he was 46 and in a valley on the Italian side hours before ascending the glacier with an unfinished bow, arrows and a dagger.

Forensic scientists and archaeologists have become detectives, conceiving and discarding theories about why and how he died. The discovery last year of an arrow blade in

'This reinforces evidence that neolithic times were quite violent. From the bones in the Alps it appears there were battles'

scotches	puts an end to
forensic scientist	a scientist who uses his or her scientific knowledge to help solve police investigations or decide court cases
hypothermia	extreme drop in body temperature
appease	satisfy, pacify
neolithic	the last period of the Stone Age
scapula	shoulder-blade

his left shoulder showed his death was
55 violent, not the result of drowning, hypothermia or a fall.

Researchers speculated he was a willing sacrifice to appease the gods or the victim of an accident or a long-range ambush. The
60 injured hand shows instead that Oetzi knew he was in danger and had time to defend himself.

One of the German hikers, Alois Pirpamer, has revealed that Oetzi's dagger
65 was not beside the corpse, as previously thought, but in his right hand, suggesting the killer was close. That detail emerged when the makers of a Discovery Channel documentary to be broadcast next month
70 introduced Mr Pirpamer to Dr Egarter Vigl. The clue prompted the scientist to re-examine the hand, revealing a 15mm-deep zig-zag wound.

"This reinforces evidence that neolithic
75 times were quite violent because from the bones found in the Alps it appears there were battles up there," said Brando Quilici, who directed the documentary.

It is thought Oetzi bled to death after
80 the arrow shattered the scapula and damaged nerves and blood vessels before lodging near the lung.

Work on the body of Oetzi the Iceman suggests that, rather than being sacrificed, he died defending himself from a knife-wielding attacker

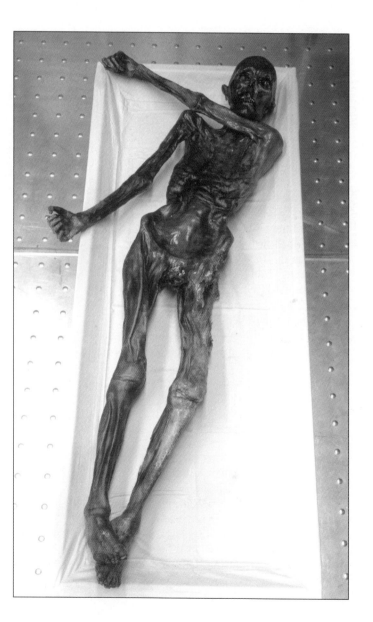

This article from the *Daily Mail* appeared on 20 March 2002.

Nearly 60 years on, a final chapter in the intriguing tale of The Man Who Never Was

By **Bill Mouland**

MBE: Mrs Naylor de Mendez

HE was perhaps the most unlikely hero of the Second World War.

In life, Glyndwr Michael was
5 a decrepit down-and-out who killed himself by drinking rat poison.

But in death, he helped save thousands of Allied lives and
10 speeded the end of the war.

In one of the greatest con-tricks in military history, the 34-year-old's body was secretly appropriated by MI5.

15 Michael was given a new identity – that of William Martin, an acting major in the Royal Marines – and dumped in the sea off Spain.

20 Fake documents on the corpse fooled Hitler over the intended focus of the Allies' invasion of Italy.

With Nazi forces massed
25 elsewhere, Allied troops met lit-tle resistance and thus suffered far fewer casualties.

The tale of the deception, codenamed Operation Mince-
30 meat, became a best-selling book and classic film – The Man Who Never Was – while the body of 'Major Martin' was laid to rest at the Cemetery of Solitude outside
35 Huelva, southern Spain.

For 50 years, his true identity was unknown. Yet red flowers were regularly laid on the grave.

In 1996, both these mysteries were solved. Amateur historian Roger Morgan discovered Glyndwr Michael's name in files at the Public Record Office in Kew, West London.

'He helped save many lives'

He is convinced MI5 used the body without the knowledge of the dead man's family.

However, agents in charge of Operation Mincemeat always insisted that the family gave permission on condition the identity of the corpse would never be revealed.

It also emerged that the flowers had been laid on the grave by British-born Isabel Naylor de Mendez.

Last night in Huelva, in possibly the final chapter to the story, Mrs Naylor de Mendez, 69, was made an MBE for tending the war graves at the cemetery.

She received her award from the British ambassador to Spain, Peter Torry.

She told how her father first put flowers on the grave of 'Major Martin' in 1946. He asked her to take on the task shortly before he died in 1966.

'My father told me that this man, whoever he might have been, saved many lives in the war and it was a sort of duty for us to keep his grave tidy,' Mrs Naylor de Mendez said.

Of her MBE, she added: 'I feel very honoured. I don't think I deserve it. It's been a great surprise and I'm very grateful.'

Mr Morgan said yesterday: 'I think it's jolly good that Mrs Naylor de Mendez is getting the MBE. She and her father had put flowers on the grave since 1946, and that had always been a bit of a mystery as well.'

The Commonwealth War Grave Commission has added Michael's name to that of the Major on the gravestone.

Mr Morgan said: 'Operation Mincemeat was a very successful tactical deception.

'Even after the war there were still highly ranked Germans who believed Major Martin was real.' Operation Mincemeat was drawn up in the spring of 1943.

With Churchill planning to invade Italy through Sicily, a ruse was needed to make the Germans believe the attack would take place elsewhere.

Intelligence agents conceived the idea of planting false papers on an officer and making it look as if he had died in a plane crash at sea.

London coroner Bentley Purchase provided them with the body of Michael, the illegitimate son of illiterate parents from a Welsh mining village, who had been found dead in a warehouse.

The cadaver was kept in cold storage while preparations continued in the minutest detail. Michael was given military papers, including a pass to Combined Operations Head-quarters, identifying him as Acting Major William Martin, an expert in amphibious warfare.

To make it as convincing as possible, there was also a letter from his father, a warning about his overdraft from his bank manager, bills for an engagement ring and a shirt, theatre ticket stubs and a letter from his solicitor.

Finally, there were love letters and a photograph of his fiancee, 'Pam' – in reality Jean Gerard Leigh, who worked as a clerk for MI5.

Michael's body was dressed in the uniform of a Royal Marines officer and the personal effects were put in a briefcase – chained to his wrist – with 'plans' showing how the Allies would invade Italy via Sardinia and Greece.

'Very successful deception'

'Major Martin' was packed in dry ice, driven to Scotland and put on a submarine.

Off the Spanish coast, the submarine captain read Psalm 39 before the body, kept afloat by a life jacket, was slipped into the sea along with an upturned life raft.

Although Spain, under the fascist control of Franco, was officially neutral, MI5 knew the information would be passed on to the Germans.

When the 'Major' was found, German agents excitedly reported the contents of the briefcase to Berlin.

Hitler poured reinforcements into Sardinia and Greece, leaving Sicily poorly defended.

In 1956 the story was made into a film starring Clifton Webb and Gloria Grahame.

b.mouland@dailymail.co.uk

MI5	the secret service
MBE	an award: Member of the Order of the British Empire
cadaver	corpse
amphibious	both on land and in the sea
Psalm 39	from the Bible, often read at funerals

Language in context

The power of language

Key features of the texts are:

1. photograph, headline and intro
2. paragraphs
3. pyramid writing

1 PHOTOGRAPH, HEADLINE AND INTRO

The **photograph** can be a key feature of a newspaper article.

a) Look at the photographs which accompany the two articles. Write a paragraph to explain what part they play in:

- attracting the reader's attention (What is there about each of the photos that makes you want to read the article?)
- adding to the interest of the story (What can the photo do that the text cannot do?)
- providing extra information (What details can you see in the photos which are not fully explained in the texts?)

Apart from the photograph, the **headline** is usually the first feature of a newspaper article to capture the reader's attention.

Headlines are often brief and eye-catching:

117 PEGS ON MY ED

(Sun)

RANGERS IN CUP OF CHEER

(Daily Express)

b) The headlines to the two articles on pages 112–15 are much longer than the examples from the *Sun* and *Daily Express*. Write a paragraph to explain how these two headlines (*How Oetzi…* and *Nearly 60 years on…*) succeed in capturing the reader's interest. Think about:

- the ways in which each one provides key facts of the story which follows
- their dramatic language (*stabbed in the back… final chapter…*)
- the element of mystery (*How Oetzi… The Man Who Never Was*)

Newspaper articles are structured so as to gain the reader's attention and then keep it. An important part of this structure is the opening, called the **intro**.

The intro will often contain a dramatic and attention-grabbing fact. For example:

Crazy Edward McKenna is facing up to stardom as a record holder after sticking 117 clothes pegs to his head… (*Sun*, 18 March 2002).

c) Reread the intros to the two articles (*Scientists … 5,300 years ago* and *He was … end of the war*). Write a paragraph commenting on the way in which the writers have grabbed the reader's attention with the intros. For example:

- Which dramatic facts have been introduced?
- What is there about each intro that makes you want to read on?

2 PARAGRAPHS

> A **paragraph** is a block of sentences linked together by one main idea or subject.

Paragraphs in **tabloid** newspaper articles tend to be shorter than paragraphs in many other kinds of writing. (The tabloids are the popular, small-format newspapers such as the *Daily Mail*, the *Mirror* and the *Sun*.) This is done in order to keep the reader's attention. For example, some paragraphs in the article on The Man Who Never Was contain no more than a single sentence each.

a) The article about Oetzi the Iceman is divided into eleven paragraphs. Each one can be given a **topic heading**: a brief title which summarises the content. For example, the first paragraph might be headed: *Discovery about how Oetzi died.*

Write a topic heading for each of the other ten paragraphs. Compare your ten topic headings with a partner and talk about any differences between your two lists. Have you focused on different ideas within particular paragraphs, for example?

b) Bill Mouland's article on The Man Who Never Was is divided into many more paragraphs than the Iceman report.

- Join some of the paragraphs together so as to reduce the total number of paragraphs to eight, with the following possible topic headings:

  1 *Who was he?*
  2 *The 'con-trick' and its legend*
  3 *Solving the mystery*
  4 *Who tended the grave?*
  5 *The success of Operation Mincemeat*
  6 *The original idea*
  7 *The result in Spain and Germany*
  8 *The film*

- List your eight new paragraphs by writing down the opening and closing phrases only. (For example, if you were doing this with the Iceman article, the opening paragraph would be written as *Scientists have discovered … 5,300 years ago.*)

- Finally, write a sentence or two about each new paragraph to explain what it contains. For example, if you were writing about the Iceman article, you might say:

  The opening two paragraphs contain the important new discovery about how Oetzi died; they introduce the account by presenting the key facts.

3 PYRAMID WRITING

> Journalists often use a method of structuring newspaper articles known as **pyramid writing**. The most striking or important information is put at the beginning of the article.

It is called pyramid writing because, of all the readers who read an article's headline, only 70 per cent will read to the end of the intro, and only 50 per cent will carry on to the end of the third or fourth paragraph. This situation can be represented in an upside-down pyramid outline:

Percentage of people who read different sections of a newspaper article

Headline 100% of readers

Intro 70% of readers

2nd, 3rd or 4th paragraphs 50% of readers

a) Write two or three paragraphs analysing the ways in which the writers of the two articles have used pyramid writing. Quote from the articles to show how the writers have:

- created an attention-grabbing headline
- included the most dramatic facts in the intro
- included the slightly less dramatic facts in the next few paragraphs
- left the more technical, or least interesting, details until the end

Writing newspaper articles

FOUNDATION TIER TASKS

1 SUMMARISING THE ARTICLE

Reread Bill Mouland's article about The Man Who Never Was.

Imagine you were a member of wartime intelligence. You have just been informed by an agent working under cover in Spain that Operation Mincemeat has been a total success.

Write a report for your Commanding Officer, summarising the main points of the operation in about 200–250 words.

Planning and drafting

You could use the following eight points as a guide (reread the paragraphs beginning with the sentences in brackets). But you might feel that you do not want to refer to all eight in your report:

- Why the operation was necessary and what they hoped to achieve (lines 100–4: *With Churchill planning…*)
- When it was planned (95–9: *Even after the war…*)
- The idea (105–9: *Intelligence agents conceived…*)
- Who the body was (4–7 and 110–15: *In life… London coroner Bentley Purchase…*)
- The first steps (11–19: *In one of the greatest… Michael was given…*)
- The fake evidence planted on the body (116–43: *The cadaver was… To make it… Finally, there were… Michael's body was…*)
- The journey by submarine (144–51: *'Major Martin' was… Off the Spanish coast…*)
- The enemy is fooled (161–3, 8–10 and 24–7: *Hitler poured… But in death… With Nazi forces…*)

You could start:
As you know, this spring, when we were still planning the invasion of Italy through Sicily, the Prime Minister asked us to find a way of…

2 WRITING A NEWSPAPER ARTICLE

Imagine you are a journalist who has just interviewed Albert Ostman about his capture by a Sasquatch (Bigfoot) – you can find the account of his experience on page 35. Use the notes you have taken to write an article for your tabloid newspaper of around 200–250 words.

NOTES TAKEN DURING INTERVIEW WITH ALBERT OSTMAN

1 Ostman – 64-year-old retired lumberman from British Columbia

2 was on camping trip near Vancouver Island

3 found that something had disturbed his supplies and food on two nights in a row

4 one night was shaken awake to find himself being carried away inside his sleeping bag

5 the opening of the sleeping bag was held shut – Ostman dragged along the forest ground for maybe 25 miles, nearly suffocating – journey took 3 hours

6 he was thrown to the ground in a heap, and emerged to find himself in the company of four Sasquatches

7 a family: father, mother and pair of offspring – one male, one female

8 adult male over eight feet tall and powerfully built, covered in dark hair all over

9 the children, though smaller, were still about seven feet tall

10 the Sasquatches chattered amongst themselves in a seemingly intelligent language

11 did not hurt or threaten him, but were determined not to let him leave

12 their lair inside a small valley enclosed by cliffs – adult male stood guard at the only apparent exit

13 Ostman may have been selected as a prospective mate for the young female

14 held captive for six days – formed bond with the younger male, who became fond of sampling Ostman's snuff

15 Ostman's escape: he offered his snuff to the adult male, which dumped the entire container into his mouth – then writhed on the ground in great discomfort. Ostman ran off

Planning and drafting

First reread Albert Ostman's story in the extract on page 35. When you plan the article, remember the rules of pyramid writing:

- think up an attention-grabbing headline
- draft a dramatic intro
- leave the least important or least interesting details to the end

Quotes from Ostman will help bring the report to life: *'To my horror I realised that something was shaking me awake,' said the terrified 64-year-old…*

You are writing for a tabloid newspaper, so the paragraphs will be short. Add a rough sketch of a photo which could accompany the article.

Your article could begin:
A retired lumberman told yesterday about his nerve-wracking six-day ordeal – abducted by a family of Sasquatches!

HIGHER TIER TASKS

1 ANALYSING THE ARTICLES

Write an analysis of the two articles to show how each one has succeeded in capturing and maintaining the reader's interest.

Planning and drafting

In your answer you should refer to the writers' use of:

- pyramid writing:
  - an eye-catching headline
  - a dramatic intro
  - less important and less interesting details left to the end
- quotes from:
  - historian Roger Morgan
  - scientist Dr Eduard Egarter Vigl
  - documentary director Brando Quilici

- paragraphing
- the photographs – what part do they play in:
  - attracting the reader's attention?
  - adding to the interest of the story?
  - providing extra information?

You could start:
The two articles are linked by the common theme of 'mysterious bodies' and the writers have fully exploited the dramatic potential of their stories…

2 WRITING A NEWSPAPER ARTICLE

Write an article for a tabloid newspaper, based on any story from history, legend or fiction.

Planning and drafting

You could choose a story from:

- **history**, for example the execution of Mary Queen of Scots or the death of a climbing boy (see pages 160–1)
- **legend**, for example the Fall of Troy or Arthur pulling the sword out of the stone
- **fiction**, for example Dr Frankenstein's creation of the monster or the story of the Hound of the Baskervilles

Remember the rules of pyramid writing.

Include quotes from eye-witnesses or other people involved. Keep the paragraphs short. Add a rough sketch of a photo which could accompany the article.

If you chose to base your report on the execution of Mary Queen of Scots (see page 160), you could start:
The lips of the dead Queen of Scots moved up and down for a quarter of an hour yesterday after…

Ice titan

In this unit you will:

- read a newspaper article and a web-page covering the same item of news
- compare their different treatments
- plan a page of a news website

On 19 March 2002, reports started to come in that a huge Antarctic ice shelf, called Larsen B, had collapsed into the sea. This is how the story was reported in the *Daily Mail* and on the *Channel 4 News* website.

The ice monster

Fears as a 50 billion-ton Antarctic mass collapses

By **Tim Utton**
Science Reporter

AN Antarctic ice sheet the size of Cambridgeshire has collapsed into the sea in the latest terrifying sign of global warming.

5   It was described by one minister yesterday as 'a wake-up call to the whole world'.

  Experts said the 50 billion-ton mass of ice had crumbled with 10 'staggering' speed, taking less than a month to break off and float away.

  The collapse of the 650ft thick shelf, called Larsen B, is due to 15 an unprecedented temperature rise of 2.5C on the Antarctic Peninsula over the last 50 years – a rate five times faster than the rest of the Earth.

20   Dr David Vaughan, a glaciologist with the British Antarctic Survey, said: 'We have increased carbon dioxide and methane in the atmosphere to levels that 25 haven't been seen on Earth for at least half a million years, and probably longer.

  'It would be surprising if we didn't see climate change as a 30 result.

  'In 1998, the BAS predicted the demise of more ice shelves around the Antarctic Peninsula. Since then, warming on the

35 peninsula has continued and we watched as, piece by piece, Larsen B has retreated.

'We knew what was left would collapse eventually, but 40 the speed of it is staggering.

'It's hard to believe 50billion tons of ice sheet have disintegrated in less than a month.

'Climate change has effective- 45 ly been "taking the bricks out of the wall" one by one.'

Larsen B, which was twice the size 15 years ago, has now disintegrated into thousands of 50 icebergs.

In response to the collapse, Environment Minister Michael Meacher called for 'dramatic and fundamental' changes to 55 address global warming.

The ice sheet's rapid decline was 'the most significant evidence of continuing climate change'.

60 Speaking at the launch of a climate change exhibition at London's Science Museum, he added: 'It's an indication of global warming which is 65 extremely stark and the implications are that we have got to arrest climate change and adapt to it. But above all, we have got to reduce it.

70 'I think it's a wake-up call to the whole world that when an ice shelf of such enormous proportions can break up, that shows the effect we are having 75 on the planet.'

demise   death (here: loss or destruction)

Language in context

The power of language

Key features of the texts are:

1. the language of writing to inform
2. adjectives
3. quotes

1 THE LANGUAGE OF WRITING TO INFORM

Writing to **inform** focuses on conveying information and ideas clearly. To achieve this, writers of information texts need to have a very accurate understanding of who their **audience** is. This audience might have to be given **statistics** and access to **further information**.

In the articles on pages 120–3, statistics include the size of the ice shelf and changes in temperature. Further information might include other examples of global warming or a selection of comments by scientists.

Audience

Both writers know that their audience is very wide: it is the general public who read the *Daily Mail* or watch *Channel 4 News*.

a) Write a paragraph to explain what methods the two texts have used in order to get across the following scientific details to a wide audience:

- the size of the Larsen B ice shelf (look at the opening paragraph of the *Daily Mail* article, for example)
- the size of the iceberg that has broken from the Thwaites Glacier (on the *Channel 4 News* web-page)
- the way in which climate change has damaged the ice sheet (the *Daily Mail* paragraph beginning *Climate change has…*)

Statistics

b) Reports of this kind can involve a great many statistics. Imagine you were creating a series of PLANET EARTH fact-cards. Read both texts and create a card on *Ice shelves and climate change*. You could use the following headings:

PLANET EARTH

ICE SHELVES AND CLIMATE CHANGE

- **EVENT:** The collapse of the Larsen B ice shelf

- **WHEN IT FORMED:** (see *Channel 4 News*, the paragraph near the end, beginning *It's been discovered…*)

- **WHERE IT WAS:** (see *Daily Mail* lines 1–4) Which continent was it part of?

- **ITS SIZE:** (see *Daily Mail*, 8–19; and *Channel 4 News*, Dr Pudsey's quote) How heavy was it? How thick? How many square kilometres?

- **WHAT CAUSED IT TO COLLAPSE:** (see *Daily Mail*, 13–27) How serious was the temperature rise?

- **HOW LONG IT TOOK TO COLLAPSE:** (see *Channel 4 News*, the paragraph beginning *Now, satellite…* and the photos on page 123)

Further information

c) In pairs, look at the *Channel 4 News* web-page. Talk about how you could access further information from this page, if you wanted to:

- find out more about global warming
- check the day's other main news stories
- see a moving-image report of ice shelves collapsing
- see still photographs of ice shelves collapsing
- read other people's comments

2 ADJECTIVES

> An **adjective** is a word which gives us information about a noun or pronoun. A group of words which does this is called an **adjective phrase**.

Both texts use adjectives and adjective phrases to get across the magnitude and seriousness of the ice shelf's collapse.

a) Find the adjectives or adjective phrases which describe:

in the *Daily Mail* article

- the latest sign of global warming (lines 1–4)
- the speed at which the ice had crumbled (8–12)
- the temperature rise which caused the collapse (13–19)
- the changes needed to deal with global warming (51–5)
- the evidence of continuing climate change (56–9)
- the indication of global warming (60–9)
- the proportions of the ice shelf (70–5)

in the *Channel 4 News* text

- the speed of the final collapse (paragraph 4)
- the two-and-a-half-degree increase in temperature (the paragraph beginning *The Antarctic…*)
- Larsen B (the paragraph beginning *Now, satellite…*)
- the iceberg that has broken from the Thwaites Glacier (the paragraph beginning *And in a…*)

b) Write two paragraphs to explain how the writers have used adjectives to get across how significant the collapse of Larsen B is.

3 QUOTES

> Journalists often use quotations (commonly called **quotes**): word-for-word comments from people closely involved with the story.

Quotes in an article can be used for a variety of purposes, for example:

- they help the reader to understand how urgent the subject is if they are spoken by someone well known or important
- they add authority, especially if they are spoken by someone who has made a close scientific study of the subject

a) *Quotes to underline the urgency*
Look at the quotes in both texts from Michael Meacher. Write a paragraph to explain why they have quoted him at length. What is his position in government, for example? Why is it important for us to read his exact words, rather than the journalist's report of what he said? (Look at the powerful adjectives he uses, for example, and the warnings he gives.)

b) *Quotes to add authority*
Write a paragraph to explain the importance of the quotes from Dr David Vaughan (in both texts) and Dr Carol Pudsey (in the *Channel 4 News* text). Look, for example, at:

- the background information provided by Dr Vaughan
- Dr Pudsey's personal reaction to the ice shelf's collapse

Compare and contrast

FOUNDATION TIER TASKS

1 SUMMARISING THE NEWS REPORTS

Reread both texts and then summarise

- what has happened to the Larsen B ice shelf
- why it has happened

Write about 200–250 words in total.

Planning and drafting

The task is in two parts.

Part 1: what has happened to the Larsen B ice shelf

Think about:

- the collapse of the ice shelf – see the *Daily Mail*, lines 1–12 and 47–50), and *Channel 4 News*, paragraph 1 and the quote from Dr Pudsey

Part 2: why it has happened

Think about:

- temperature rises in Antarctica – see the *Daily Mail*, 13–19
- global warming – *Daily Mail*, 20–30, and *Channel 4 News*, Dr Vaughan's quote

> You could start:
>
> *In March 2002, news suddenly came in of a dramatic event in Antarctica. The Larsen B ice shelf…*

2 WRITING A SPEECH

Imagine that you are going to take part in a debate about the future of the planet. Your task in the debate is to argue that something urgently needs to be done about global warming and its effects. Write your speech.

Write about 200–250 words.

Planning and drafting

You could first give an example of the effects of global warming: the collapse of the Larsen B ice shelf. Explain what happened and why it happened. (Use the points that you summarised in task 1.)

You might then want to use Michael Meacher's quotes as a basis for some of your own arguments:

- the Larsen B collapse is an extremely important sign:
  the most significant… It's an indication…
- something has to be done about climate change:
  the implications are… But above all…
- everyone around the world needs to take notice:
  I think it's a…

> You could start:
>
> *Ladies and gentlemen, events in Antarctica in recent years have shown once and for all that we can no longer fail to take action against global warming. In March 2002, a huge ice shelf…*

HIGHER TIER TASKS

1 ANALYSING THE TEXTS

Write an analysis of the two texts, comparing how effective they are in informing their audiences about the collapse of the Larsen B ice shelf and explaining how serious an event it is.

Planning and drafting

Remember that both texts are reporting on the same event and both journalists have access to the same facts.

Think about:

- the writers' awareness of audience
- their methods of helping the audience to understand scientific concepts and statistics
- the possibility of accessing further information
- their use of adjectives and adjective phrases to get across the magnitude and seriousness of the event
- their use of quotes

Look back through the previous unit (pages 112–19) so that you can also comment on how effectively the two texts have used:

- photographs/moving images, headlines and intros
- paragraphs
- pyramid writing

> You could start:
> *Both of these texts are reports of the same event: the collapse of the Larsen B ice shelf in March 2002…*

2 PLANNING A WEB-PAGE

Use the *Channel 4 News* text as a model to plan your own web-page on an item in the news. You could use something that has actually just happened or base your web-page on information from one of the texts in this book, such as the sighting of a Bigfoot (pages 34–5), the opening of the Gemini South telescope (pages 40–1) or the new discoveries concerning Oetzi the Iceman (pages 112–13).

Planning and drafting

Think about:

- your audience (who do you think will access this site?)
- the ways in which you convey scientific concepts and statistics
- the links to other related pages
- the use of photographs and video

Decide whether you want to use:

- adjectives which help to convey a particular impression
- quotes from authorities and eye-witnesses

You could use the design of the *Channel 4 News* web-page as a model, or study others, such as the BBC website at **www.bbc.co.uk/news**

No-one wants jigging mouses!

In this unit you will:

- study a television advertisement
- examine the techniques of moving-image advertising
- plan an advertisement

This is the storyboard for a thirty-second television advertisement for the Aero chocolate bar. It was shown in Spring 2002.

SHOT NO.	TIME IN SECONDS	SOUND EFFECTS	DESCRIPTION OF SHOT	SHOT	DIALOGUE
1	00–02	Busy traffic	Delivery man (DM) walks from the back of his lorry up to the shop door. He carries two boxes.		
2	02–04	Faint traffic noise from outside	Inside the shop, the owner (O) is standing behind the counter, contentedly eating an Aero bar.		DM: *Hello, mate. It's your new Honeycomb Aero and a hundred promotional items.*
3	04–06		DM puts the boxes on the floor.		

4	06–07		O's face drops.		O: *Mouses? No-one wants jigging mouses!*
5	07–08		Close-up of shop counter, as O throws his Aero down angrily. DM's eyes peer over the top.		
6	08–09		O turns angrily to the cupboards in the wall behind him.		
7	09–10		O opens the doors one by one, to reveal dozens of mice, all dancing and playing with hula-hoops.		O: *All they want is bubbly…*
8	10–12		His voice fades away as he turns back to DM.		…*chocolate!*

9	12–13		His jaw drops in amazement as he watches DM…		
10	13–15		…who turns round and opens his hand to reveal…		DM (smugly): *These are from…*
11	15–17	Singing in Chinese from the mouse	…a dancing mouse standing up on his palm, which then sings in Chinese and dances.		*…Taiwan!*
12	17–19		A woman customer (C) walks behind O, just as the mouse is jumping onto his hand. Not noticing the mouse, she picks an Aero off the display…		C (looking at the Aero): *Oh, lovely!*
13	19–20		Hearing her enthusiastic comment, O turns round to her, smiling, while DM comments over his shoulder.		DM: *Off your hands before you can say…*

14	20–23		C starts to open the Aero, but a look of horror strikes her face as she sees the mouse. She screams.		C (screams)
15	23–27	Thud as she hits the floor.	Shot of DM and O from over C's shoulder. As she drops from view, their eyes follow her descent to the floor.		
			DM says goodbye and leaves. O watches his departure in dismay.		DM: *Cheerio!*
16	27–28		Cut to the Aero display box on the counter with the mouse standing next to it.		Voice-over: *Honeycomb Aero* *All bubble…*
17	28–30		Closer shot of the Aero display box – cutting out the mouse.		*…No squeak!*

Promotional items are free gifts, given away with a product. These are often made, very cheaply, in Far East countries such as Taiwan.

Language in context

The power of language

Key features of the texts are:

1 moving-image techniques

2 awareness of target groups

3 message and slogan

1 MOVING-IMAGE TECHNIQUES

Film, television, video, computer-generated moving images and similar technologies are known as **moving-image media**. Anybody creating a moving-image text has to think about **vision** (what the audience see), **sound** (what they hear, including sound effects and music) and **duration** (timing: how long the audience will watch each part of the text).

Vision

A single uninterrupted run of the camera is called a **shot**. A single individual picture is called a **frame** (and a photograph taken from a film frame is known as a **still**).

When you are filming a scene, you have a choice from a variety of different camera-shots, such as the close-up, the close-shot, the medium-shot and the long-shot. The Aero advertisement uses the following shots:

a) In pairs, study the storyboard and discuss the following questions:

- What can you show the audience with a close-up, which can't be achieved with other shots?
- What can you achieve with a long-shot?
- What kind of shot is useful for showing two or three people's expressions in a single frame?
- What kind of shot is used most frequently in the Aero advertisement? Why is it so useful in filming this scene?

The skill of placing people or objects in a particular place within the edges of the film frame is called **framing**.

Directors use framing to gain particular effects. For example, in this advertisement the mouse from Taiwan fills almost the whole of frame 11 so that we can see it in detail and be impressed by its amazing performance.

b) Write down how the framing helps to show:

- where the story is about to take place and what is happening (frame 1: note that the framing allows us to see the lorry with its tail down, the delivery man carrying boxes from it, and the shop entrance)
- the shop owner's reaction to the phrase 'promotional items' (frame 4)
- the actions of the customer (frame 12)
- the customer's reactions to seeing the mouse (frame 14)
- the shop owner's reaction when the customer faints and the delivery man makes a hasty departure (frame 15)
- the product (frame 17)

Extreme close-up	Close-up	Close-shot	Long-shot

The camera can also take shots from different directions and different heights, such as looking up at an object, or viewing it from above. These views are called **camera angles**.

c) Write down what camera angle you could use if you wanted to:
- show people waiting on a platform as a train comes in
- make the villain in a film look menacing
- show the full effect of a massive traffic-jam in one shot

d) What effect does the camera angle have in frame 5 of the advertisement?

Changing from one shot to another is called **cutting**.

For example, the director of this advertisement cuts from a shot of the cheerful shop owner (frame 2) to a shot of the delivery man depositing the boxes on the floor (frame 3).

e) In pairs discuss how the cutting helps to contrast the shop owner's feelings with the delivery man's (on two occasions: frames 2–5 and 9–10).

Sound

Music and **sound effects** are extremely important in creating a mood and in helping to tell the story.

f) There are only a few special sounds used in the Aero advertisement (think about the singing mouse and the thud as the woman hits the floor). Write down why each one is important. What part does it play in helping the audience to understand the story that is being told? How does it add to the humour?

g) The advertisement only once uses **voice-over** (a voice heard without the speaker being seen). Where is it used and what is its effect?

Duration

A key difference between print-media texts (anything that appears on a printed page) and moving-image texts is **duration**: the fact that a moving-image text takes a set amount of time to be experienced by the audience.

h) In pairs:
- talk about the overall length of the Aero advertisement (how long is it, how does that length compare with the average television advertisement in your opinion?)
- think about the duration of the shots – pick two or three examples of one-second shots which illustrate the fact that a great deal can be conveyed in a very short piece of action
- find the shot which the director holds for the longest time and discuss why you think the camera stays with that shot as long as it does.

2 TARGET GROUPS

All advertisements are aimed at a particular audience. They are known as the **target group**.

For example, television advertisements for disposable nappies are aimed mainly at women in the 16–35 age group. When a new advertisement is being planned, the makers have to ask themselves at least two questions:
- which **gender** are we aiming at: male, female, both?
- which **age group** are we aiming at: up to 15, 16–24, 25–35, 36–55, over 55?

a) Look at the images and the humorous approach of the Aero advertisement – as well as the product itself – and decide which target groups (gender and age) it is aimed at. Write a paragraph to explain your decision.

3 MESSAGE AND SLOGAN

The **message** of an advertisement is the main point that the advertisers are trying to get across. The message is often underlined in a **slogan** – a short, catchy phrase designed to stick in the memory.

a) Write a paragraph to explain what you think the message of the Aero advertisement might be and how the slogan (heard in voice-over at the end) helps to sum it up or put it into words.

133

Creating a TV advertisement

FOUNDATION TIER TASKS

1 SUMMARISING THE ADVERTISEMENT

Imagine you were telling a friend about this advertisement. Summarise what happens in 200–250 words.

Planning and drafting
- Use the seventeen storyboard frames, and the individual shot descriptions, as a guide.
- Write in the present tense (*he places the boxes on the floor… she looks up…*).
- Avoid repeating yourself (*In the first shot… in the third shot…*).

You could start:
As the advertisement starts, a delivery man is seen unloading some boxes from his lorry, which is parked in a busy street. He carries the boxes…

2 CREATING A STORYBOARD

Draw six frames of a storyboard for a television advertisement. (Either choose an advertisement that you know well or make up your own.) Then write a paragraph to explain how your six frames fit into the advertisement as a whole.

Planning and drafting

You could choose to draw the opening or concluding six frames, or any six from the middle of the advertisement.

Drawing up the storyboard
Use the same storyboard framework as the one which represents the Aero advertisement on pages 128–31. Include:
- the shot number
- the duration of that particular shot
- any sound effects or music
- a brief description of the shot
- a rough outline sketch of the shot

- any dialogue

Writing an explanatory paragraph
Start by explaining what the overall message of the advertisement is. Then explain what part your six frames play in the advertisement as a whole. For example, do they introduce the situation and the characters, or round off the advertisement, underlining the message with a slogan?

Your explanatory paragraph could start:
I have chosen to represent the opening six shots of the television advertisement for Woolworths. These six shots introduce the main character – a woman shopper – and the Woolworths store itself. The message of the advertisement is…

HIGHER TIER TASKS

1 ANALYSING THE ADVERTISEMENT

Write an analysis of the Aero advertisement, commenting on its effectiveness in getting its message across and encouraging us to buy the product.

Planning and drafting

In your analysis you could comment on the effectiveness of the use of the moving-image techniques you looked at on pages 132–3.

You could also address the following questions:
- How successfully does the advertisement attract its target group?
- What is its message and how effectively is it conveyed (through the storyline and the slogan)?
- Would the advertisement encourage you to buy the product?

You could start:
The television advertisement for Honeycomb Aero employs a number of moving-image techniques…

2 PLANNING AN ADVERTISING CAMPAIGN

Imagine you were part of an advertising team given the job of promoting a new product. Write a 'brief' for the customer (the manufacturer or owner of the product), in which you explain your plans for a television advertisement.

Planning and drafting

- First invent a product. It could be anything from a chocolate bar to trainers, a deodorant to a theme park.

- Then write an introduction in which you address questions of target group, message and whether or not to use humour.

- Follow up the introduction with a section in which you describe the proposed advertisement. Refer to vision, sound and music, and overall length.

- Then explain how the moving-image techniques you looked at on pages 132–3 (varying the shots, framing etc) will help to get the message across and attract buyers.

- You could include sketches of two or three frames if it helps to explain visual effects.

> You could start:
> *In devising this new television advertisement for Parker's Instant Pizza, we first of all conducted some research on our target group. Interviewing a broad sample of shoppers, we discovered that…*

Self assess

These are the main language features that you have learned about in this section. Decide how confident you feel about:

- commenting on the effects of the **photographs**, **headline** and **intro** in a newspaper article
- understanding the **paragraph structure** in a newspaper report
- explaining **pyramid writing** and its uses

- understanding why writers have to be aware of **audience**
- identifying **adjectives** and **adjective phrases** and discussing their uses
- commenting on the uses of **quotes**

- identifying **moving-image techniques**, such as the use of different **shots**, **framing**, **camera angles** and **cutting**
- understanding the importance of **duration** as a feature of a moving-image text
- explaining **target groups** and their importance in advertising
- commenting on the link between an advertisement's **message** and the **slogan**

What do you feel you need to revise?

Lifeboat!

In this unit you will:

- study the website of a charity organisation
- learn about multi-genre texts
- create a multi-genre text

These two screens are from the website of the Royal National Lifeboat Institution (RNLI). Below is the home-page.

This link-page provides an account of the charity and its work: *The RNLI in Brief*.

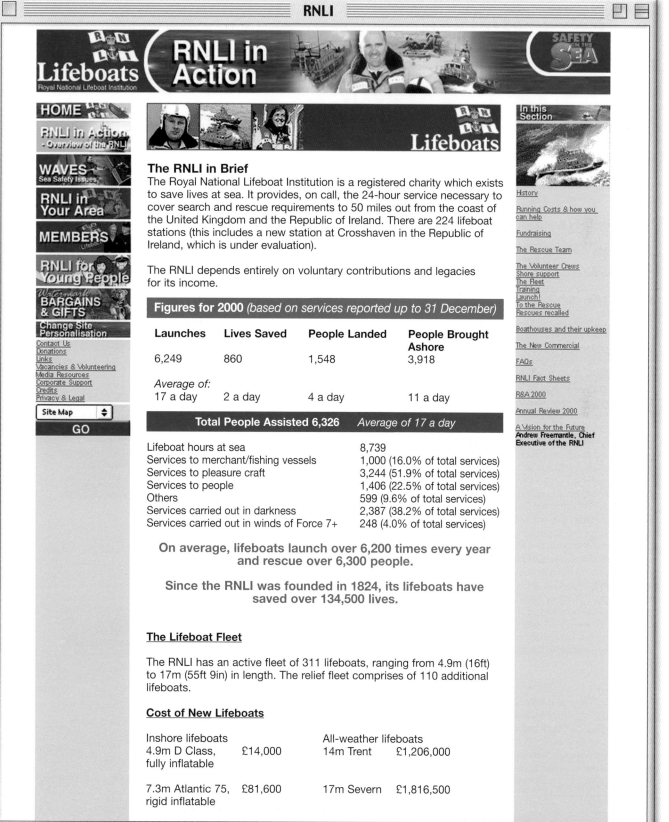

The RNLI in Brief

The Royal National Lifeboat Institution is a registered charity which exists to save lives at sea. It provides, on call, the 24-hour service necessary to cover search and rescue requirements to 50 miles out from the coast of the United Kingdom and the Republic of Ireland. There are 224 lifeboat stations (this includes a new station at Crosshaven in the Republic of Ireland, which is under evaluation).

The RNLI depends entirely on voluntary contributions and legacies for its income.

Figures for 2000 *(based on services reported up to 31 December)*

Launches	Lives Saved	People Landed	People Brought Ashore
6,249	860	1,548	3,918
Average of:			
17 a day	2 a day	4 a day	11 a day

Total People Assisted 6,326   *Average of 17 a day*

Lifeboat hours at sea	8,739
Services to merchant/fishing vessels	1,000 (16.0% of total services)
Services to pleasure craft	3,244 (51.9% of total services)
Services to people	1,406 (22.5% of total services)
Others	599 (9.6% of total services)
Services carried out in darkness	2,387 (38.2% of total services)
Services carried out in winds of Force 7+	248 (4.0% of total services)

On average, lifeboats launch over 6,200 times every year and rescue over 6,300 people.

Since the RNLI was founded in 1824, its lifeboats have saved over 134,500 lives.

The Lifeboat Fleet

The RNLI has an active fleet of 311 lifeboats, ranging from 4.9m (16ft) to 17m (55ft 9in) in length. The relief fleet comprises of 110 additional lifeboats.

Cost of New Lifeboats

Inshore lifeboats		All-weather lifeboats	
4.9m D Class, fully inflatable	£14,000	14m Trent	£1,206,000
7.3m Atlantic 75, rigid inflatable	£81,600	17m Severn	£1,816,500

Navigation/menu items within the website image:

HOME

RNLI in Action - Overview of the RNLI

WAVES Sea Safety Issues

RNLI in Your Area

MEMBERS

RNLI for Young People

BARGAINS & GIFTS

Change Site Personalisation

Contact Us
Donations
Links
Vacancies & Volunteering
Media Resources
Corporate Support
Credits
Privacy & Legal

Site Map

GO

In this Section

History
Running Costs & how you can help
Fundraising
The Rescue Team
The Volunteer Crews
Shore support
The Fleet
Training
Launch!
To the Rescue
Rescues recalled
Boathouses and their upkeep
The New Commercial
FAQs
RNLI Fact Sheets
R&A 2000
Annual Review 2000
A Vision for the Future
Andrew Freemantle, Chief Executive of the RNLI

This is a further selection of the link-pages which can be accessed from the RNLI home-page.

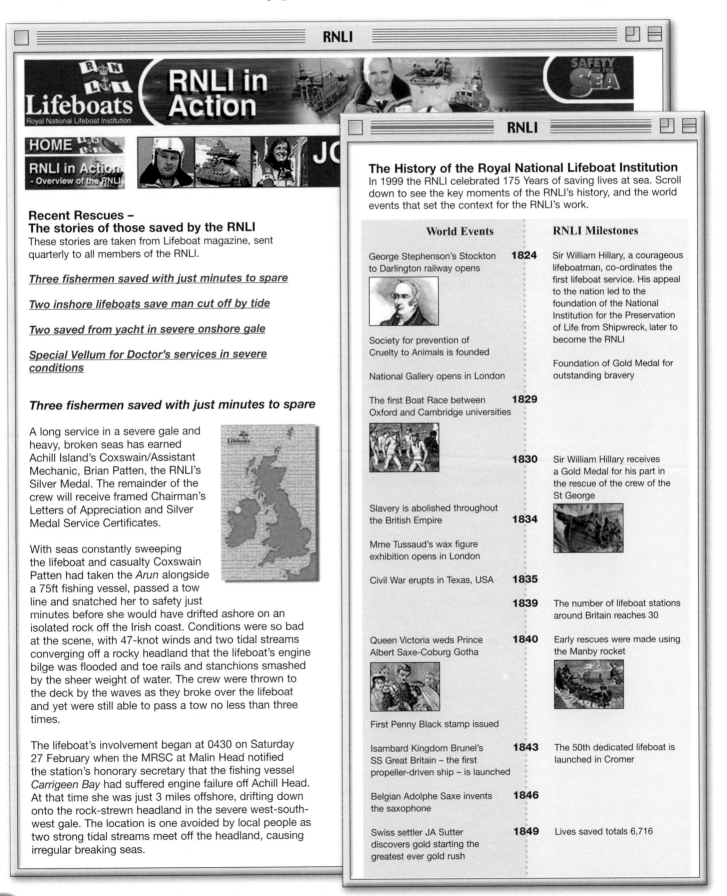

RNLI

![Lifeboats - Royal National Lifeboat Institution | RNLI in Action | SAFETY ON THE SEA](banner)

HOME

RNLI in Action
- Overview of the RNLI

JC

Recent Rescues –
The stories of those saved by the RNLI

These stories are taken from Lifeboat magazine, sent quarterly to all members of the RNLI.

Three fishermen saved with just minutes to spare

Two inshore lifeboats save man cut off by tide

Two saved from yacht in severe onshore gale

Special Vellum for Doctor's services in severe conditions

Three fishermen saved with just minutes to spare

A long service in a severe gale and heavy, broken seas has earned Achill Island's Coxswain/Assistant Mechanic, Brian Patten, the RNLI's Silver Medal. The remainder of the crew will receive framed Chairman's Letters of Appreciation and Silver Medal Service Certificates.

With seas constantly sweeping the lifeboat and casualty Coxswain Patten had taken the *Arun* alongside a 75ft fishing vessel, passed a tow line and snatched her to safety just minutes before she would have drifted ashore on an isolated rock off the Irish coast. Conditions were so bad at the scene, with 47-knot winds and two tidal streams converging off a rocky headland that the lifeboat's engine bilge was flooded and toe rails and stanchions smashed by the sheer weight of water. The crew were thrown to the deck by the waves as they broke over the lifeboat and yet were still able to pass a tow no less than three times.

The lifeboat's involvement began at 0430 on Saturday 27 February when the MRSC at Malin Head notified the station's honorary secretary that the fishing vessel *Carrigeen Bay* had suffered engine failure off Achill Head. At that time she was just 3 miles offshore, drifting down onto the rock-strewn headland in the severe west-south-west gale. The location is one avoided by local people as two strong tidal streams meet off the headland, causing irregular breaking seas.

RNLI

The History of the Royal National Lifeboat Institution

In 1999 the RNLI celebrated 175 Years of saving lives at sea. Scroll down to see the key moments of the RNLI's history, and the world events that set the context for the RNLI's work.

World Events		RNLI Milestones
George Stephenson's Stockton to Darlington railway opens	**1824**	Sir William Hillary, a courageous lifeboatman, co-ordinates the first lifeboat service. His appeal to the nation led to the foundation of the National Institution for the Preservation of Life from Shipwreck, later to become the RNLI
Society for prevention of Cruelty to Animals is founded		
National Gallery opens in London		Foundation of Gold Medal for outstanding bravery
The first Boat Race between Oxford and Cambridge universities	**1829**	
	1830	Sir William Hillary receives a Gold Medal for his part in the rescue of the crew of the St George
Slavery is abolished throughout the British Empire	**1834**	
Mme Tussaud's wax figure exhibition opens in London		
Civil War erupts in Texas, USA	**1835**	
	1839	The number of lifeboat stations around Britain reaches 30
Queen Victoria weds Prince Albert Saxe-Coburg Gotha	**1840**	Early rescues were made using the Manby rocket
First Penny Black stamp issued		
Isambard Kingdom Brunel's SS Great Britain – the first propeller-driven ship – is launched	**1843**	The 50th dedicated lifeboat is launched in Cromer
Belgian Adolphe Saxe invents the saxophone	**1846**	
Swiss settler JA Sutter discovers gold starting the greatest ever gold rush	**1849**	Lives saved totals 6,716

RNLI

Lifeboats
Royal National Lifeboat Institution

RNLI for YOUNG PEOPLE

SAFETY ON THE SEA

Home

Around the Coast

GAMES

Some great games for you to play – all to do with the sea

STUFF

Welcome to the RNLI Young People's Site

Brring, brring! Don't forget to check with whoever pays the telephone bill before getting into the Internet!

RNLI - LATEST NEWS

RNLI TO PUT MORE CHILDREN IN STORM FORCE CONDITIONS!

In an effort to engage more young people in its lifesaving work at sea, the RNLI is releasing a brand new membership pack for Storm Force

CALLING ALL BUDDING VAN GOGHS, REMBRANDTS GOYAS

We have an exciting new competition for our young supporters.

Introducing Stormy Stan

Get Splashed

STORM FORCE

Storm Force - the young people's membership for the RNLI

Join Up

Educational Resources

RNLI

Lifeboats
Royal National Lifeboat Institution

DONATIONS

Lifeboats

HOME

RNLI in Action - Overview of the RNLI

WAVES
Sea Safety Issues

RNLI in Your Area

MEMBERS

RNLI for Young People

BARGAINS & GIFTS

SEARCH & EXPLORE

Contact Us
Donations
Links
Vacancies & Volunteering
Media Resources
Corporate Support
Credits
Privacy & Legal

Site Map

GO

In the 30 seconds or so it will take you to read this sentence, the cost of maintaining the nation's maritime rescue service will have been **over £95** – not a penny of which comes from the government.

The RNLI is funded entirely by voluntary donations and legacies. For us to continue to save lives at sea and fund our plans for the future, we need your help.

Your donation will help us save lives

£8	A pair of gloves for a lifeboat crewmember
£15	A mouth to mouth resuscitator
£22	A pair of crewmember's boots
£63	A pair of protective trousers for a crewmember
£184	A lifejacket for our all-weather lifeboat crew
£245	A first aid kit

I would like to give £ 0 to help the lifeboat crews

Gift Aid
Increase your gift by one third!
Tick here so we can reclaim the tax you have already paid on your donation

Send your donation:

Download form (pdf)

RNLI

Lifeboats
Royal National Lifeboat Institution

Watermark The Gift Catalogue of the RNLI

RNLI GIFTS

HOME

Jump to section

Flip through the on-line catalogue

View Basket & Purchase

Order catalogue

Watertight Guarantee

ORDER HELPLINE
01202 663333

If you have any questions about ordering from the Watermark catalogue, or about an order which you have already placed, please telephone our Customer Service Helpline.

THAWTE
Authentic Site
Secured by SSL

Lifeboatman Bear

Lifeboatman Bear to the rescue. This lovable 240 mm (9.5") high Teddy Bear likes to keep everything on board shipshape, and he is dressed for the part too, in a coxwain's cap, spotted neckerchief, and jumper, embroidered with the RNLI logo.

Code	Description	Price (£)
BUYME W12050	Bear	£9.99

Language in context

The power of language

Key features of the texts are:

1 genre

2 purpose and audience

3 register

1 GENRE

> **Genre** is the name given to a particular kind of writing with its own special and recognisable features. Texts which include a variety of genres are called **multi-genre texts**.

Multi-genre texts

Magazines are good examples of multi-genre texts. For example, the *Radio Times* for 23–9 March 2002 contained sections on the following subjects, each one in a different genre:

Subject	Genre
a column by presenter John Peel	*opinion column*
an article about *Hornblower* star Ioan Gruffudd	*biographical article*
My kind of day	*autobiographical article*
an article about French and Saunders	*commentary*
answers to questions from the actor Simon Callow	*question and answer column*

a) That week's *Radio Times* also contained the following genres, among others:

sports writing   letters
recipes   advertisements
advice texts   reviews

In pairs, decide which of these six genres each of the following *Radio Times* items belongs to. Each one has been identified by a headline or opening phrase.

- *Just watched the first episode of* Black Books *and have to write and say…*
- *Ford Galaxy: designed for living. Engineered to last.*
- *The World Cup clock is ticking as England face Italy…*
- 20,000 Leagues under the Sea. *This is a marvellously designed and fabulously cast…*
- *Alan Titchmarsh's* How to Be a Gardener…
- *Bursting with the flavour of summer, strawberries and oranges make perfect partners for a refreshing fruit salad, says Gary Rhodes…*

b) In pairs, talk about a magazine that you know well and make a list of the different genres included in its contents, giving an example of each one. Use the *Radio Times* genres listed above to start you off, as some of the genres in your magazine may be the same.

2 PURPOSE AND AUDIENCE

> Whatever we write – whether it is a shopping list or a short story – it is essential to have a **purpose** and an **audience** in mind.

Genre and purpose

The National Curriculum for English lists twelve purposes for writing and also gives examples of genres which suit the various purposes.

These purposes and genres are:

Purposes for writing	Genres
writing to imagine, explore and entertain	*stories, poems, play scripts, autobiographies, screenplays, diaries*
writing to inform, explain and describe	*memos, minutes, accounts, information leaflets, news articles, prospectuses, plans, records, summaries*
writing to persuade, argue and advise	*brochures, advertisements, editorials, speeches, articles, opinion letters, campaign literature, polemical essays*
writing to analyse, review and comment	*reviews, commentaries, articles, essays, reports*

a) Find as many examples as you can of (a) different purposes for writing and (b) genres in the various pages of the RNLI website. Write down the section in which each example is to be found. Enter your findings in three columns like this:

Section	Purpose for writing	Genre
RNLI in Brief	to inform	factual account

Genre and audience

Audience is the term given to the people who are expected to read or see a text – the group to whom that text is addressed.

The RNLI website appeals to a number of different audiences.

b) Write a few sentences to explain which sections of this website might be aimed at each of the following audiences:
- the general public who do not know much about the RNLI but would like to find out more
- people who might be thinking about making a donation
- people considering joining a lifeboat crew
- anybody wanting to buy RNLI gifts
- sea-fishermen

For example, if the audience were the under-tens, you might say:

The section headed 'RNLI for Young People' is aimed at the under-tens. We can tell this, not just from the title of the section, but from its contents (drawing competitions, etc), and also from the language (Introducing Stormy Stan... 'Brring, brring!').

3 REGISTER

Anyone writing for a website has to make decisions about which **register** to use. Register is the term given to the style of language which suits a certain kind of subject matter or is appropriate to a particular situation or social context.

The author's choice of register will be influenced by the **purpose** of the writing and the **audience** it is aimed at. An informal register will tend to include examples of colloquial language (similar to everyday speech); a formal one will usually be more like standard written English.

At different times people might use, for example:
- a scientific register (for writing about new research)
- a technical register (to explain how a machine works)
- a religious register (when writing about their faith)

a) Reread the extracts from the three web-pages on *Recent Rescues*, *RNLI for Young People* and *RNLI Gifts*. For each one, write down:
- the audience (e.g. *the general public*)
- the purpose (e.g. *to persuade*)
- the register (e.g. *informal*)

Writing multi-genre texts

FOUNDATION TIER TASKS

1 SUMMARISING THE FACTS

Use the information on the web-pages to write an account of the RNLI and the work that it does.

Write 200–250 words.

> #### Planning and drafting
>
> You could divide your account into three sections.
>
> *Section 1: the history of the RNLI*
> - Write a paragraph on who founded it and when it was founded.
>
> *Section 2: the purpose of the RNLI*
> Look at *RNLI in Action: the RNLI in Brief*
> - Explain why the RNLI exists.
> - Describe what kind of service it provides.
>
> (Don't include too many statistics.)
>
> *Section 3: an example of the RNLI's work*
> Look at *RNLI in Action: Recent Rescues*
> - Describe Brian Patten's achievement (or access the website and find examples of other lifeboat crews' successes).

> You could start:
> *The RNLI was founded in …… by …… He was himself a brave lifeboatman who…*

2 WRITING A MAGAZINE ADVERT

Write the text for a full–page magazine advertisement, persuading people to give a donation to the RNLI.

Write 200–250 words.

> #### Planning and drafting
>
> You could:
> - explain what the RNLI does (use the information you collected for question 1)
> - give some examples of its recent achievements (look at *RNLI in Action: the RNLI in Brief*)
> - persuade people to make a donation (perhaps using some of the figures on the *Donations* web-page).
>
> Make sure that you have taken into account the **purpose** of your advert and its intended **audience** (the general public).
>
> Your advertisement could have a striking **headline** or you could use the RNLI **slogan** (see page 62), which is: *Safety on the Sea*.

> The first section (below the heading) could begin:
> *Every year the RNLI saves …… people in the seas around our coasts…*

HIGHER TIER TASKS

 1 ANALYSING THE TEXT

Write an analysis of the RNLI website, showing how effective it is in explaining what the organisation does and in encouraging people to support it.

Planning and drafting

Genres and registers

You could begin by describing the RNLI website as a multi-genre text, explaining how different genres and registers are used because they are suitable for the range of purposes and audiences:

- Which different genres and registers are to be found on the website?
  Look at the examples of information texts, advertisements, poetry and letters, for example.

- In what ways are the genres suitable for the range of purposes and different audiences?
  Compare the genres and registers which have been chosen for the *Young People* page with the genre and register used to describe the Achill Island rescue, for example.

Design

- How useful is the range of link-pages? What kind of information can be accessed?
  Look at the links along the outer columns of the home-page.

- How effective is the combination of image and text?
  Refer to the design of the link-pages on history, young people and gifts.

> You could start:
> *The RNLI website is a good example of a multi-genre text. From the home-page we can see that…*

2 PLANNING PAGES FOR A CHARITY WEBSITE

Plan a home-page and five link-pages for a website of a charity (such as Plan International UK, pages 60–1) or a campaign (such as Rainforest Concern, page 79)

- Draw a sketch-plan to show what the home-page will look like.
- Describe the contents of the five planned link-pages, explaining which different genres will be included and which registers will be used.

Planning and drafting

The sketch-plan

First draw an outline sketch of the home-page; you could base it on the RNLI home-page, which has:

- a **banner** across the top featuring the charity's name and some images
- a **centre column**, which includes:
  an introduction: what the charity does
  several links to *Latest News*
- **side columns** on the left and right showing the links to major areas of interest, for example:
  the history of the charity and its achievements
  the activities of the charity in your area
  bargains and gifts
  a page aimed at young people
  how to join or make a donation

The description of the planned link-pages

Look back at page 140 to consider the different genres that might be represented. Then write a sentence or two on each of your five planned link-pages, explaining:

- which aspect of the charity they feature
- which genre and register they are written in

> You could base the opening of your description of one of the link-pages on the following:
>
> *The first link-page, Friends of the Earth in Action, is a chronological account, written in a formal register, of the charity's achievements. It covers the…*

Two thousand years of history...

In this unit you will:

- compare a number of leaflets advertising historic buildings
- examine their design and language
- plan an advertising leaflet

This is part of a leaflet advertising Warwick Castle.

WARWICK CASTLE

A thousand years of history in the making

Come and take a look inside Warwick Castle - and step back in time!

Warwick Castle – with history, drama and excitement, it's a great day out for everyone!

Encounter over 1,000 years of mystery and intrigue at Warwick Castle. From the days of William the Conqueror to the splendour of the Victorian era, the Castle has been a mighty force in English history.

Experience the sights and smells of a mediaeval household in 'Kingmaker – a preparation for battle' or feel the weight of a sword in 'Death or Glory'. Take a step forward in time and marvel at the elegant splendour of the Great Hall, State Rooms and the Victorian 'Royal Weekend Party, 1898'.

Warwick Castle is a great day out for all the family, with plenty to see and do all year round – see our calendar inside for all our special events taking place throughout the year.

Food and drink facilities are available at the Castle from the Coach House and the Undercroft, where delicious hot meals, snacks, morning coffee, afternoon tea, children's meals, wine and beer are offered.

Visit our gift shops where you will discover Warwick Castle themed gifts, plus our more unique ranges. Turn your child into a fair maiden or deadly archer or treat yourself to one of our tapestries, books or jewellery sets.

Death or Glory

Our armoury attraction is home to some magnificent displays, all grouped into three distinct historical periods of the last 1,000 years. You'll get the chance to try on a helmet and discover the sheer amount of strength needed to lift a sword.

The Dungeon and Torture Chamber

Why not venture underground to the eerie silence of the Mediaeval Dungeon or enter into our grisly Torture Chamber.

Grounds and Gardens

With 60 acres of grounds and gardens, there's always plenty to see outside as well as in; whatever time of the year you visit. Wander around our beautiful Peacock Garden and enter our 18th century Conservatory, filled with an array of exotic plants. Then take a trip to our Victorian Rose Garden where the delicate English flowers bloom during late June.

Towers and Ramparts

Marvel at the impressive Towers and Ramparts and survey the panoramic views of the Castle grounds and Warwick Town. Initially used as mighty defence systems, the Towers were later converted into sumptuous apartments for affluent and powerful visitors, many of which can be viewed as part of our special events during January to March – see our calendar of events inside for further details.

Kingmaker

Witness a mediaeval household in 'Kingmaker – a preparation for battle'. The year is 1471 and preparations are being made for what will be Richard Neville's, Earl of Warwick, final battle.

See how weapons would have been made, watch the seamstresses hard at work, come face to face with the Earl's warhorse and feel the incredible weight of the armour worn.

Royal Weekend Party

Step back in time to the splendour of the Victorian period at Warwick Castle. Meet the beautiful Daisy, Countess of Warwick, preparing for one of her spectacular parties, with her impressive guest list consisting of royalty and future prime ministers. Watch as day passes to evening and witness the guests in twelve rooms of the former private apartments preparing for the celebrations. See and hear for yourself the British aristocracy at play.

Great Hall and State Rooms

Deep in the heart of the Castle, enter the grandeur of the Great Hall before stepping through into the State Rooms surrounded by superb collections of family treasures from around the world.

Ghost Tower

Enter our spooky Ghost Tower and hear the chilling tale of the murder of Sir Fulke Greville, whose restless soul is said to still haunt these rooms.

To book fast-track entry tickets or for further information please call 0870 442 2000 or book on-line at www.warwick-castle.co.uk

This is the inside of a leaflet advertising Tower Bridge in London.

Tower Bridge Experience

THE BRIDGE OF VIEWS

Over 100 years ago the Victorians built the bridge which has become a symbol of London to the world. High level walkways let pedestrians cross the Thames even while its roadway is split and lifted to let tall ships through. These walkways gave Londoners a new vista across their ever-changing city skyline.

Today, these views are more spectacular than ever. At the Tower Bridge Experience you can look out across London from this unique vantage point and witness the rich history and bold engineering invention that made one of the world's most famous bridges.

Have fun and learn with the interactive computer displays on the high level walkways

Enjoy panoramic views across the city and down-river

Visit the original engine rooms; discover how a "bascule" bridge works

Tour the exhibitions inside the towers and see how the bridge was built

Allow around 60 minutes for the whole Experience

Station X was the name given to Bletchley Park, the home of the codebreakers in the Second World War. The leaflet below describes what visitors can see there today.

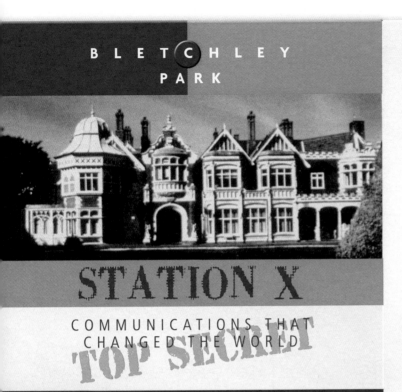

BLETCHLEY PARK

STATION X

COMMUNICATIONS THAT CHANGED THE WORLD

TOP SECRET

Home of the world's first programmable electronic computer - Colossus

Bletchley Park

Bletchley Park, also known as 'Station X', was home to the famous codebreakers of the Second World War and the birthplace of modern computing and communications. It is now a heritage site run by a charitable Trust, with historic buildings, exhibitions and tours for visitors, community activities and non-residential conference facilities.

The Mansion

Bought in 1883 by Sir Herbert Leon as his family home, the Mansion is the centrepiece of Bletchley Park. Its exterior reflects his changing tastes, each addition being a different architectural style, whilst the opulence of the wood-panelled interior and gilded ballroom is indicative of the status of a wealthy Victorian businessman.

The Mansion's first reprieve from demolition was its acquisition in 1938 by the Government Code and Cypher School. The wooden huts and brick blocks were added until over 12,000 people worked within the Park.

The extensive Churchill Memorabilia Collection, the Toy Museum and the Post Office famous for its First Day Covers are all located within the Park.

The 'Bombe' machine was devised by Alan Turing to assist in breaking 'Enigma' codes.

The Grounds

The Bletchley Park heritage site occupies 30 acres. Within this area there are a number of different exhibitions and displays covering, amongst others:

- Uniforms & WWII Memorabilia
- WWII aircraft recovery
- Wartime fire engines and historic vehicles
- US, German & British Re-enactment groups
- Wartime electronics and amateur radio station
- Model railway layouts
- Model boats (displays often take place on the lake)
- Military vehicles
- Historic cinema projectors

Displays frequently change so there is always something new to see.

Enjoy a picnic by the lake or a visit to the 'Hut 4' bar and café when you are ready to 'take a break'. Snacks available in the museum complex.

The Cryptology Trail

This fascinating experience enables you to follow the trail of a coded message from its interception to decode and interpretation. With its complex system of outposts and intercept stations, the wireless system was the forerunner of the Worldwide Web.

The need for speed, accuracy and secrecy was paramount, so very few knew the whole story. After following the Cryptology Trail you will know the secrets of Bletchley Park almost as well as those who worked here!

Enigma

The Enigma machine was the main decoding device for German armed forces and rail system. They believed its codes were unbreakable. Some of the finest brains in Britain were assembled at Bletchley Park for the sole purpose of breaking the Enigma codes.

One of the leading figures was Alan Turing, a brilliant mathematician considered to be the father of the modern computer. During your visit you will see working examples of Enigma and other coding machines, plus a replica of the 'Turing Bombe' deciphering device.

The Tour

No visit to Bletchley Park is complete without a guided tour. Experienced guides give you a real insight into the work that went on here and the secrecy surrounding it until just a few years ago.

The tours are optional and run at regular intervals. Your guide will first give you the background to the Park and then take you around the main buildings. Your guide will explain what went on at key locations and illustrate the story with a few amusing anecdotes of their own.

The tour takes about one hour.

The Internet

Take a virtual tour of Bletchley Park through our website at **www.bletchleypark.org.uk** This will help you get more out of your visit and also keep you up-to-date with many different special events taking place on Open Weekends.

CABINET WAR ROOMS

The nerve centre of Britain's war effort

SECRET
KEPT UNDER LOCK AND KEY.

Left and below are the front cover and the inside of a leaflet advertising the underground rooms used by the Cabinet during the Second World War.

Cabinet War Rooms

Air Raid Reports

CENTRAL SECTOR.

Churchill inspecting damage caused by a bomb that just missed the Cabinet War Rooms on 30th September 1940.

Wartime pictures of life and work in the Cabinet War Rooms.

On His Majesty's Service

MOST SECRET

Copy No.

In August 1939, one week before war began, the Cabinet War Rooms became operational in a former government storage basement. In the twenty-one rooms of this cramped and Spartan refuge, the most senior figures of Britain's government and its armed forces worked and slept and survived the ferocious air attacks on London during the Second World War.

They have been kept exactly as they were before the lights were finally extinguished after six years of war. Visitors can now step back in time as they walk through the actual rooms, experiencing the atmosphere and conditions of those times and witnessing where Winston Churchill took decisions crucial to the survival of the nation.

URGENT

The Map Room, the focal point for information about the progress of the war.

The Cabinet Room, where Churchill and his Ministers continued the work of Government during bombing raids

GO TO IT

DAILY EXPRESS
8th June 1940

Language in context

2 **VOCABULARY**

> **Vocabulary** is the term given to a writer's choice of words.

The vocabulary in these leaflets has been chosen with the aim of getting across certain ideas and associations. For example, the Tower Bridge leaflet contains the phrase *witness the rich history*…
In this phrase, the **verb**, **adjective** and **abstract noun** have all been carefully chosen for their effect on the reader.

- The verb *witness* is an example of an imperative (see question 1); it suggests that we will see something important and worth remembering.
- The adjective *rich* suggests the wealth of exciting and interesting things in our past.
- The abstract noun *history* is the 'product' that these tourist attractions are 'selling'.

> An **adjective** is a word which gives us information about a noun or pronoun.
> A group of words which does this is called an **adjective phrase**.

a) Look at the Tower Bridge leaflet, which describes the attraction as *one of the world's **most famous** bridges*. Pick out the other adjectives and adjective phrases that describe the following nouns (listed in the order in which they appear in the text):

- the walkways (an adjective phrase)
- ships
- the vista across London
- the city skyline
- the views (an adjective phrase)
- the vantage point
- the views across the city

The power of language

Key features of the texts are:

1. imperatives
2. vocabulary
3. the combination of text and image

1. **IMPERATIVES**

> We use the **imperative** form of the verb when we want to give a command, issue a warning, make a request or persuade someone to do something.

Imperatives for persuasion

Imperatives are widely used in leaflets of this kind. Most often, they are used as a way of persuading you to visit the place being advertised:
***Come** and **take** a look inside Warwick Castle – and **step** back in time!*

a) Write down examples of imperatives used in:

- the left-hand panel of the Warwick Castle leaflet (*Warwick Castle – with history…*)
- the final section of the Station X leaflet (headed *The Internet*)
- the right half of the Tower Bridge leaflet

b) The Warwick Castle leaflet is full of imperatives. Reread the sections on page 145 headed *Kingmaker* and *Royal Weekend Party*. Make a note of all the imperatives, starting with *Witness*…

Write a paragraph to explain how effective the imperatives are in persuading the reader that there will be plenty of things to see and do on a visit to Warwick Castle.

b) Each of the adjectives you have just found helps to describe the same feature. Which special attraction of Tower Bridge are they focusing on? Write a sentence or two to comment on the message that the writers of the leaflet were trying to convey with these adjectives. What in particular are they trying to 'sell'?

c) Write a paragraph commenting on the following adjectives and adjective phrases in the leaflet about the Cabinet War Rooms:

*this **cramped** and **Spartan** refuge… the **most senior** figures… the **ferocious** air attacks… the **actual** rooms… decisions **crucial** to…*

How do they help to convey:

● what the rooms must have been like to work in?

● what part the rooms played in the war?

> An **abstract noun** is the label we give to something we cannot touch, such as an emotion, feeling or idea.

d) Reread the section of the Station X leaflet headed *The Cryptology Trail*. The first half (up to …*Web*) contains the following abstract nouns:

experience, message, interception, decode (here an abstract noun, but more usually a verb), *interpretation, system, forerunner, Worldwide Web*

Find the abstract nouns in the rest of the section (down to …*worked here!*).

e) The section headed *The Cryptology Trail* is about three features of Station X:

● Station X's work with codes

● the system they built up

● the qualities which were most important to them

Divide the abstract nouns from *The Cryptology Trail* into three groups, showing how each noun helps us to understand one of these three features.

3 TEXT AND IMAGE

> Explanatory texts will often use a combination of **text** (words) and **image** (photographs and illustrations).

a) In pairs, talk about the following images. What message or messages does each one get across?

● The photograph of Station X at the top of the leaflet (what atmosphere does it conjure up?).

● The round photograph in the top right-hand corner of the Tower Bridge leaflet.

● The photograph at the top of the Warwick Castle leaflet (page 144).

b) Study the front cover and inside panels of the leaflet on the Cabinet War Rooms. Make notes on which ideas and facts are explained:

● through the **text** alone
Look at the inside centre panel and the captions accompanying the photographs.

● through the **illustrations** alone
Look at the use of:

  ● **realia** (the term given to real documents and historical objects), such as:
  the photographs and newspaper cartoon from the Second World War
  the labels
  the leather file

  ● modern photographs

c) Write a paragraph or two commenting on the ways in which the spread uses a combination of text and image in order to give us an idea of how interesting and important the Cabinet War Rooms are. In your writing, explain the choices made about the overall **design concept** (the main design idea which aims to get across a particular impression or message). Which central idea holds the whole design together?

Compare and contrast

FOUNDATION TIER TASKS

1 SUMMARISING THE ATTRACTIONS

Summarise in your own words what Bletchley Park (Station X) is and what its attractions are to visitors.

Write 200–250 words.

Planning and drafting

You could write a short paragraph on each of the following:

- Introduction: why Station X is important (see the section headed *Bletchley Park*).
- A summary of the attractions: what visitors can see and enjoy there (see *The Grounds* and *The Cryptology Trail*).
- An explanation of its most important exhibit: the Enigma machine and its importance (see *Enigma*).

> You could start:
> *Bletchley Park was an important centre in World War 2. Also known as 'Station X', it was…*

2 WRITING A LETTER

Write a letter to a friend in which you recommend her or him to visit a particular historic building. You could choose:

- a site that you have visited yourself
- one of the buildings advertised in the leaflets on pages 144–7
- Hadrian's Wall (using the information on the opposite page)

Planning and drafting

In your letter, you could refer to:

- the building itself
- the attractions
- visitor facilities (such as cafés, picnic areas and access for the disabled)

Choose **adjectives** and **abstract nouns** (see pages 148–9) to make your letter sound enthusiastic, and to get across how dramatic and interesting your visit was.

> You could start:
> *Dear ……………,*
> *Have you ever been to …………………… ?*
> *It's amazing! I suppose I had been expecting…*

HIGHER TIER TASKS

1 COMPARING THE LEAFLETS

Write a comparison of the four leaflets. First describe which language features they have in common, using examples to illustrate your points. Then explain which of the four is most effective in your opinion, again referring closely to the texts as you give your reasons.

Planning and drafting

In describing the typical language features, explain the effectiveness of:

- the widespread use of **imperatives**
- careful choice of vocabulary, particularly **adjectives** and **abstract nouns**
- the combination of **text** and **image**
- the overall **design concept**

In comparing the effectiveness of the four leaflets, ask yourself which ones use the language features most successfully to:

- describe the overall site clearly, so that you know exactly what is there
- select particularly attractive features
- explain what facilities there are for visitors

> You could start:
> *All four leaflets advertise sites of particular interest and importance in British history. Each one…*

2 PLANNING A LEAFLET

Plan the cover and the three inside panels of a leaflet to advertise a site of historic interest. Either pick somewhere that you know well, or base your ideas on the information about Hadrian's Wall provided on the right.

First write 100–200 words describing the overall design. State the main messages that you want to convey and explain the overall design concept.

Then draft the text.

Finally explain how the text and the images will combine for maximum effect.

Planning and drafting

The overall design

You could:

- make the building exterior the centre of your design (Tower Bridge) or focus on the interior only (Cabinet War Rooms)
- combine a wide selection of photographic images (Tower Bridge) or choose very few (Station X)
- reflect the nature of the historic site in an overall design concept (Cabinet War Rooms)

The text

- Remember to use the typical language features of leaflets.
- You could use the following information about Hadrian's Wall.

Text and image

- Think carefully about how best to combine text and images.

You could start your text with a sentence used in an actual visitor guide to Hadrian's Wall:

Wherever you go, or whatever you do, you will be able to see why the Romans stayed here, but it may be more difficult to work out why they left…

INFORMATION ABOUT HADRIAN'S WALL

The wall itself

- was built by Hadrian to mark the boundary of the Roman Empire
- was constructed between 120 and 128 Common Era
- is a series of frontier installations running from west to east, over 73 miles from coast to coast
- stood some six metres high
- was garrisoned (occupied) by troops in forts and turrets along its entire length
- had milecastles (forts at intervals of a mile, garrisoned by 10–20 men)

What to see

- the central section, which crosses the Northumberland National Park, is the best preserved
- there are good milecastles at Cawfields and Poltross Burn
- Housesteads is the best-preserved fort, with spectacular views
- current excavations at Vindolanda are revealing a great deal about Roman life
- the bathhouse at Chesters fort shows how advanced and civilised the Romans were

What to do

- the Roman Army Museum has models and is a great learning experience for children
- walk the wall, a National Trail from Once Brewed National Park Visitor Centre
- stroll around Corbridge Roman site on a tape tour

Other attractions nearby

- the National Thyme Collection at Hexham Herbs
- Bardon Mill Pottery
- The Garden Station at Langley – a restored Victorian railway station

People are ...

In this unit you will:

- study a series of three advertisements
- examine the combination of image and text
- plan an advertisement

The three advertisements on these pages are all encouraging people to think about a career in social work.

People can be fascinating, mystifying, rewarding. They're never boring. Social work is work with people, it's that simple and that complicated. To find out more about training to be a qualified social worker call for a career booklet on 0845 604 6404 or visit www.socialworkcareers.co.uk (minicom: 0845 601 6121)

social work
it's all about people.

autism	autistic people have difficulty in relating to others and their language does not develop normally
congenital deficiency	a weakness in the genes inherited from your parents
cerebellum	the part of the brain which controls muscular movements, balance and co-ordination
traumas	harmful experiences
social isolation	being cut off from other people

Language in context

The power of language

Key features of the texts are:

1. use of narrative
2. typography
3. graphic novel techniques

1 NARRATIVE

A **narrative** is another term for a story or account. Biographies, autobiographies, novels and short stories are all examples of **narrative texts**.

Advertisements in print media (newspapers, magazines etc) mainly use two kinds of writing:

- writing to inform (giving you details about the product)
- writing to persuade (encouraging you to buy it)

A good example is the advertisement for Plan International UK (pages 60–1). But these three *People are…* advertisements are unusual because they are mainly narrative texts: they each tell a story.

a) In pairs, look back at the three advertisements and pick out examples of:

- writing to inform (giving you information about social work as a career)
- writing to persuade (encouraging you to train as a social worker)
- narrative writing (telling a story)

2 TYPOGRAPHY

Typography is the name given to the way words are written, drawn or printed. It is a term used in **graphics** (the art of combining images and lettering for particular effects).

Graphic artists put as much thought into typography as writers do into choosing the right words. For example, look at the way *Station X* is printed on the front cover of the Bletchley Park leaflet (page 146). It is made to look like old-fashioned typewriter print. Beneath it, the words *TOP SECRET* look as though they have been made with an ink stamp. The typography has been chosen to fit the image of Bletchley Park and its association with wartime decoding.

a) Write a short paragraph on each of the following examples of typography from *People are terrifying*. For each example, describe the typography used and explain why you think it was chosen. (Use the explanation of the *Station X* typography (above) as a model for your comments.)

- the word *terrifying* in the title, and the text in the bottom left-hand corner (*Mother screams at you…*)
- the words *you get a message from a GP*
- the words *unlucky thirteen*
- the words *social work* in the bottom right-hand corner

3 GRAPHIC NOVEL TECHNIQUES

> A **graphic novel** is a story which is told through a combination of words and images. It closely resembles a cartoon-strip in its method of telling the story.

Graphic novels are similar in design to children's comics. But they are different in the following ways:

- they are much longer
- they deal with adult issues
- they contain a single, extended story
- they use a wide range of images – not just line drawings
- the drawing styles are adult
- the images are a very important part of the narrative – some frames contain no words at all

a) Look at the frames and images from the three advertisements listed in the right-hand column. In pairs, discuss how the illustration alone helps to tell the story in each case. For example, the text about Errol (*People are proud*) says: *as he tells you he's had a good life.*

The illustration gives much more information about him in a way that also shows how fanatical he has always been about cricket.

People are proud

- frame 8: What does the road sign suggest about the location of, and the attitude of, Errol's family?
- frame 10: What does this image suggest? Look particularly at the way the word *home* has been reproduced.
- frame 11: How does the image of the umpire help to convey the idea that death itself was *a small thing to Errol*?
- frame 5 onwards: Which other images help to show Errol's obsession with cricket? How do they get it across?

People are terrifying

- frame 2: What evidence did the doctor have, apart from the sight of the bruising?
- frame 3: The girl on the horse doesn't look like the girl in the story – is it the same girl? Why has this picture been included?

People are mystifying

- What story is being told through the set of three frames near the bottom of the page (starting with the text *the rewards*)? For example, why does the adult look exactly the same while the child has changed?
- What fact is being illustrated by the two frames of the cathedral at the bottom?

b) In pairs, talk about the way in which you first read the three advertisements. For example, did you find yourself looking at the images first, then the writing, or the other way round? What do you notice now that you look at them for the second or third time? What do you like about the graphic novel style of narrative? What can it do that traditional novel narrative cannot do?

c) After your discussion, write a paragraph headed *Graphic novel style*. Explain what it is and how a graphic novel text might be read differently from a traditional novel or short story.

Creating a multi-genre advertisement

FOUNDATION TIER TASKS

1 SUMMARISING THE NARRATIVE

Imagine you are a social worker whose job it is to help Errol (in *People are proud*). You visit him for the first time and have a long talk. Draft the brief report that you write up after your meeting.

Write 200–250 words.

Planning and drafting

Use the story told on page 153 as a basis for your report. First check what you wrote down in answer to question 3a on graphic novel techniques (page 157). That will remind you which parts of the narrative are told through the illustrations rather than the text.

Write about:

- your impressions of Errol when you first saw him (get some ideas from the three frames on the top line)
- what he told you about his background:
  - his age
  - his family life
  - his employment history (you could make up details about what jobs he had done)
- his view of his past life (was he cheerful or sad, for example?)
- his passion for cricket (mention the way he describes life in cricketing terms)
- his current difficulties and needs

Then write a section headed *Action*. State briefly what you plan to do to help Errol, including:

- practical changes in his home
- home-helps and visitors

> You could start:
> *I visited Errol Jones at his home on ....
> (date). As soon as he opened the door I got the impression of a man who...*

2 WRITING A LETTER

Write a letter to your local MP explaining why you think social workers are doing an excellent job. Use the three stories from the *People are...* advertisements as evidence.

Planning and drafting

You could include the following facts about social workers.

Social workers can help...

- old peope who live a long way from their families
- young people who are being abused (such as the thirteen-year-old girl)
- people suffering from autism – and their families

Social workers can give practical help, such as...

- helping old people to manage on their own at home
- helping people to make friends and rebuild their lives
- working alongside local doctors who suspect abuse, and approaching parents directly
- supporting families with autistic children and helping them to feel that they are not alone

> You could start:
> *Dear .... (name of your MP),*
> *I am writing to you in support of the many social workers in our local community. I don't think many people appreciate...*

HIGHER TIER TASKS

1 ANALYSING THE ADVERTISEMENTS

Write an analysis of the three *People are…* advertisements explaining what methods they use in persuading people to consider social work as a career.

Planning and drafting

In your analysis, refer closely to the text and graphics and include examples from all three advertisements to illustrate your points.

- You could begin by stating what it is that links the three advertisements (think about purpose, form, audience and topic).
- You could then explain that the methods used involve both language and images (refer to the different kinds of writing used, typography, the part played by the illustrations, and graphic novel style).

> You could start:
> *These three advertisements are linked by a common purpose, form, audience and topic…*

2 PLANNING AN ADVERTISEMENT

Plan a full-page advertisement which encourages people to consider a similar career to social work, such as nursing, teaching or the police. Use the same graphic novel style as the *People are…* series.

Planning and drafting

- Decide which career you want to advertise and think up a brief story which illustrates the kind of work that this career involves.
- Remember some of the key features of the graphic novel style.

> If you choose to advertise nursing, for example, you could start with a heading *Patients are terrified…* The opening frame might then show a young child being brought into a hospital ward looking extremely frightened, the text reading *You meet Sam…*

Self assess

These are the main language features that you have learned about in this section. Decide how confident you feel about:

- explaining what **genre** is and picking out a genre's typical features
- understanding the links between a text's **genre**, its **purpose** and its **audience**
- understanding **register** and its links to **purpose** and **audience**

- commenting on the ways in which **imperatives** can be used to persuade
- discussing the uses of **adjectives**, **adjective phrases** and **abstract nouns** in writing to persuade
- commenting on the effects of combining **text** and **image**

- understanding what **narrative** is and identifying a **narrative text**
- explaining the uses of **typography**
- defining a **graphic novel** and understanding how it works

What do you feel you need to revise?

Horrors of the past

In this unit you will:

- compare two accounts from past centuries
- examine the language of reporting
- write a report of an event

EXECUTION

In 1587, after being found guilty of plotting against Queen Elizabeth I, Mary Queen of Scots was condemned to death. This is an account of her beheading, written by an eye-witness, Robert Wynkfielde.

The Execution of Mary Queen of Scots
8 February 1587

ROBERT WYNKFIELDE

Her prayers being ended, the executioners, kneeling, desired her Grace to forgive them her death: who answered, 'I forgive you with all my heart, for now, I hope, you shall make an end of all my troubles.' Then they, with her two women, helping her up, began to disrobe her of her apparel...

All this time they were pulling off her apparel, she never changed her countenance, but with smiling cheer she uttered these words, 'that she never had such grooms to make her unready, and that she never put off her clothes before such a company'.

Then she, with a smiling countenance, turning to her men servants, as Melvin and the rest, standing upon a bench nigh the scaffold, who sometime weeping, sometime crying out aloud, and continually crossing themselves, prayed in Latin, crossing them with her hand bade them farewell, and wishing them to pray for her even until the last hour.

Then the two women departed from her, and she kneeling down upon the cushion most resolutely, and without any token or fear of death, she spake aloud this Psalm in Latin, *In Te Domine confido, non confundar in eternam*, etc. Then, groping for the block, she laid down her head, putting her chin over the block with both her hands, which, holding there still, had been cut off had they not been espied. Then lying upon the block most quietly, and stretching out her arms cried, *In manus tuas, Domine*, etc., three or four times. Then she, lying very still upon the block, one of the executioners holding her slightly with one of his hands, she endured two strokes of the other executioner with an axe, she making very small noise or none at all, and not stirring any part of her from the place where she lay: and so the executioner cut off her head, saving one little gristle, which being cut asunder, he lift up her head to the view of all the assembly and bade *God save the Queen*. Then, her dress of lawn falling from off her head, it appeared as grey as one of threescore and ten years old, polled very short, her face in a moment being so much altered from the form she had when she was alive, as few could remember her by her dead face. Her lips stirred up and down a quarter of an hour after her head was cut off.

Then one of the executioners, pulling off her garters, espied her little dog which was crept under her clothes, which could not be gotten forth but by force, yet afterward would not depart from the dead corpse, but came and lay between her head and her shoulders...

apparel	clothing
countenance	facial expression
make her unready	help her to undress
In Te Domine...	I have faith in you, O Lord, that I will not be damned for eternity...

had been cut off	would have been cut off
In manus tuas, Domine...	Into your hands, O Lord...
dress of lawn	covering or blindfold of fine linen
threescore and ten	seventy
polled	cropped

DEATH OF A CLIMBING BOY

In 1817 a Parliamentary Committee of the House of Commons listened to evidence concerning the use of 'climbing boys' – children sent down chimneys by sweeps. This story is one of the accounts offered in evidence. Having heard many stories like this one, the Committee recommended that the use of climbing boys should be prohibited. No-one took any notice.

Death of a Climbing Boy, 29 March 1813

EVIDENCE TAKEN BEFORE THE PARLIAMENTARY COMMITTEE ON CLIMBING BOYS, 1817

In 1817 a Committee of the House of Commons recommended that the use of climbing boys be prohibited, but the recommendation was not carried into effect.

On Monday morning, 29 March 1813, a chimney sweeper of the name of Griggs attended to sweep a small chimney in the brewhouse of Messrs Calvert and Co. in Upper Thames Street; he was accompanied by one of his boys, a lad of about eight years of age, of the name of Thomas Pitt. The fire had been lighted as early as 2 o'clock the same morning, and was burning on the arrival of Griggs and his little boy at eight. The fireplace was small, and an iron pipe projected from the grate some little way into the flue. This the master was acquainted with (having swept the chimneys in the brewhouse for some years), and therefore had a tile or two broken from the roof, in order that the boy might descend the chimney. He had no sooner extinguished the fire than he suffered the lad to go down; and the consequence, as might be expected, was his almost immediate death, in a state, no doubt, of inexpressible agony. The flue was of the narrowest description, and must have retained heat sufficient to have prevented the child's return to the top, even supposing he had not approached the pipe belonging to the grate, which must have been nearly red hot; this however was not clearly ascertained on the inquest, though the appearance of the body would induce an opinion that he had been unavoidably pressed against the pipe. Soon after his descent, the master, who remained on the top, was apprehensive that something had happened, and therefore desired him to come up; the answer of the boy was, 'I cannot come up, master, I must die here.' An alarm was given in the brewhouse immediately that he had stuck in the chimney, and a bricklayer who was at work near the spot attended, and after knocking down part of the brickwork of the chimney, just above the fireplace, made a hole sufficiently large to draw him through. A surgeon attended, but all attempts to restore life were ineffectual. On inspecting the body, various burns appeared; the fleshy part of the legs and a great part of the feet more particularly were injured; those parts too by which climbing boys most effectually ascend or descend chimneys, viz. the elbows and knees, seemed burnt to the bone; from which it must be evident that the unhappy sufferer made some attempts to return as soon as the horrors of his situation became apparent.

brewhouse	building where beer is brewed
flue	the main chimney passage through which the smoke escapes
suffered	allowed
not clearly ... inquest	not discovered for certain at the official inquiry into the death
induce	encourage, persuade
viz.	in other words

Language in context

The power of language

Key features of the texts are:

1. emotive reporting
2. factual reporting
3. audience and purpose

1 EMOTIVE REPORTING

> Writing which has an impact on the reader's feelings is said to have an **emotive** effect. This effect can be achieved through the use of particular words and phrases (e.g. **quoting** what people said), or through careful selection of the details that the writer chooses to present to the reader (**emotive description**).

Emotive quoting

a) Reread Robert Wynkfielde's account of the execution of Mary Queen of Scots.

Make a note of the things Mary is recorded as having said. It will be easiest to draw up three columns in which you record:

- what she said in each case (her actual words, or as Wynkfielde reports her)
- who she was addressing
- how she said it (if we are told)

b) Write a paragraph explaining what impression you have formed of Mary from this evidence. For example, how is she approaching her death? What kind of relationship does she seem to have had with her women and servants? What do they feel about her?

Emotive description

c) Make a list of the other details Wynkfielde has selected which help the reader to form an impression of Mary as an individual, rather than merely an anonymous victim.

For example, look at references to:

- Mary's clothes
- her religious behaviour
- her appearance after death
- her pet dog

d) Write a paragraph to explain how much sympathy or admiration you think Wynkfielde has for Mary. Look particularly at the details that you have been studying in questions a–c.

e) In small groups, find evidence in the account of Thomas Pitt's death that the writer was probably in favour of prohibiting the use of climbing boys.

Look, for example, at the emotive details and language in the sentences beginning:

- *He had no sooner extinguished…*
- *Soon after his descent…*
- *On inspecting the body…*

2   FACTUAL REPORTING

> Many kinds of reporting need to be **factual** rather than emotive: for example, official reports, minutes of meetings or legal documents.

a) Imagine that you had been asked by Queen Elizabeth's chief minister to witness the execution of Mary Queen of Scots and to write a brief report of what happened. These are your instructions:

- keep it brief (maximum 200 words)
- include only the main facts
- leave out all emotive details
- do not report Mary's exact words

Write your report.

b) Because it was used as evidence for a Parliamentary Committee, the report of the death of the climbing boy, Thomas Pitt, is full of facts. Use them to write a numbered, step-by-step summary, in note form, of exactly how the boy died.

- Use your own words.
- Accompany your summary with an annotated diagram which shows the grate, the flue and the roof.

3   AUDIENCE AND PURPOSE

> **Audience** is the term given to the people who are expected to read or see a text – the group to whom that text is addressed. All texts are written for a particular **purpose** or range of purposes.

For example, the intended audience of the second text was a Parliamentary Committee on climbing boys. One purpose was to give a factual account of the death of Thomas Pitt.

a) In pairs, discuss who, in your opinion, Robert Wynkfielde's intended audience or audiences might have been. Consider each of the following possibilities and grade each one on a scale from 5 (very likely) to 1 (very unlikely), making a note of evidence from the text which supports your judgement.

a) supporters of Queen Elizabeth
b) supporters of Mary
c) neutrals
d) people who would have known the reason for Mary's execution
e) people who would not have known the reason for Mary's execution
f) a small group of readers
g) a wide readership
h) Robert Wynkfielde's contemporaries
i) people who might read the account in future centuries

b) Having considered Robert Wynkfielde's audience, now discuss what you think his purpose or purposes might have been. Discuss the following possibilities, for example. As you did before, grade each one on a scale from 5 (very likely) to 1 (very unlikely), making a note of evidence from the text which supports your judgement.

a) to write a vivid and entertaining piece of journalism
b) to leave a true record
c) to persuade people that Mary's execution was right and just
d) to gain sympathy for Mary

Writing to report

FOUNDATION TIER TASKS

1 FILMING THE EXECUTION

Imagine you were making a film about Mary Queen of Scots.

- Use the account on page 160 to create a sequence of six frames of a storyboard which shows her execution.
- Then write a paragraph or two to explain the decisions you have made.

Planning and drafting

1 Make notes on what happens in the sequence that you want to show.

2 Copy six frames like the one below, showing in each one:
   - a sketch of what the audience will see
   - a note of any music or sound effects
   - any dialogue

3 Write a comment on each frame to explain decisions you have made about:

   shots
   camera angles
   framing
   cutting
   (See pages 132–3.)

You could start, for example, at the moment when Mary lays her head on the block:

2 WRITING A LETTER

Use the report of Thomas Pitt's death to write a letter to a newspaper arguing for the use of climbing boys to be made illegal.

Write 200–250 words.

Planning and drafting

You could refer to the following points in your letter:

- Thomas Pitt's age
- how long the fire had been burning
- the size and shape of the chimney flue
- the boy's words when he realised he was stuck
- the state of his body when the surgeon examined it
- his attempt to escape

You could start:

31 March, 1813

Sir,

The monstrous and inhuman use of boys to climb down chimneys must be prohibited immediately. Yesterday I heard a report…

HIGHER TIER TASKS

1 ANALYSING THE TWO REPORTS

Both writers have written reports on dramatic and horrifying events. Comment on the similarities and differences between the two accounts.

Planning and drafting

The task is in two parts.

Part 1: the similarities

You could comment on:

- the dramatic subject matter (an execution and a fatal accident)
- the clear and vivid reporting in both reports

Part 2: the differences

You could comment on:

- emotive reporting
- factual reporting
- audience and purpose

Use the point–evidence–comment method when you analyse the texts (see page 89).

You could start:
The main similarity between the two accounts is that both deal with a dramatic and horrifying death…

2 WRITING A REPORT

Write a brief account of Mary's execution from the viewpoint of one of her enemies, a supporter of Queen Elizabeth.

Imagine you have been given the following instructions by one of Elizabeth's ministers:

- Your intended **audience** is the general public.
- Your **purpose** is to prevent the public having any sympathy for Mary.
- The account will be printed and circulated around inns and other public places; the **form** you write in will therefore be a political leaflet.

Write 200–250 words.

Planning and drafting

Remember that you do not want to present Mary as a heroine, but as a traitor justly paying for her crimes.

You could:

- leave out any emotive detail that might cause a reader to have sympathy with her (e.g. her pet dog)
- emphasise the reason for her death (she had been found guilty of plotting against Queen Elizabeth)
- distort her behaviour at the block (e.g. by misrepresenting what she said to her followers or the executioner)
- mock her appearance after death (e.g. by presenting it comically)

You could choose to:

- write in modern English, or
- give the language a flavour of Elizabethan English, without trying to make it completely authentic.

You could start:
Yesterday the realm of England was cleansed of a traitor! Justly convicted of conspiring in the death of…

Women and the Great War

In this unit you will:

- compare two letters written by women in the Great War
- examine the language of letter-writing
- write a persuasive letter

A MOTHER'S LETTER FROM HOME

After the initial wave of patriotism at the start of the First World War, it did not take long for ordinary soldiers in the front line to become angry by the wasteful loss of so many young lives. One of these men, writing anonymously as 'A Common Soldier', sent a letter to the *Morning Post*, calling for a stop to the war. The reply to his letter from 'A Little Mother', printed opposite, was so popular that the editor of the newspaper decided to publish it separately as a pamphlet. Within a week, seventy-five thousand copies had been sold.

A MOTHER'S ANSWER TO "A COMMON SOLDIER."

TO THE EDITOR OF THE MORNING POST

SIR, – As a mother of an only child – a son now in training and waiting for the age limit to do his bit – may I be permitted to reply to Tommy Atkins, whose letter appeared in your issue of the 9th inst.? Perhaps he will kindly convey to his friends in the trenches, not what the government thinks, not what the Pacifists think, but what the mothers of the British race think of our fighting men. It is a voice which demands to be heard, seeing that we play the most important part in the history of the world, for it is we who "mother the men" who have to uphold the honour and traditions, not only of our Empire, but of the whole civilised world.

To the man who pathetically calls himself a "common soldier", may I say that we women, who demand to be heard, will tolerate no such cry as "Peace! Peace!" where there is no peace. The corn that will wave over land watered by the blood of our brave lads shall testify to the future that their blood was not spilt in vain. We need no marble monuments to remind us. We only need that force of character behind all motives to see this monstrous world tragedy brought to a victorious ending. The blood of the dead and the dying, the blood of the "common soldier" from his "slight wounds" will not cry out to us in vain. They have all done their share, and we, as women, will do ours without murmuring and without complaint. Send the Pacifists to us and we shall very soon show them, and show the world, that in our homes at least there shall be no "sitting at home warm and cosy in the winter, cool and 'comfy' in the summer". There is only one temperature for the women of the British race, and that is white heat. With those who disgrace their sacred trust of motherhood we have nothing in common. Our ears are not deaf to the cry that is ever ascending from the battlefield from men of flesh and blood whose indomitable courage is borne to us, so to speak, on every blast of the wind. We women pass on the human ammunition of "only sons" to fill up the gaps, so that when the "common soldier" looks back before going "over the top" he may see the women of the British race on his heels, reliable, dependent, uncomplaining.

The reinforcements of women are, therefore, behind the "common soldier". We gentle-nurtured, timid sex did not want the war. It is no pleasure to us to have our homes made desolate and the apple of our eye taken away. We would sooner our lovable, promising, rollicking boy stayed at school. We would have much preferred to have gone on in a light-hearted way with our amusements and our hobbies. But the bugle call came, and we have hung up the tennis racquet, we've fetched our laddie from school, we've put his cap away, and we have glanced lovingly over his last report, which said "Excellent" – we've wrapped them all in a Union Jack and locked them up, to be taken out only after the war to be looked at. A "common soldier", perhaps, did not count on the women, but they have their part to play, and we have risen to our responsibility. We are proud of our men, and they in turn have to be proud of us. If the men fail, Tommy Atkins, the women won't.

> Tommy Atkins to the front,
> He has gone to bear the brunt.
> Shall "stay-at-homes" do naught but snivel and
>   but sigh?
>   No, while your eyes are filling
>   We are up and doing, willing
> To face the music with you – or to die!

Women are created for the purpose of giving life, and men to take it. Now we are giving it in a double sense. It's not likely we are going to fail Tommy. We shall not flinch one iota, but when the war is over he must not grudge us, when we hear the bugle call of "lights out", a brief, very brief, space of time to withdraw into our own secret chambers and share with Rachel the Silent the lonely anguish of a bereft heart, and to look once more on the college cap, before we emerge stronger women to carry on the glorious work our men's memories have handed down to us for now and all eternity. – Yours, &c.,

A LITTLE MOTHER
August 14.

Tommy Atkins	the nickname given to the ordinary English soldier at that time
the 9th inst.	the 9th of this month
Pacifists	people who were opposed to war
not ... one iota	not a jot, not the slightest bit

A DAUGHTER'S LETTER FROM THE FRONT

The feelings of women serving in the front line were often very different from
those of the mother who wrote to the *Morning Post*. Angry at women who were
so ready to send their sons to their deaths – people like her own mother and a
Mrs Evans-Mawnington – Helen Zenna Smith wrote the following letter, based
on her experiences of serving as an ambulance driver in the battle zone.

Letter from Helen Zenna Smith

A war to end war, my mother writes. Never. In twenty years it will repeat itself. And twenty years
after that. Again and again, as long as we breed women like my mother and Mrs. Evans-
Mawnington. And we are breeding them–

Oh, come with me, Mother and Mrs. Evans-Mawnington. Let me show you the exhibits
5 straight from the battlefield. This will be something original to tell your committees, while they
knit their endless miles of khaki scarves – something to spout from the platform at your
recruiting meetings. Come with me. Stand just there.

Here we have the convoy gliding into the station now, slowly, so slowly. In a minute it will
disgorge its sorry cargo. My ambulance doors are open, waiting to receive. See, the train has
10 stopped. Through the occasionally drawn blinds you will observe the trays slotted into the sides
of the train. Look closely, Mother and Mrs. Evans-Mawnington, and you shall see what you shall
see. Those trays each contain something that was once a whole man … the heroes who have done
their bit for King and country … the heroes who marched blithely through the streets of London
Town singing 'Tipperary', while you cheered and waved your flags hysterically. They are not
15 singing now, you will observe. Shut your ears, Mother and Mrs. Evans-Mawnington, lest their
groans and heart-rending cries linger as long in your memory as in the memory of the daughter
you sent out to help win the War.

See the stretcher-bearers lifting the trays one by one, slotting them deftly into my ambulance.
Out of the way quickly, Mother and Mrs. Evans-Mawnington – lift your silken skirts aside … a
20 man is spewing blood, the moving has upset him, finished him – He will die on the way to
hospital if he doesn't die before the ambulance is loaded. I know … All this is old history to me.
Sorry this has happened. It isn't pretty to see a hero spewing up his life's blood in public, is it?
Much more romantic to see him in the picture papers being awarded the V.C., even if he is minus
a limb or two. A most unfortunate occurrence!

25 That man strapped down? That raving, blaspheming creature screaming filthy words you
don't know the meaning of … words your daughter uses in everyday conversation, a habit she
has contracted from vulgar contact of this kind. Oh, merely gone mad, Mother and Mrs. Evans-
Mawnington. He may have seen a headless body running on and on, with blood spurting from
the trunk. The crackle of the frost-stiff dead men packing the duckboards watertight may have
30 gradually undermined his reason. There are many things the sitters tell me on our long night
rides that could have done this.

No, not shell-shock. The shell-shock cases take it more quietly, as a rule, unless they are
suddenly startled. Let me find you an example. Ah, the man they are bringing out now. The one
staring straight ahead at nothing … twitching, twitching, twitching, each limb working in a

'Tipperary'	a popular soldiers' song
the V.C.	the Victoria Cross, the highest British award for bravery in war
blaspheming	uttering oaths against God
duckboards	wooden walkways placed over the mud
shell-shock	mental breakdown caused by experience of battle
white feathers	tokens given to men accused of cowardice
haloed	talked about as though she were 'a saint'

35 different direction, like a Jumping Jack worked by a jerking string. Look at him, both of you. Bloody awful, isn't it, Mother and Mrs. Evans-Mawnington? That's shell-shock. If you dropped your handbag on the platform, he would start to rave as madly as the other. What? You won't try the experiment? You can't watch him? Why not? *Why not?* I have to, every night. Why the hell can't you do it for once? Damn your eyes.

40 …Gaze on the heroes who have so nobly upheld your traditions, Mother and Mrs. Evans-Mawnington. Take a good look at them … The heroes you will sentimentalise over until peace is declared, and allow to starve for ever and ever, amen, afterwards. Don't go. Spare a glance for my last stretcher … that gibbering, unbelievable, unbandaged thing, a wagging lump of raw flesh on a neck, that was a face a short time ago, Mother and Mrs. Evans-Mawnington. Now it might be

45 anything … a lump of liver, raw bleeding liver, that's what it resembles more than anything else, doesn't it? We can't tell its age, but the whimpering moan sounds young, somehow. Like the fretful whimpers of a sick little child … a tortured little child … puzzled whimpers. Who is he? For all you know, Mrs. Evans-Mawnington, he is your Roy. He might be anyone at all, so why not your Roy? One shapeless lump of raw liver is like another shapeless lump of raw liver. What do

50 you say? why don't they cover him up with bandages? How the hell do I know? I have often wondered myself … but they don't. Why do you turn away? That's only liquid fire. You've heard of liquid fire? Oh, yes. I remember your letter… *'I hear we've started to use liquid fire, too. That will teach those Germans. I hope we use lots and lots of it.'* Yes, you wrote that. You were glad some new fiendish torture had been invented by the chemists who are running this war. You were delighted to think

55 some German mother's son was going to have the skin stripped from his poor face by liquid fire … Just as some equally patriotic German mother rejoiced when she first heard the sons of Englishwomen were to be burnt and tortured by the very newest war gadget out of the laboratory.

Don't go, Mother and Mrs. Evans-Mawnington … don't go. I am loaded, but there are over

60 thirty ambulances not filled up. Walk down the line. Don't go, unless you want me to excuse you while you retch your insides out as I so often do. There are stretchers and stretchers you haven't seen yet … Men with hopeless dying eyes who don't want to die … men with hopeless living eyes who don't want to live. Wait, wait, I have so much, so much to show you before you return to your committees and your recruiting meetings, before you add to your bag of recruits – those

65 young recruits you enroll so proudly with your patriotic speeches, your red, white, and blue rosettes, your white feathers, your insults, your lies … any bloody lie to secure a fresh victim.

What? You cannot stick it any longer? You are going? I didn't think you'd stay. But I've got to stay, haven't I? … I've got to stay. You've got me out here, and you'll keep me out here. You've got me haloed. I am one of the Splendid Young Women who are winning the War…

Language in context

The power of language

Key features of the texts are:

1 emotive language

2 irony

3 polemical writing

1 EMOTIVE LANGUAGE

> Words and phrases which have an impact on the reader's feelings are called **emotive language**.

To remind yourself about emotive language, look back at page 162.

a) Find the following nouns and noun phrases in *A Mother's Answer*:

- *the British race*
- *our fighting men*
- *the history of the world*
- *the honour and traditions*, not only of *our Empire*, but of *the whole civilised world*
- *land* watered by *the blood of our brave lads*
- *We need no* ***marble monuments***
- *force of character*
- *their sacred trust of motherhood*

Now find the following groups of emotive adjectives and make a note of the nouns that they describe:

reliable, dependent, uncomplaining
gentle-nurtured, timid
lovable, promising, rollicking

Write a paragraph to explain what emotions the writer hopes to stir in the reader by using this language. Think about emotive concepts such as nationalism, heroism and motherhood.

2 IRONY

> When we say the opposite of what we mean or adopt an opposite tone in order to make a point, we are using **irony**.

For example, if somebody tries to help but actually makes things worse, people sometimes say, *Well, that's a great help! Thank you very much!*

Irony is a major feature of Helen Zenna Smith's letter. It is used in the following ways.

Presenting the horror as an interesting exhibition

At the beginning of the second paragraph Helen Zenna Smith addresses her mother and Mrs Evans-Mawnington as though she were a guide giving people a pleasant conducted tour around a museum or art gallery:

> *Oh, come with me, Mother and Mrs. Evans-Mawnington. Let me show you the exhibits straight from the battlefield.*

a) Jot down examples of moments where horrifying sights are introduced as though they were merely interesting museum exhibits. For example, look at paragraph 3, beginning *Here we have the convoy…*

b) In pairs, discuss what point Helen Zenna Smith is making by describing the sights in this way. What attitudes of women back in Britain is she exposing and attacking?

For example, think about the references in *A Mother's Answer* to:

> *the blood of the "common soldier" from his "slight wounds"…*
>
> *We women pass on the human ammunition of "only sons" to fill up the gaps…*
>
> *We are up and doing, willing / To face the music with you – or to die!*

Addressing the readers in a polite and calm tone of voice

> Helen Zenna Smith's **tone** is exaggeratedly polite and calm throughout much of this letter. But this serves only to make us feel how angry and bitter she really is.

c) Write a paragraph commenting on her use of ironic politeness and restraint. How does this tone help us to understand her real anger?

For example, think about:

- the frequent **repetition** of *Mother and Mrs. Evans-Mawnington*. It sounds polite at first, but after a few times?
- the **understatement** of:

   They are not singing now, you will observe. Oh, merely gone mad…
   A most unfortunate occurrence!

   What are the real facts behind each of these ironic understatements?
- the **ironic apology** in *Sorry this has happened*. How sorry is she, in reality?

d) In pairs, find the two or three best examples, in your opinion, of where disgusting sights are ironically described with a tone of exaggerated politeness and restraint. Experiment with reading them aloud in this tone.

Quoting

Helen Zenna Smith also attacks the views of her mother by simply quoting what she has said.

e) Look at the following phrases. Each one is a comment by her mother, here quoted ironically. For each one, write down (a) what her mother meant when she first used the phrase, and (b) why Helen Zenna Smith is quoting it ironically, why she feels that the phrase deserves to be mocked:

   heroes who have done their bit for King and country
   That will teach those Germans. I hope we use lots and lots of it.
   Splendid Young Women (note the capitals)

For example, she ironically quotes the phrase *A war to end war.* You could say that: (a) people like her mother thought that the war would be over quickly and bring lasting peace, and (b) Helen Zenna Smith quotes the phrase ironically, in the knowledge that this conflict will not 'end war' – it will lead to other wars in the near future. She is attacking her mother's complacent optimism.

3 POLEMICAL WRITING

> **Polemic** is the name given to an argumentative attack on someone else's opinions. Politicians and pressure-groups, for example, often use **polemical** speech and writing.

Both of these letters contain the typical elements of **polemical** writing:

- shocking details
- strong language

a) Find examples in Helen Zenna Smith's letter of:

- vivid and gruesome details (e.g. *shapeless lump of raw liver… retch your insides out…*)
- strong language (e.g. *Bloody awful… Damn your eyes*)
- personal reference (e.g. *For all you know … he is your Roy*)

Write two or three paragraphs commenting on these three features and explaining why each one would be likely to shock Helen Zenna Smith's mother and Mrs Evans-Mawnington.

Letter writing

FOUNDATION TIER TASKS

1 SUMMARISING THE ARGUMENT

Reread *A Mother's Answer* on page 167. Then summarise the main arguments she puts forward in reply to 'A Common Soldier'.

Use your own words as far as possible. Write 200–250 words.

Planning and drafting

As you make preparatory notes, think about her central points. Writing as a mother of an only child, she argues that:

- women's opinions deserve to be heard
- victory will bring peace
- women must make their contribution, just as the men are doing
- although women are at home, they understand the sacrifices that are being made
- women are ready to provide their sons to fight in the war
- women did not want the war – it was hard to part with their sons
- women are proud of the men and will stand by them

You could start:

In replying to the letter from 'A Common Soldier', the woman writes as 'A Little Mother'. She introduces her letter by informing us that she herself has an only son who…

She argues that it is time to listen to what the women at home have to say, and she expresses her belief that…

2 WRITING A POLEMICAL LETTER

Write your own polemical letter to a national newspaper. Choose a subject that you feel strongly about and express your argument forcefully.

Write 200–250 words.

Planning and drafting

Think about an issue over which you have strong feelings. It could be a national issue, such as vivisection (experiments on living animals), or a local issue, such as a plan to build a motorway through nearby countryside.

You could use some of the language features found in the two Great War letters:

- emotive language: *this plan is an attack on our British way of life…*
- emotive details: *the Thompsons, a retired couple who will be turned out of their homes…*
- ironically polite address: *you would be more than welcome to spend a night next to the motorway…*
- ironic quoting: *your proposed 'county-wide development scheme' is…*
- ironic mocking of your opponents' behaviour and attitudes: *when you go back to your management boards and finance committees…*
- shocking details and strong language: *three children have already been killed on this road, thanks to your incompetence…*

You could start:

I am writing to express my objections to the proposal to extend the M9 motorway through open moorland.

You could then quote the opposition ironically: *You call it 'a development scheme'; but for those of us living by the side of this proposed motorway, it will be…*

…and use emotive language: This is nothing less than the destruction of our natural heritage…

HIGHER TIER TASKS

1 WRITING 'A SOLDIER'S ANSWER'

Field–Marshal Sir Douglas Haig was the Commander-in-Chief of the British Armies in France. On 11 April 1918, he sent out this *Special Order of the day* to all British troops.

SPECIAL ORDER OF THE DAY
By FIELD-MARSHAL SIR DOUGLAS HAIG
K.T., G.C.B., G.C.V.O., K.C.I.E.
Commander-in-Chief, British Armies in France

To ALL RANKS OF THE BRITISH ARMY IN FRANCE AND FLANDERS

Three weeks ago to-day the enemy began his terrific attacks against us on a fifty-mile front. His objects are to separate us from the French, to take the Channel Ports and destroy the British Army.

In spite of throwing already 106 Divisions into the battle and enduring the most reckless sacrifice of human life, he has as yet made little progress towards his goals.

We owe this to the determined fighting and self-sacrifice of our troops. Words fail me to express the admiration which I feel for the splendid resistance offered by all ranks of our Army under the most trying circumstances.

Many amongst us now are tired. To those I would say that Victory will belong to the side which holds out the longest. The French Army is moving rapidly and in great force to our support.

There is no other course open to us but to fight it out. Every position must be held to the last man: there must be no retirement. With our backs to the wall and believing in the justice of our cause each one of us must fight on to the end. The safety of our homes and the Freedom of mankind alike depend upon the conduct of each one of us at this critical moment.

General Headquarters
Thursday, April 11th 1918.

Commander-in-Chief
British Armies in France

> The war was to drag on for precisely seven months after the issuing of Haig's *Special Order*.

Write *A soldier's answer* to Haig's *Special Order*, to be published in the *Morning Post*.

Planning and drafting

First, think about the points you want to reply to and the main arguments you want to get across to readers at home.

For example, you might have views on the statements and orders by Haig:

- at the end of paragraph 2 (*he has…*)
- in the final paragraph (*…to the end*)

You could write in an ironically polite tone, as Helen Zenna Smith does (see page 171).

If you want to quote Haig ironically (see page 171), you could use:

- *We owe this to the determined fighting and self-sacrifice of our troops.*
- *the splendid resistance offered by all ranks of our Army under the most trying circumstances.*
- *Many amongst us now are tired.*

Remember that polemical writing often contains shocking details and strong language.

> You could start:
> *Yesterday morning, as the first shells started to whistle over our dugout, my mates and I received a Special Order from the Commander-in-Chief. 'Words fail me' to describe how much it lifted our spirits! You will hardly believe how delighted we were to hear that…*

2 COMPARING THE TEXTS

Compare the two texts in favour of the war (*A Mother's Answer* and Haig's *Special Order*) with the letter by Helen Zenna Smith. What are the main differences between the two pro–war texts and the one anti-war text?

Planning and drafting

Think about both the content and the language.

Content
- Who are the three writers? What accounts for their very different perspectives on the war?
- What are the main differences in the arguments they are putting forward?

The language of the two pro-war texts
- emotive language
- emotive description

The language of Helen Zenna Smith's letter
- ironic presentation of the horror
- ironic address
- ironic quoting
- mocking of people's behaviour and attitudes
- shocking details and strong language

> You could start:
> *The two women writers have totally different perspectives on the war…*

Outsiders

In this unit you will:

- compare two extracts about childhood
- examine the language of biography and autobiography
- write a biographical article

The two extracts which follow are both about childhood in the middle of the twentieth century.

BILLY

Billy is a biography of the Scottish comedian and actor Billy Connolly, written by his wife Pamela Stephenson. In this extract she describes a period in the early 1950s when Billy was nine and had joined the scouts.

Later on, when Billy graduated to becoming a Scout, he found the boys were divided into patrols that had animal names. He had fancied himself as a Cobra or a Buffalo and was embarrassed to be placed among the Peewits. However, being a Scout gave him a love of the outdoors that has never left him. Billy still jokes about the novelty of a country visit for Glasgow city children of the time: 'They take you to the countryside once a year. It's supposed to be good for you. The teachers say: "See that green stuff over there? Grass. See the brown things walking about on it? Cows. Don't break them and be back here in half an hour."'

It was such a relief to be able to escape from home and visit his pals who lived in other towns. Billy McKinnel came from Bearsden, an up-market district in north-west Glasgow. It was absolute luxury to sit watching television on Mrs McKinnel's white-and-gold, floral sofa in its squeaky, plastic covering. The Glaswegian comedian Chic Murray, a hefty riot of a man with a tartan suit and a cloth cap, came on the box one day, telling a story about two men called 'Simmet' and 'Drawers' – 'simmet' means singlet in Scotland and, of course, 'drawers' are underpants. Chic's tale was all wordplay and absolutely the funniest thing Billy had ever heard. Mr and Mrs McKinnel were roaring along with the boys. In the story, the Drawers' son had just announced to his father that he wanted to go and live in America, and his father was admonishing him: 'Don't let the Drawers down!'

At that moment, Billy slid over the arm of the couch, for he lost all mastery over his body. He lay on the floor completely convulsed, and Billy says he knew right then, without a shadow of a doubt, that he would spend his life being a funny man. The only comedians he'd previously heard were radio stars like Ted Ray, who all had English accents. Chic Murray, and the variety theatre comic Jimmy Logan, had a profound effect on Billy because they spoke with Glaswegian accents and talked about things that were familiar to him.

One afternoon in March 2001, spluttering laughter from a thousand mourners violates the sombre atmosphere of Glasgow Cathedral. Billy has stepped into the pulpit, nicely understated in a black suit, with bright orange Buddha beads and a diamanté scarf. 'I bet you never thought you'd see me here!' He smirks at the largely Protestant congregation.

Billy glances down at Jimmy Logan's Saltire-draped coffin lying beneath him in the nave. 'I made him laugh one lunchtime,' he boasts. 'There was ham on the menu so I told him, "You've been doing it for years, so you might as well have a bit!"'

admonishing	telling off
convulsed	creased up with laughter
diamanté	a brightly sparkling material
largely Protestant	Billy was brought up a Catholic
Saltire-draped	covered with the Scottish flag
ham	it can also mean overacting

MY PLACE

Australian writer and artist Sally Morgan wrote her autobiography
My Place as a celebration of her aboriginal grandparents. In this
extract she describes the moment at school when she first
understood that the children in her class had different backgrounds,
even though they were all from the same town of Manning.

It was early in Grade Three that I developed my infallible Look At The Lunch method for telling which part of Manning my class-mates came from. I knew I came from the rough-and-tumble part, where there were teenage gangs called Bodgies and Widgies, and where hardly anyone looked after their garden. There was another part of Manning that, before I'd started school, I had been unaware of. The residents there preferred to call it Como. The houses were similar, only in better condition. The gardens were neat and tidy, and I'd heard there was carpet on the floors.

Children from Como always had totally different lunches to children from Manning. They had pieces of salad, chopped up and sealed in plastic containers. Their cake was wrapped neatly in grease-proof paper, and they had real cordial in a proper flask. There was a kid in our class whose parents were so wealthy that they gave him bacon sandwiches for lunch.

By contrast, kids from Manning drank from the water fountain and carried sticky jam sandwiches in brown paper bags.

The kids at school had also begun asking us what country we came from. This puzzled me because, up until then, I'd thought we were the same as them. If we insisted that we came from Australia, they'd reply, 'Yeah, but what about ya parents, bet they didn't come from Australia'.

One day, I tackled Mum about it as she washed the dishes.

'What do you mean, "Where do we come from?"'

'I mean, what country. The kids at school want to know what country we come from. They reckon we're not Aussies. Are we Aussies, Mum?'

Mum was silent. Nan grunted in a cross sort of way, then got up from the table and walked outside.

'Come on, Mum, what are we?'

'What do the kids at school say?'

'Anything. Italian, Greek, Indian.'

'Tell them you're Indian.'

I got really excited, then. 'Are we really? Indian!' It sounded so exotic.

'When did we come here?' I added.

'A long time ago', Mum replied. 'Now, no more questions. You just tell them you're Indian.'

It was good to finally have an answer and it satisfied our playmates. They couldn't quite believe we were Indian, they just didn't want us pretending we were Aussies when we weren't.

Language in context

The power of language

Key features of the texts are:

1. direct speech
2. juxtaposition
3. biographical and autobiographical writing

1 DIRECT SPEECH

There are two ways of reporting what somebody says: direct speech and indirect speech. **Direct speech** uses the speaker's actual words. In **indirect** (or **reported**) **speech**, the writer reports what the speaker has said but does not use the speaker's exact words.

For example:

'Write this down,' she said. (direct speech)
She told us to write it down. (indirect or reported speech)

The writers of both extracts use direct speech, but the effects are different.

a) Find the examples of direct speech in the extract from *Billy*. They come from three phases of Billy's life:

- his time in the scouts
- an occasion in childhood when he watched television at a friend's house
- an episode in his adult life when he spoke at a funeral

b) Write a paragraph to explain why you think Pamela Stephenson decided to use direct speech in recounting these three incidents. In other words, why was it important for us to read the speaker's exact words in each case?

Think, for example, about:

- the language used by the teachers and the instructions they issued
- the wordplay in Chic Murray's tale
- Billy's wordplay at the funeral
- the fact that Billy has spent most of his adult life as a comedian

c) Reread the second section of the extract from *My Place*. Most of it is in direct speech.

In groups of three, redraft the section from *The kids at school…* to *…tell them you're Indian* as though it were two short scenes from a television drama – scene one, the playground; scene two, the kitchen.

You could start:

Scene one: *the playground*
A group of children have gathered round Sally and her brother and sister.

CHILD 1 So where d'ya come from?
SALLY (*puzzled*) Australia.
CHILD 2 Yeah, but what about…

When you have completed the play script, act it out (don't feel that you have to imitate Australian accents). Then discuss how realistic the dialogue sounds.

d) Redraft the discussion in the kitchen (from *One day…*) wholly in *indirect* speech. You could start:
One day, when I tackled Mum about where we had come from, she asked what I meant…

e) Now write a paragraph to explain why direct speech is more effective than indirect speech at this point in Sally's story. Think about:

- the realistic sound of the school children's reply: *Yeah, but…*
- Sally's explanation that *Where do we come from?* means *What country?*
- her use of the word *Aussies*
- Nan's grunt and departure from the room
- Sally's insistence: *Come on, Mum, what are we?*
- Mum's brief reply: *Tell them you're Indian.*
- Mum's *Now, no more questions…*

2 **JUXTAPOSITION**

> **Juxtaposition** is the placing of one item next to another for particular effect.

Writers of biography and autobiography often juxtapose incidents or facts in order to make a particular point.

a) Write a paragraph to explain what point Pamela Stephenson is making when she juxtaposes the account of Billy watching television as a child with the funeral of the Scottish comedian Jimmy Logan. How does the juxtaposition help us to understand the kind of person Billy Connolly has become and the events that influenced him?

b) Juxtaposition can be used very effectively to point out a contrast. Look back at the first three paragraphs of the extract by Sally Morgan (*It was early … brown paper bags.*). Write a paragraph to explain how Sally Morgan contrasts the two neighbourhoods of Manning by juxtaposing descriptions.

For example, look at the contrasts she points out by juxtaposing:

- the account of her own neighbourhood (*I knew I came from…*) with the account of the other part of Manning (*The residents there…*) – think about names (*Bodgies, Como*), houses and gardens
- the descriptions of the children's lunches

3 **BIOGRAPHICAL AND AUTOBIOGRAPHICAL WRITING**

> In a **biography**, an author writes about someone else's life; an **autobiography** is an account of the writer's own life.

- Because biographies are accounts of someone else's life, they are written mainly in the **third person**: *Later on, when **Billy graduated** to becoming a Scout, **he found** the boys were divided into patrols that had animal names.*
- Autobiographies are written from the subject's own point of view and are therefore mainly in the **first person**: *I knew I came from the rough-and-tumble part…*

a) Write down three important sentences from *Billy*, written in the third person, and from *My Place*, written in the first person.

b) Biographies are not written wholly in the third person, and autobiographies are not written wholly in the third. Find examples in *My Place* where Sally Morgan uses the third person in order to convey other people's feelings. For example, look at sentences about:

- the residents in the other part of Manning
- the children at school
- Mum
- Nan

Although Pamela Stephenson's biography is mainly in the third person, most of the account is told from Billy's **viewpoint**. For example:
It was such a relief to be able to escape from home and visit his pals who lived in other towns.

c) Write down other examples of sentences which, although in the third person, give Billy's viewpoint. Look, for example, at accounts of:

- joining a scout patrol
- visiting the countryside
- watching television on the McKinnels' sofa
- Chic Murray's tale and Billy's reaction to it

Writing biography

FOUNDATION TIER TASKS

1 WRITING A BIOGRAPHY

Write a short biography of a well-known person for a children's encyclopedia.

Write 200–250 words.

Planning and drafting

Pick a person you are interested in and know something about. For example, you could choose to write about someone who is historically important or a sportsperson or someone from the world of entertainment.

First make some notes. The following are examples of notes which could be made in preparation for writing an entry on Nelson Mandela.

NELSON MANDELA

- born 1918, at Umtata in the Transkei, South Africa
- called Rolihlahla as a child – means 'stirring up trouble'
- spent childhood herding cattle
- sent away to school
- married his first wife, Evelyn
- qualified as a lawyer
- became angry about the system of apartheid
- 1944: joined the African National Congress
- 1952: put in charge of the ANC's peaceful protests
- thousands of ANC supporters arrested in the 1950s
- 1956: tried for treason
- 1960: after 69 protestors killed in the Sharpeville Massacre, he helped to form Umkhonto we Sizwe (Spear of the Nation) – secret organisation to plan sabotage against the government
- married his second wife, Winnie
- 1962: arrested and sentenced to five years in prison
- 1964: second trial – given life sentence
- became a worldwide symbol of resistance to apartheid
- 11 February 1990: released
- 1991: end of apartheid
- 1994: became first black President of South Africa

If you decide to write about Nelson Mandela, you could start:
Nelson Mandela was born in 1918 at Umtata in the Transkei, South Africa. Called Rolihlahla – which means 'stirring up trouble' – he spent his childhood herding cattle, until being sent away to school…

2 WRITING AN AUTOBIOGRAPHY

Write about an episode from your own life. Choose a single moment or incident in which something important happened.

Write 200–250 words.

Planning and drafting

Use the extract from Sally Morgan's autobiography as a model.

For example, you could write about:

- the moment when you realised something important about your school, your neighbourhood or your friends (as Sally Morgan does in paragraphs 1 to 3)
- a time when you had an important conversation with your parents or other adults (as she does in the second section of the extract)

Think about using:

- direct speech to record people's exact words (look back at question 1a, page 176)
- juxtaposition, to highlight contrasts (question 2b, page 177)
- first- and third-person sentences, for variety (questions 3b and 3c, page 177)

You could start:
It was in my third year at primary school that I first realised…

or

One day I decided to ask my grandmother why…

HIGHER TIER TASKS

1 ANALYSING THE LANGUAGE

Explain how Pamela Stephenson and Sally Morgan, through their content and use of language, provide insights into life as it was in 1950s Glasgow and 1960s Western Australia.

Planning and drafting

Think about the ways in which they provide local background details.

Refer, among other things, to their use of:
- direct speech (e.g. the instructions issued by Billy's teachers, and Sally's conversation with her mother)
- juxtaposition
- first- or third-person sentences

You could start:
Both writers have chosen to describe the experiences of people who, for different reasons, did not have easy childhoods. For example…

2 WRITING A BIOGRAPHY

Write a section from a biography of a well-known person who interests you. You could choose a figure you have studied at school, for example, or somebody from the world of sport or entertainment.

Planning and drafting

Pick an important moment in their adult life or an episode from childhood which has significance for the kind of person they were to become.

Self assess

These are the main language features that you have learned about in this section. Decide how confident you feel about:

- explaining the effects of **emotive writing**
- using **factual writing** for reports
- explaining the different **audiences** and **purposes** for which a text might be written

- identifying **irony** and explaining how it can be used
- explaining what **polemic** is and commenting on its use

- distinguishing between **direct** and **indirect speech** and commenting on their uses
- explaining the effects of **juxtaposition**
- defining **biography** and **autobiography**
- understanding the uses of **first person** and **third person**

What do you feel you need to revise?

Glossary

Abstract noun The label we give to something we cannot touch, such as an emotion, feeling or idea, e.g. *a thriving **family** and **community** that has **skills** and **resources**.*   (p. 63, p. 82, p. 149)

Active and **passive** In an active sentence, the subject performs the action; in a passive sentence, the subject is on the receiving end of the action, e.g. *Ostman **had** no choice…* (active), *the story **was picked up** by other papers…* (passive).   (p. 37)

Adjective A word which gives information about a noun or pronoun. A group of words which does this is called an **adjective phrase**, e.g. ***gruesome** deaths, **savage** butchery, a **horrific** scene.*   (p. 49, p. 82, p. 125, pp. 148–9)

Adverbials Words or phrases which add important information to a sentence, answering questions such as When? How? and Where? e.g. ***Meanwhile**, a witness, Ellen Stanton, told police she had seen Alfred Stratton … tearing **at high speed away from the shop**.*   (pp. 48–9, pp. 74–5)

Angles Camera shots from different directions and heights.   (p. 133)

Anticlimax (also known as **bathos**) A deliberate let-down, often for comic effect, after a build-up to something important or dramatic, e.g. *…with a fearful savage dignity – but mad.*   (p. 23)

Audience The people who are expected to read or see a text – the group to whom that text is addressed. The term can refer to readers, listeners, film/television audiences, or users of information technology.   (p. 43, p. 109, p. 124, pp. 140–1, p. 163)

Autobiography A written account of the writer's own life.   (p. 177)

Biography A written account of someone else's life.   (p. 177)

Blank verse *See **Metre***

Chronological writing Writing in which events are described in the order in which they happened.   (p. 36)
*See also **Non-chronological writing***

Colloquial language Informal, everyday speech and writing. Particular examples are called **colloquialisms**, e.g. *if you are dumb enough… Clever kid.*   (p. 100)

Conditional sentence A sentence in which one thing depends upon another. The conditional clause in the sentence will usually begin with the words *if* or *unless*, e.g. *If you do not have a smoke alarm, fit one. Do not open the front door unless…*   (p. 75)

Cutting The action of changing from one film shot to another.   (p. 133)

Determiner *See **Noun***

Directive *See **Imperative***

Direct speech A speaker's exact words reproduced in writing. In **indirect** (or **reported**) **speech**, we report what was said but do not use the speaker's exact words, e.g. '*…and don't break anything!*' (direct speech), *Ostman said the Sasquatches chatted among themselves* (reported speech).   (p. 176)

Duration The set amount of time for an audience to experience all or part of a moving-image text.   (p. 133)

Ellipsis The term given to an omission in language. **Ellipsis points** (three dots…) can show that something has been left out of a sentence or that it is unfinished, e.g. *This clearly would not do for perishable products, but for coal, concrete, brick, wood…* **Suspension points** (also three dots…) are used to suggest a pause, e.g. *Dug with sweat and blood and … and … shovels.*   (p. 23)

Emotive language Words and phrases which have a particular effect on our feelings and emotions, e.g. *land watered by the blood of our brave lads.*   (p. 88, p. 162, p. 170)

Exclamation mark Punctuation used at the end of exclamations, strong assertions and the expression of powerful emotions, e.g. *Listen to me!* (p. 23)

Frame A single image on a strip of film, or a 'frozen' television image. A photograph taken from a film or television frame is known as a **still**. (p. 132)

Framing The skill of placing people or objects in different positions within the edges of the film frame to get particular effects. (p. 132)

Genre A particular kind of book or film with its own special and recognisable features – such as horror, western or science fiction. (A comedy film or book which mocks a particular genre is called a **parody**.) (p. 10, p. 31, pp. 140–1)

Graphic novel A story which is told through a combination of words and images. It closely resembles a cartoon-strip in its style and narrative. (p. 157)

Graphics The art of putting images and lettering together for a special effect. (p. 156)

Iambic pentameter *See* **Metre**

Image An illustration, such as a photograph or a drawing, used by an advertiser to achieve a particular effect. (p. 42, p. 56, p. 63, p. 83, p. 116, p. 149)
See also **Imagery**

Imagery The collective term for metaphors and similes. An image in poetic language is a picture in words which helps to get across an idea. (p. 17)

Imperative The form of the verb used to give a command, issue a warning or make a request. The imperative form is used in **directives** – sentences which ask/tell someone to do something, e.g. *Be prepared, Don't engage in conversation, share a taxi with a friend* (p. 74, p. 148)

Intro The opening paragraph or sentence of a newspaper article. (p. 116)

Irony Saying the opposite of what you mean, or adopting an opposite tone, in order to make a point, e.g. *Sorry this has happened…* (pp. 170–1)

Juxtaposition Placing one item next to another for particular effect. Writers often juxtapose incidents or facts in order to make a particular point. (p. 177)

Metaphor A way of comparing things without using the words *like* or *as*, where the writer writes about something as if it really were something else, e.g. *Or else my kingdom stands on brittle glass.* (p. 11)
See also **Simile**

Metre The pattern of light and heavy stresses in a line of poetry. A verse line can be divided into **feet** (the equivalent of bars in music). A five-feet line is known as **pentameter**. A foot which contains an unstressed syllable followed by a stressed one is called an **iamb**. Verse which has five iambs per line as its standard rhythm is therefore called **iambic pentameter**. Iambic pentameter which does not rhyme is also known as **blank verse**. (p. 16)

Multi-genre texts Texts which include a variety of genres. (pp. 136–59)

Narrative Another term for a story or account. Biographies, autobiographies, novels and short stories are all examples of **narrative texts**. (pp. 8–33, pp. 152–9, pp. 174–5)

Neologism A newly invented word or phrase, e.g. *has been **outed** as a lawbreaker.* (p. 100)

Non-chronological writing Writing which organises events in a different order from the one in which they happened. (p. 48)
See also **Chronological writing**

Noun A word which labels a person, place or thing. **Common nouns** are the labels given to people, places and things in general. **Proper nouns** are the names of particular people, places or things. **Abstract nouns** are the labels we give to things we cannot touch, such as emotions, feelings or ideas. The way a noun is used in a sentence is decided by **determiners** such as the **articles** *a, an, the* or words such as *some, those, this, that.* (pp. 42–3, p. 63, p. 82, p. 149)

Paragraph A block of sentences linked together by one main idea or subject. (p. 68, pp. 88–9, p. 117)

Parenthesis A word or phrase inserted into a sentence to provide additional information, placed between commas, brackets or dashes, e.g. *Then, in 1910, the murder of two miners…* (p. 37)

Passive *See* ***Active***

Person *See* ***Verb***

Polemic An argumentative attack on someone else's opinions. Politicians and pressure groups, for example, often use polemical speech and writing. (p. 171)

Quote Someone's word-for-word comment reported in a news article, e.g. *Dr David Vaughan said, 'We have increased carbon dioxide'.* (p. 109, p. 125, p. 162, p. 171)

Register The style of language chosen to suit a particular situation, social context or subject matter. (p. 94, p. 141)

Rhetorical language Language used for particular effects, especially in important speeches. It includes structures such as lists (e.g. *government of the people, by the people, for the people*) and repetition (e.g. *afraid of today, afraid of tomorrow and … afraid of each other*). (p. 69)

Sentence A group of words which makes sense. Sentences can be structured in three ways: they can be **simple**, **compound** or **complex**. A simple sentence contains only one clause. Sentences which do not conform to a regular pattern are called **minor sentences**, e.g. *Too flat and flabby. No weapon.* (p. 31)

Shot In moving-image media, a single uninterrupted run of the camera. Shots include **close-ups**, for example, where the camera is very near to the subject, or **long-shots**, taken from further away. (p. 132)

Simile A way of comparing things in an unusual or unexpected way, in which the writer creates an image in the reader's mind. A simile uses the words *like* or *as*, e.g. *her hair stood out from her head like a crest of serpents*. (p. 11)
See also ***Metaphor***

Slang A form of language used by particular groups in informal situations, often to add vividness and immediacy, e.g. *knocking back one cherry brandy over the odds*. (p. 100)

Slogan A short, catchy phrase designed to stick in the memory, most often used in advertising, e.g. *making a world of difference*. (p. 62, p. 133)

Suspension points *See* ***Ellipsis***

Target group The particular audience at which an advertisement is aimed. (p. 133)

Tense The form of the **verb** which shows *when* something happens − either the past, the present or the future, e.g. *Our fathers **brought forth*** (past), *Now we **are engaged*** (present), ***shall*** *not **perish** from the earth* (future). (p. 57, p. 68)

Typography A term used in graphics for the way words are written, drawn or printed. (p. 156)

Verb A word that expresses an action, a happening, a process or a state. Verbs can be in the **first person** (*I hope to, We soon learned*), the **second person** (*You'll see*) or the **third person** (*It's a great way, She enjoyed herself, Conservation can be hard work*). (p. 83, p. 95, p. 101, p. 177)

Vocabulary The term given to a writer's choice of words. (p. 88, pp. 148–9)

Voice-over In moving-image media, a voice heard without the speaker being seen. (p. 133)